Generative AI for Multimedia Content Processing, Security and Privacy

Other related titles:

You may also like

- PBPC084 | Kolekar | Generative AI for Video Surveillance Applications (Multimedia Book Series) | contracted April 2025
- PBSE029 | Rani | Machine Learning and Deep Learning Driven Techniques for Multimodal Data Security in the Internet of Multimedia Things (Multimedia Book Series) | contracted 2024
- PBPC0762 | Ramamurthy | Generative AI Unleashed: Advancements, transformative applications, and future frontiers | June 2025
- PBPC066 | Srivastava | Federated Learning for Multimedia Data Processing and Security in Industry 5.0 (Multimedia Book Series) | Jan 2025
- PBPC061 | Lv | Access Control and Security Monitoring of Multimedia Information Transmission (Multimedia Book Series) | pub date Dec 2023

We also publish a wide range of books on the following topics:
Computing and Networks
Control, Robotics and Sensors
Electrical Regulations
Electromagnetics and Radar
Energy Engineering
Healthcare Technologies
History and Management of Technology
IET Codes and Guidance
Materials, Circuits and Devices
Model Forms
Nanomaterials and Nanotechnologies
Optics, Photonics and Lasers
Production, Design and Manufacturing
Security
Telecommunications
Transportation

All books are available in print via https://shop.theiet.org or as eBooks via our Digital Library https://digital-library.theiet.org.

IET COMPUTING SERIES 082

Generative AI for Multimedia Content Processing, Security and Privacy

Fundamentals, advances and applications

Surjeet Dalal, Umesh Kumar Lilhore,
Shalini Bhaskar Bajaj and Momina Shaheen

The Institution of Engineering and Technology

About the IET

This book is published by the Institution of Engineering and Technology (The IET).

We inspire, inform and influence the global engineering community to engineer a better world. As a diverse home across engineering and technology, we share knowledge that helps make better sense of the world, to accelerate innovation and solve the global challenges that matter.

The IET is a not-for-profit organisation. The surplus we make from our books is used to support activities and products for the engineering community and promote the positive role of science, engineering and technology in the world. This includes education resources and outreach, scholarships and awards, events and courses, publications, professional development and mentoring, and advocacy to governments.

To discover more about the IET, please visit https://www.theiet.org/.

About IET books

The IET publishes books across many engineering and technology disciplines. Our authors and editors offer fresh perspectives from universities and industry. Within our subject areas, we have several book series steered by editorial boards made up of leading subject experts.

We peer review each book at the proposal stage to ensure the quality and relevance of our publications.

Get involved

If you are interested in becoming an author, editor, series advisor or peer reviewer, please visit https://www.theiet.org/publishing/publishing-with-iet-books/ or contact author_support@theiet.org.

Discovering our electronic content

All of our books are available online via the IET's Digital Library. Our Digital Library is the home of technical documents, eBooks, conference publications, real-life case studies and journal articles. To find out more, please visit https://digital-library.theiet.org.

In collaboration with the United Nations and the International Publishers Association, the IET is a Signatory member of the SDG Publishers Compact. The Compact aims to accelerate progress to achieve the Sustainable Development Goals (SDGs) by 2030. Signatories aspire to develop sustainable practices and act as champions of the SDGs during the Decade of Action (2020–2030), publishing books and journals that will help inform, develop, and inspire action in that direction.

In line with our sustainable goals, our UK printing partner has FSC accreditation, which is reducing our environmental impact on the planet. We use a print-on-demand model to further reduce our carbon footprint.

British Library Cataloguing in Publication Data

A catalogue record for this product is available from the British Library

ISBN 978-1-83724-208-5 (hardback)
ISBN 978-1-83724-209-2 (PDF)
ISBN 978-1-80705-147-1 (EPUB3)

Typeset in India by MPS Limited

Cover image: BlackJack3D/E+ via Getty Images

The IET International Book Series on Multimedia Information Processing and Security – Call for Authors

Multimedia data (and more generally multimodal data) stands as one of the most demanding and exciting aspects of the information era. The processing of multimedia has been an active research area with applications in secure multimedia contents on social networks, digital forensics, digital cinema, education, secured e-voting systems, smart healthcare, automotive applications, the military, insurance and more. The advent of the Internet of Things (IoT), big data, Cyber-Physical systems (CPSs), robotics, as well as personal and wearable devices now provide many opportunities for the multimedia community to reach out and develop synergies.

This book series comprehensively defines the current trends and technological aspects of multimedia research with a particular emphasis on interdisciplinary approaches. The authors will review a broad scope to identify challenges, solutions and new directions. The published books can be used as references by practicing engineers, scientists, researchers, practitioners and technology professionals from academia, government and industry working on state-of-the-art multimedia processing, analysis, search, mining, management and security solutions for practical applications. It will also be useful to senior undergraduate and graduate students.

Proposals for coherently integrated internationally co-authored or multi-authored edited research monographs will be considered for this book series. Each proposal will be reviewed by the book series editors with additional peer reviews from independent reviewers. Please contact:

- Dr. Amit Kumar Singh, Department of Computer Science & Engineering, National Institute of Technology Patna, India; Emails: amit_245singh@yahoo.com; amit.singh@nitp.ac.in
- Prof. Stefano Berretti, Media Integration and Communication Center (MICC) & Department of Information Engineering (DINFO), University of Florence, Italy; E-mail: stefano.berretti@unifi.it

Contents

List of acronyms

Acronym	Full Form
AI	Artificial Intelligence
ASR	Automatic Speech Recognition
API	Application Programming Interface
CNN	Convolutional Neural Network
CTGAN	Conditional Tabular Generative Adversarial Network
DL	Deep Learning
DSP	Digital Signal Processing
FID	Fréchet Inception Distance
GAN	Generative Adversarial Network
GAI / GenAI	Generative Artificial Intelligence
GDPR	General Data Protection Regulation
GNN	Graph Neural Network
HIPAA	Health Insurance Portability and Accountability Act
IP	Intellectual Property
IoT	Internet of Things
LLM	Large Language Model
ML	Machine Learning
NLP	Natural Language Processing
ONNX	Open Neural Network Exchange
OSI	Open Source Initiative
RL	Reinforcement Learning
SMC / SMPC	Secure Multi-Party Computation
SSIM	Structural Similarity Index
VAE	Variational Autoencoder
VR	Virtual Reality

Foreword

Multimedia (and more generally multimodal data) stands as one of the most demanding and exciting aspects of the information era. The processing of multimedia has been an active research area with applications in secure multimedia contents on social networks, digital forensic, digital cinema, education, secured e-voting systems, smart healthcare, automotive applications, the military, finance, insurance and more. The advent of the Internet of Things (IoT), Cyber-Physical Systems (CPSs), robotics, as well as personal and wearable devices, now provides many opportunities for the multimedia community to reach out and develop synergies.

Our book series comprehensively defines the current trends and technological aspects of multimedia research with a particular emphasis on interdisciplinary approaches. The authors will review a broad scope to identify challenges, solutions and new directions. The published books can be used as references by practicing engineers, scientists, researchers, practitioners and technology professionals from academia, government and industry working on state-of-the-art multimedia processing and security in Industry 5.0 applications. It will also be useful to senior undergraduate and graduate students, as well as PhD students and Postdoc researchers.

The book entitled *"Generative AI for Multimedia Content Processing, Security and Privacy: Fundamentals, Advances and Applications"* offers a comprehensive study of generative artificial intelligence techniques and their impact on multimedia systems. It critically analyses security and privacy issues of using state-of-the-art generative models like GANs, VAEs, and diffusion architectures for image, video, and audio processing. The book covers technological foundations, legislative frameworks, and ethical issues while introducing advanced mitigation solutions. Generative model architectures, multimedia content authentication, privacy-preserving AI, and collaborative open-source projects are covered. The book simplifies this quickly changing area by merging mathematical underpinnings, system models, and experimental investigation. This book targets multimedia processing, AI, cybersecurity, and data protection researchers, engineers, and graduate students. It also addresses politicians, digital rights experts, and regulatory professionals interested in generative AI's multimedia implications.

We hope the readers will find this book of great value in its visionary words.

Dr. Amit Kumar Singh, Book Series Editor
Department of Computer Science and Engineering
National Institute of Technology,
Patna 800005, India

Prof. Stefano Berretti, Book Series Editor
Department of Information Engineering
University of Florence,
Florence 50139, Italy

About the authors

Surjeet Dalal is a researcher and professor in the Computer Science and Engineering Department (CSE) at Amity University Haryana, India. He has published over 100 articles in SCI and Scopus-indexed journals in the fields of artificial intelligence, computer security and Cloud computing. He has written two books and filed 14 patents. He is a member of the International Association of Engineers (IAENG). He received his PhD in artificial intelligence from Suresh Gyan Vihar University, Jaipur and his master's degree in CSE from PDM College of Engineering, India.

Umesh Kumar Lilhore is a researcher in the Department of Computer Science and Engineering, as well as a leading member of the Research Center at Galgotias University, India. He holds a PhD and postdoctoral degree in Computer Science and Engineering, along with an MTech in CSE, showcasing his comprehensive expertise in the field. With over 100 publications in top-tier SCI and Scopus-indexed journals, his research has made pioneering contributions to artificial intelligence, machine learning, deep learning, and computer security. In addition to his research accomplishments, Professor Lilhore has authored five influential books and holds 20 patents, underscoring his innovative approach to solving complex problems. As a Senior Member of IEEE, Professor Lilhore actively engages with the global academic and professional communities. He serves as an esteemed editor for Springer *BMC Medical Informatics and Decision Making*, influencing research discussions at the intersection of technology and healthcare. His involvement in organisations such as the Computer Society of India (CSI) and ACM further demonstrates his commitment to advancing knowledge and collaboration in the field of computer science. Throughout his illustrious career, Professor Lilhore has mentored numerous students and researchers, guiding the next generation of leaders in CSE. His interdisciplinary work bridges cutting-edge technology with real-world applications across academia and industry practices.

Shalini Bhaskar Bajaj is a researcher, professor and head of the Department of Computer Science and Engineering at Amity University, Haryana, India. Her research focuses on artificial intelligence, machine learning and data analytics. She has published over 100 research papers in SCI and Scopus peer-reviewed journals. She is editor-in-chief of the *Journal of Data Science and Cybersecurity* (JDSCS). She is a fellow of the Institution of Engineers (India) (FIE) and a member of the International Association of Engineers (IAENG). She completed her PhD in

Information Technology from IIT Delhi and her ME degree in Computer Technology and Applications from Delhi University, India.

Momina Shaheen is a senior lecturer in computing at the University of Roehampton, London, UK. She has led several projects in the areas of artificial intelligence, machine learning, data science, agent-based modelling, cognitive sciences and distributed systems. She has published 35+ research papers in computing and cutting-edge technologies and has authored two books. She earned her PhD degree in artificial intelligence at the University of Management and Technology, and her master's degree in software engineering from Bahria University, Islamabad, Pakistan.

Chapter 1

Introduction to generative AI for multimedia content processing

This chapter is about generative AI and how it shakes up multimedia content processing. It focuses on the key technologies that bring generative models to life: bi-directional attention, Generative Adversarial Networks (GANs), Variational Autoencoders (VAEs), and transformers. These machines can write, paint, or compose remarkable content of artistry and entertainment through a bewildering gamut across different media (text, photos, soundtracks from wearable camera activities). So, this chapter takes it from the field. The use of generative AI in the wild. That includes generating textual and visual content, audio content, and visual output. It also talks about the ethics surrounding these technologies, all the way from misinformation to information-ownership issues. By the end of this chapter, readers will have a thorough understanding of how generative AI will transform both the creation and consumption of multimedia content in our present industries as well as what future development might be like.

1.1 What is generative AI?

Generative AI is a set of artificial intelligence concerned with generating new content, e.g., images, text, audio, and video that are similar to, but different from, forms seen in training. Whereas traditional AI largely does tasks such as classification or prediction conditioned on the existing data, generative AI models are coded to produce new data similar to the input they have been trained on, as presented by Figure 1.1.

A classic example of generative AI is the manipulation by machine learning models of images, text, or even sound to generate photorealistic images, but not direct, contiguous copy-paste of training data, but things that have been imagined based on what was learnt [1]. We adopt models like GANs and VAEs to train such models. These models could be used in a variety of fields, including the art world, writing, medical research, product design, generating synthetic training data for other AI models, and much, much more. Table 1.1 presents the key features and advantages of generative AI.

1.1.1 Purpose and scope of generative AI

- **Purpose of generative AI:** Generative AI is designed to produce content, information, or knowledge that looks, reads, or appears as if it were generated

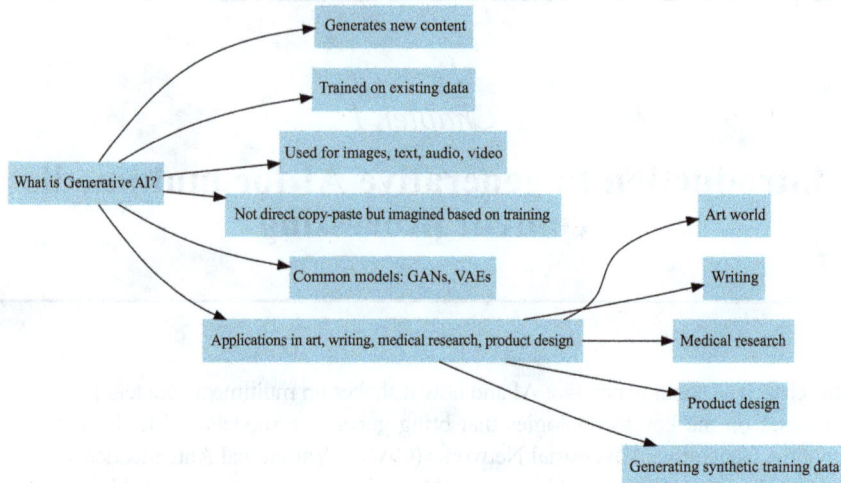

Figure 1.1   Generative AI overview

Table 1.1   Key features and advantages of generative AI

Generative AI	Developer/ Organisation	Key capabilities	Main applications	Advantages
AlphaCode	DeepMind	Solves complex programming challenges	Algorithm crafting, code optimisation	Exceptional in competitive coding scenarios; addresses advanced coding problems adeptly
ChatGPT	OpenAI	Conversational AI with versatile functions (e.g., text generation, summarisation, translation)	Content assistance, Q&A, translation, tutoring, virtual support, and coding help	Easy to use, rich knowledge base, highly adaptive, and suitable for diverse tasks in content and communication
Claude	Anthropic	Text generation focused on ethical AI practices	Customer service, content generation, virtual assistance, research	Emphasises safety and ethics, proficient in handling complex queries, designed to be transparent and non-harmful
DALL-E 2	OpenAI	Creates images from text descriptions	Marketing visuals, illustrations, product concept art	Generates high-quality, diverse images; known for creativity in style and conceptual output

(Continues)

Table 1.1   (*Continued*)

Generative AI	Developer/ Organisation	Key capabilities	Main applications	Advantages
GPT-4	OpenAI	Multimodal with advanced reasoning and improved safety	Complex problem-solving, content creation, and coding	Highly versatile, improved accuracy, and stronger safety mechanisms
Perplexity AI	Perplexity AI	Conversational AI with source-citing capability	Answering questions, researching, fact-checking, and generating referenced summaries	Provides cited sources, enhancing information credibility, and synthesises answers from multiple references for informed responses

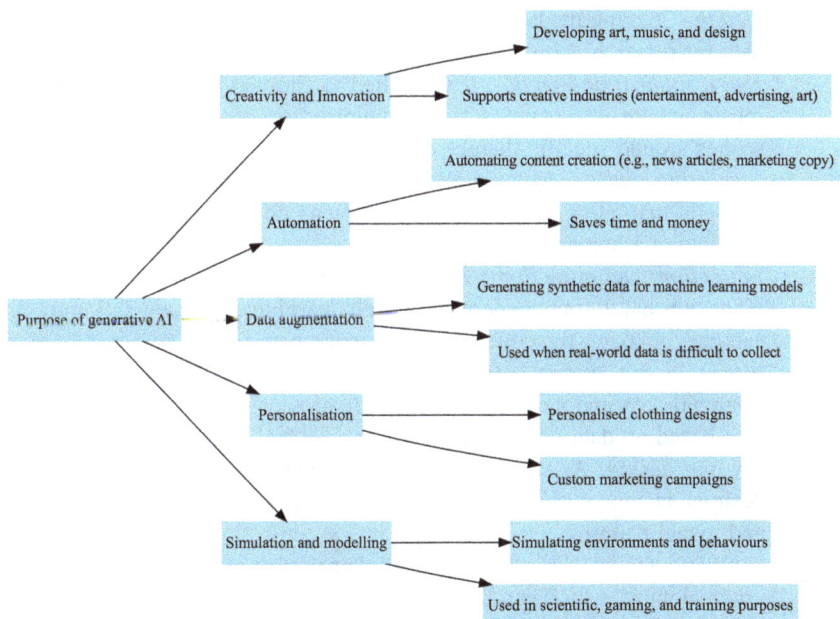

Figure 1.2   Purpose of generative AI

by a person. Its output can be accepted as realistic and generate value in several industries [2,3]. The intended result is a boost in creative capacity, productivity, and the possibility for automation in sectors that have, until now, been dependent on human interaction to create content (Figure 1.2). Generative AI has a few important roles:

- ○ *Creativity and innovation:* It can help in developing new works of art, music, and design and can potentially support creative industries such as the entertainment and advertising industries and art.
- ○ *Automation:* Using generative AI, businesses in the content creation industry (such as those that write news articles or marketing copy) may automate the production of high-quality material with little human intervention, saving both time and money.
- ○ *Data augmentation*: In situations where collecting real-world data is difficult or impossible, it might generate synthetic data that could be used to train other machine learning models.
- ○ *Personalisation:* This could range from generative AI for personalised clothing designs to custom marketing campaigns.
- ○ *Simulation and modelling:* It can be used to simulate environments and behaviours for scientific, gaming, or training purposes (virtual environments, medical simulation).

- **Scope of generative AI:** Generative AI encompasses a wide range of areas, including those touching upon the following industries and niches (Figure 1.3):
  - ○ *Health:* Creating medical images, drug discovery, and synthesising patient data for research. AI can also create simulated medical worlds for training.
  - ○ *Entertainment and media:* It is applied to filmmaking, video games, and music, where AI creates scripts, soundtracks, video content, and whole scenes around specific themes or prompts.
  - ○ *Marketing and advertising*: Writing ad copy and product design, personalised marketing messages, and even customer service chatbots mimicking a human counterpoint [4,5].
  - ○ *Education:* Not quite in the Zoom sense, but AI-generated courses, lesson plans, virtual tutors, and personalised learning materials fall into this category, making the education experience better [6].
  - ○ *Business and finance:* In business and finance, AI models produce financial data and simulate market scenarios or generate business strategies based on data-driven analysis.
  - ○ *Art and design:* AI can also be used to generate visual art, architectural designs, fashion designs, and the like. It can produce new styles, products, and visual patterns.
  - ○ *Synthetic media:* Developing technology, such as deepfake videos or voice cloning, which can be used for good and for ill.
  - ○ *Research and development:* AI is making it possible to generate hypotheses, simulate experiments, and synthesise datasets to produce new insights.

1.1.2   How generative AI works?

In this line, generative AI learns in a systematic pipeline from training to generation. Here is a closer look at the steps (Figure 1.4):

- *Collection and preprocessing of information:* To function, a generative model needs a massive amount of data to learn. This data could be text, images, audio, or

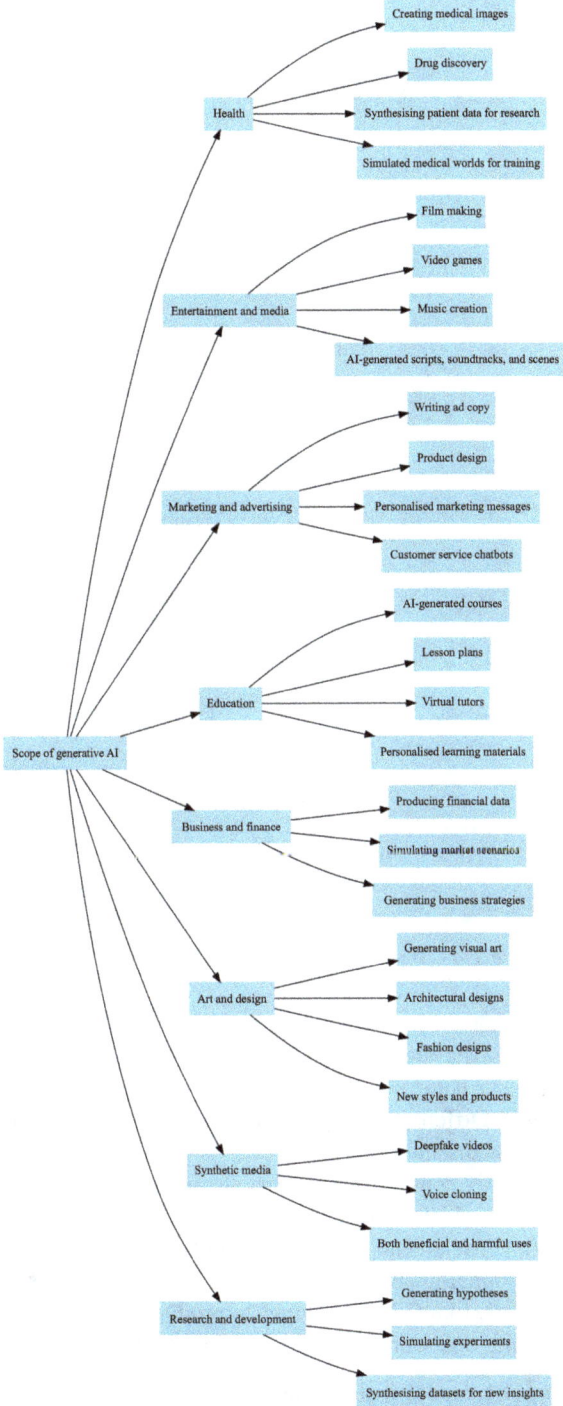

Figure 1.3   Scope of generative AI

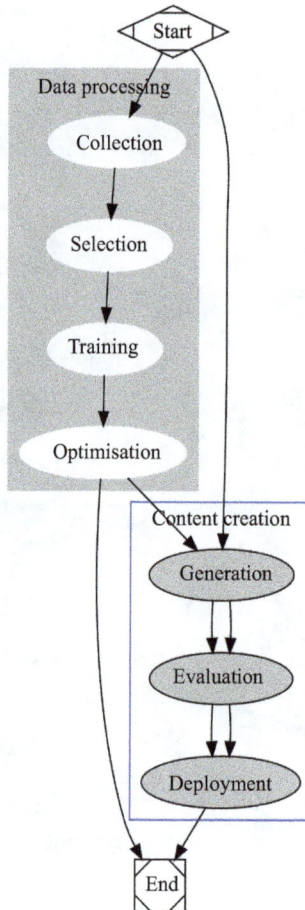

Figure 1.4   Workflow of generative AI development

whatever kind of data the model is intended to produce. The data is then pre-processed to remove noise, normalise it, and make it more usable to the model [7–9].

- *Model selection:* Different generative models are more applicable to different types of data. For instance:
  - GANs: A GAN consists of two separate neural networks, a generator and a discriminator, which cooperate to produce increasingly convincing fake data.
  - VAEs: They use an encoder-decoder architecture to construct data from a low-dimensional latent space.
  - Transformers, like GPT, are wired to produce sequences, like a sentence, by predicting one word after another based on the context.

The selection of a model will depend on the nature of your data and the outcome of interest.

- *Training the model:* In this stage, the model takes the formatted data and learns how to identify patterns or relationships in the data. In text generation, for instance, a model like GPT learns grammar, sentence structure, and the context of a word to generate the next one.
- *Optimisation:* The means of the model parameters (e.g., weights and biases in neural networks) are updated to minimise the error between model outputs and the data during training. These are done with algorithms of optimisation, like gradient descent, which adjusts the model prediction.
- *Content generation:* After learning, the model can write original content. Something is given to it as input (a text phrase or some random noise vector), and it generates new data that is like the training data.
- *Evaluate and refine:* Evaluate the quality of this content created. It could be done by humans or another model that considers realism and quality. If the results are disappointing, then you need to adjust your model until the results become better or retrain it completely for improved output [10].
- *Deployment:* The final step is to put the model into some actual situation. In fiction writing, for example, it can be turning out story lines on demand and, depending on user reactions, doing that processing in real time or not.

1.1.3   Key characteristics of generative AI

The main functionalities of generative AI are presented in Figure 1.5; the details are as follows.

- Content generation: Generative AI tends to create new kinds of content on the fly, as opposed to traditional systems, which are usually tuned to a very specific use case (i.e., prediction, classification). So that could include things like writing and creating poetry, visual art, and music.
- *Content based on pattern/structure from familiar data*: Content produced by generative AI models is based on patterns and structures learnt from producing vast amounts of data. All that matters is getting them to output at a level that mimics the complexities of human creativity [11–13].
  - o *Flexibility:* Generative AI has broad applications across various industries, including:
  - o *Media and writing media:* Writing compelling articles, news reports, and social media content.
  - o *Design:* Designing logos, site designs, and visual concepts to help with graphic design.
  - o *Marketing:* Tailored marketing messages and advertisements in accordance with each individual's profile.
  - o *Entertainment:* Entertainment from music production to script writing to level design for games.
  - o *Creative process automation:* Generative AI automates sections of the creative process, allowing the creator to focus on more abstract ideas and principles. That could lead to greater efficiency and new creative horizons.

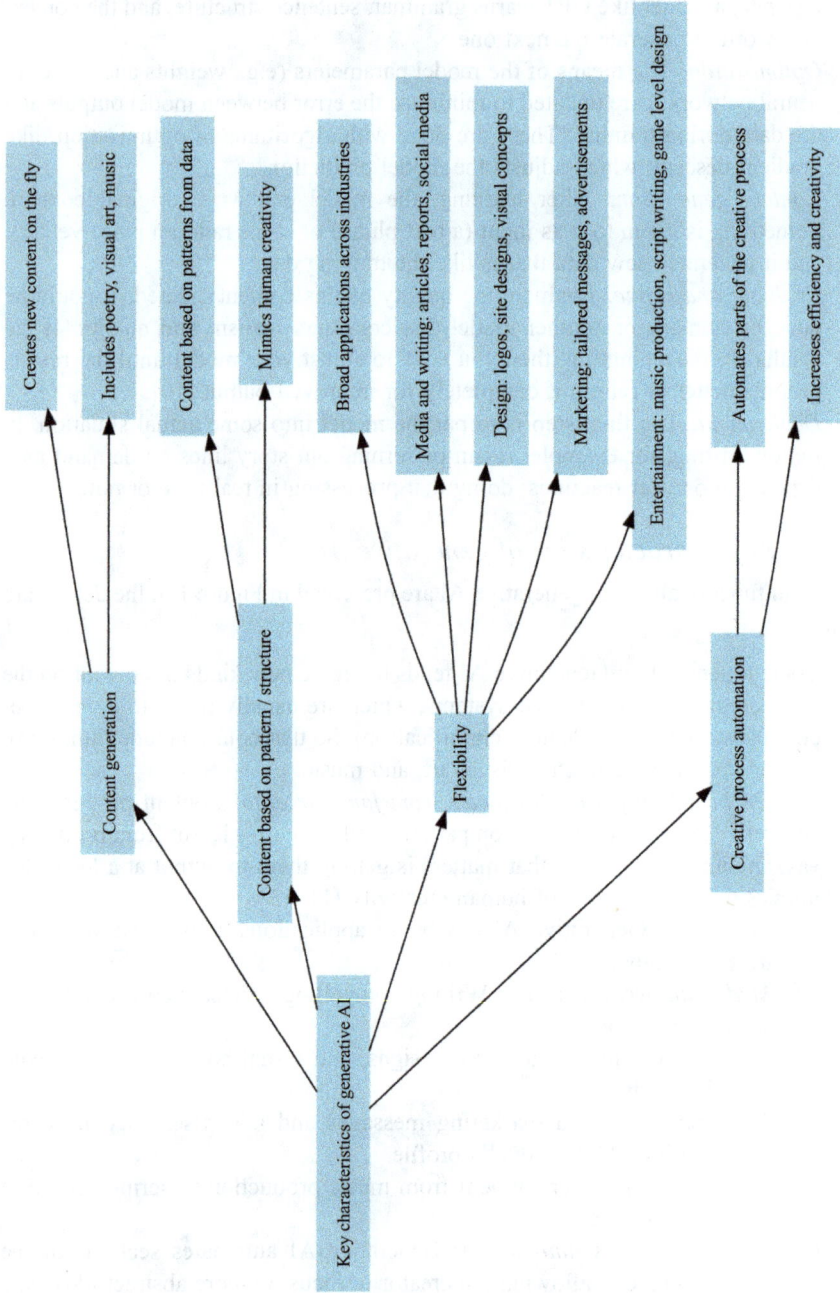

Figure 1.5 Key characteristics of generative AI

1.1.4   Evolution of generative AI

Generative AI has improved significantly, from traditional machine learning to state-of-the-art deep learning, now allowing us to produce complex content. Here is a summary of its evolution (Table 1.2 and Figure 1.6):

- *Early generative models:* AI models started with basic generative tasks where they could generate a basic image or text. The models were typically linear and could not generate very sophisticated or realistic imagery.
- *Neural networks and backpropagation:* The advent of backpropagation enabled deep learning networks to learn and optimise weights across multiple layers, enhancing the potential of generative models.
- *GANs:* Created in 2014, GANs were born to change generative AI. GANs brought in the system of two players: a generator, which produces content, and a discriminator, which decides whether the content is real or not. As a result of this adversarial training procedure, GANs generate good material like images, audio, and video [14–16].
- *VAEs and transformers:* VAEs and transformer models strengthened generative skills. VAEs made it easier to model complex data structures, and transformers, such as GPT-3 and BERT, advanced the science of natural language processing and text generation using massive amounts of data.

1.1.5   Real-world examples of generative AI

Here are just some examples of how generative AI is already being used in businesses, organisations, and even among individuals:

- *Text generation*: OpenAI's GPT-3 can write human-like text, essays, translations between languages, and nonsense verse.
- *Image generation*: OpenAI's DALL-E is a programme that can take in text to produce images, so it can be used to create new visual work as well.

Table 1.2   Evolution of generative AI

Generative model	Description	Applications
Generative Adversarial Networks (GANs)	Uses two neural networks, a generator and a discriminator, that work together to create realistic data.	Image generation, video creation, art synthesis.
Variational Autoencoders (VAEs)	Encodes high-dimensional data into a compact latent space and decodes it back to the original data.	Image compression, generative art, anomaly detection.
Transformers (e.g., GPT-3)	Uses self-attention mechanisms to process sequences, enabling efficient and scalable generation.	Text generation, translation, and summarisation.
Autoregressive Models	Generates content step-by-step, conditioning each part on the previous one.	Music generation, speech synthesis.

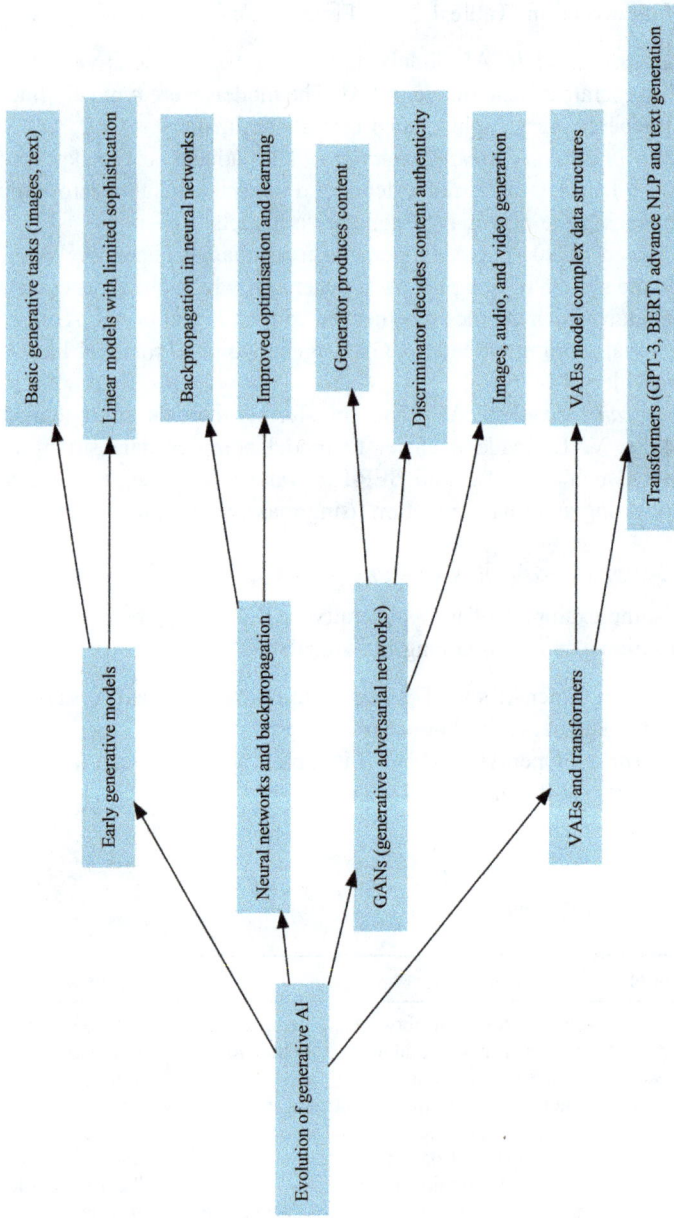

Figure 1.6 Evolution of generative AI

- *Audio synthesis: WaveNet* – synthesising human-like speech with uses for virtual assistants and audiobooks – developed by DeepMind.
- *Video generation:* GAN-based methods such as deepfake generate realistic videos that are employed for entertainment purposes and (sadly) disinformation.

1.2   The role of generative AI in multimedia content

Information in different forms that consists as word, pictorial, vocal, and video information, must be delivered via digital networks. Simply, generative AI is a significant enabler in automating the creation, improvement, and transformation of information (text/images/audio). This assists not only in its fast, innovative, cost-effective execution, but it also leaps industries in a direction that is soon to be taken independently (Figure 1.7).

Figure 1.7 is from some of the research and was analysed from some of the industry reports and papers to represent the contribution of generative AI. For instance, image creation, which utilises model families GAN and VAE to change the way images are created and open innovation in visual media for companies like design, advertising, and entertainment, is currently utilising 40% of the token allotment.

Moreover, OpenAI and Gartner research the impact of AI and configurations for visual content; in simple words, you cannot ignore it. Recent advances in natural language processing, particularly in text generation using large language models, have significantly accelerated the adoption of AI-driven content creation tools. The 30% share for text generation shows the rise of applications using large language models (LLMs) such as GPT-3 to automate content generation in journalism, marketing, and customer support, according to Stanford University and Forrester Research.

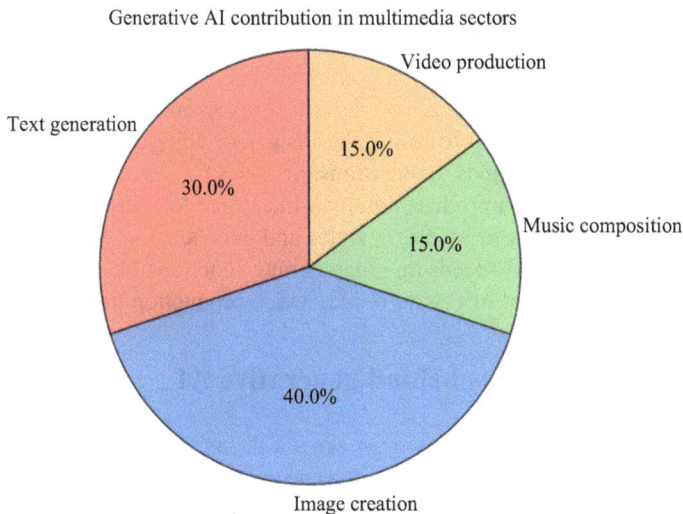

Figure 1.7   Role of generative AI in multimedia content

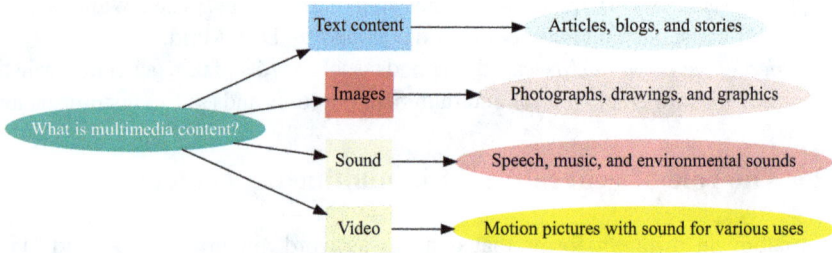

Figure 1.8   Multimedia content overview

The other relatively new use of AI is in music composition and video making (MuseNet for music, Deepfake for music) (15%). These come from research firms and the AI companies themselves, all of them in a scramble to get a read on this new and broadly adopted generative AI and its effects on various parts of the economy [17,18].

1.2.1   What is multimedia content?

Multimedia is the union of content types, such as (Figure 1.8):

- *Text content:* Text-based body of content, including articles, blogs, and stories.
- *Images:* Visual representations such as photographs, drawings, and graphics.
- *Sound*: To include speech, music, and environment.
- *Video:* Motion pictures with sound that can be projected for viewing or photographed with balance and response control for use in webcasts, overhead, security, monitoring, etc.

1.2.2   AI technology for multimedia creation

Generative AI revolutionises multimedia productions:

- *Contents:* AI can write articles, summarise documents, or generate SEO-optimised content without too much human involvement.
- *Image creation:* AI can create lifelike images or edit your existing images. It can add new backgrounds, expressions, or styles.
- *Audio:* AI content can produce a human-like voice for virtual assistants or can create music influenced by preset styles and genres.
- *Video production:* AI speeds up video editing functions like colour correction, trimming, and special effects to reduce video production timelines.

1.3   Core technologies behind generative AI

The generative AI models are based on state-of-the-art machine learning and deep learning techniques. These models are built on neural networks, a type of computational system that imitates the neurons and connections of the human brain (Figure 1.9).

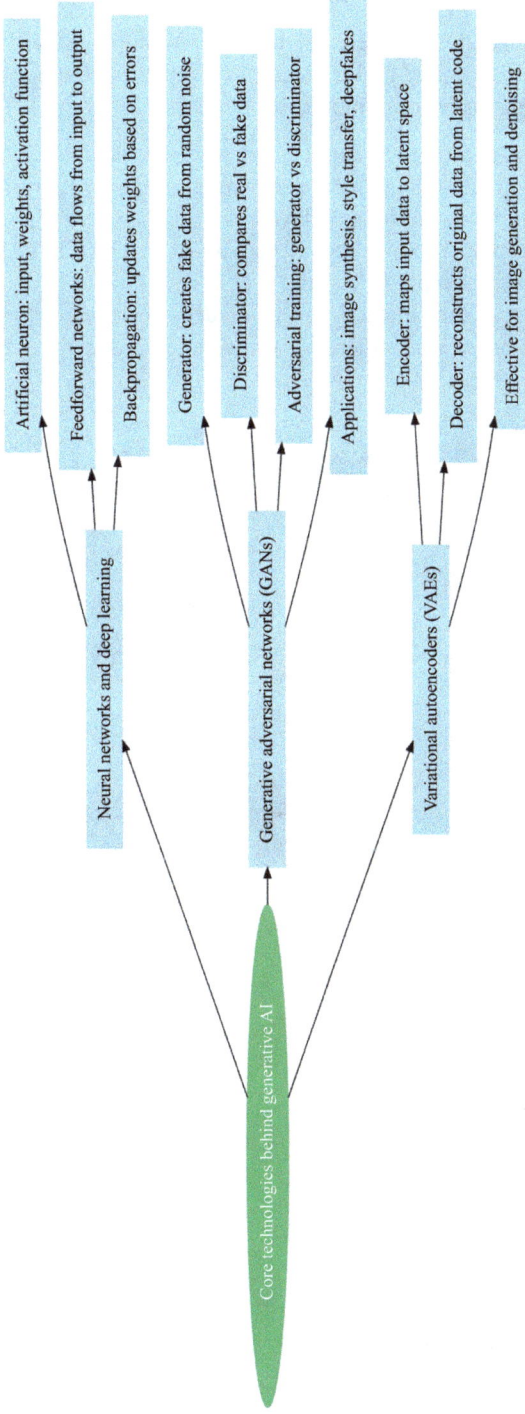

Figure 1.9   Core technologies behind generative AI

1.3.1   *Neural networks and deep learning*

Deep learning and generative models are built upon neural networks. They are composed of structured layers of nodes (neurons) that process the information, one layer at a time, through layers of computation (Figures 1.10 and 1.11).

- *Artificial neuron:* An artificial neuron is like a small colour-changing light that receives an input, processes the input using weights and an activation function, and passes the output on to the next layer.
- *Feedforward networks:* Simple neural networks, in which data flows in the forward direction from input to output.
- *Backpropagation:* A fundamental aspect of deep learning, this is a way of updating weights based on gradients of errors, allowing learning to occur.

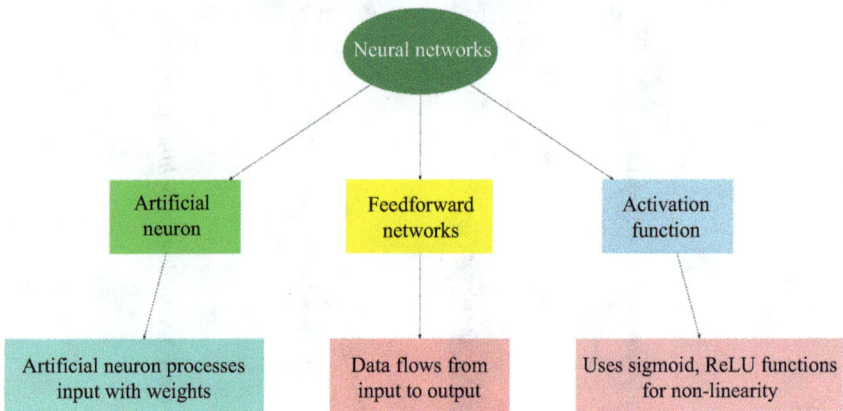

Figure 1.10   Neural network overview

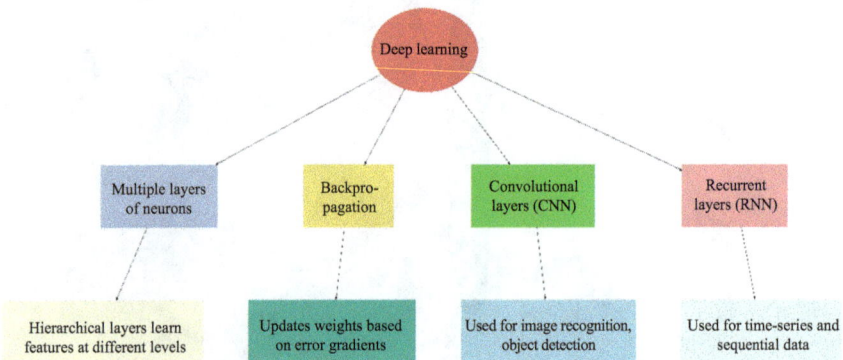

Figure 1.11   Overview of deep learning

1.3.2 Generative Adversarial Networks

Generative Adversarial Networks were one of the most important advances in generative AI. At the top, GANs are two competing neural networks:

- *Generator:* This model creates fake data (e.g., images) from random noise.
- *Discriminator:* This is the network that compares synthetic data to real data, determining its authenticity.

This training process is adversarial—the generator competes against the discriminator and tries to fool it while the discriminator tries not to be fooled by the fake data. Through adversarial competition, GANs "learn" to create high-quality data. GANs are broadly applied in fields such as:

- Image synthesis
- Style transfer (applying the style of one image onto another)
- Deepfakes (altering faces in videos)

The mathematical representation of GANs is given by (1.1).

$$Ex_{\sim pdata(x)}[\log D(x)] + Ez_{\sim pz(z)}[\log(1 - D(G(z)))] \tag{1.1}$$

Where:

- $D(x)$ is the estimated probability that x is real by the discriminator.
- $G(z)$ Is the generator's output for a given random input z.

1.3.3 Variational Autoencoders (VAEs)

VAEs are a type of generative model that are trained to encode data into a latent space in such a way that allows for easy generation of data from the space. This latent space can subsequently be sampled to produce new content.

- *Encoder:* Encodes the given input data onto a probability distribution in the latent space.
- *Decoder:* The reverse of the encoder, which brings back the original data from code.

VAEs are especially effective for image generation and denoising, therefore being suitable for the generation of new, realistic data from noisy or incomplete data.

1.4 Generative AI in multimedia

There have been several applications of generative AI in multimedia content design. Generative AI is shaking up the corporate world, transforming everything from media production to content generation across industries—not just text, but optical, audio, and video content too. Some of the exciting and influential innovations in using generative AIs in multimedia production and manipulation are listed below (Figure 1.12):

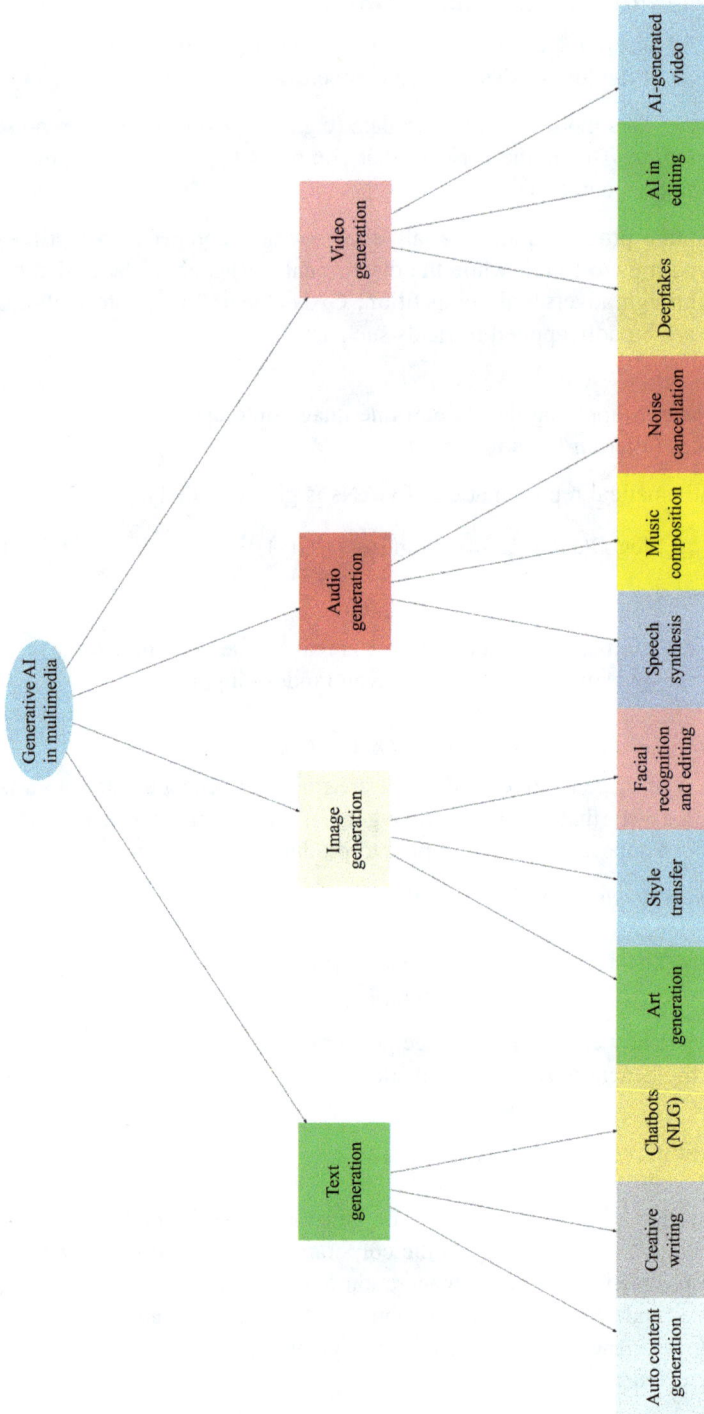

Figure 1.12 Generative AI in multimedia

1.4.1 Text generation

Text generation has recently become one of the most transformative applications of generative AI, driven by the progress of NLP. Examples like Generative Pre-trained Transformer 3 (GPT-3) can now generate human-like text, which could potentially be used for a variety of applications in many areas.

- **Applications of text generation:**
  - *Auto content generation:* Generative AI itself can generate news articles, blogs, product descriptions, and social media posts. It can also save your team a million hours of building that content they know will be on-brand and consistent. For example, in recent times, journalism companies are also creating titles or articles with the help of algorithms using AI and data.
  - *Creative writing:* AI is also entering the creativity sector and helping the creators write poems, short stories, movie scripts, and so on. These models not only analyse writing styles and understand context but also combine the two to write both creative yet logical and coherent stories, taking the creation of creative content into the next generation.
  - *Chatbots:* Perhaps the most well-known application of text generation is the AI-powered chatbots. These bots use natural language generation (NLG) to offer helpful answers, answer questions, and make conversations more interesting. It can be used to allow virtual assistants like Siri, Alexa, and Google Assistant to understand the question a user asks and also respond.

1.4.2 Auto image generation

Finally, GANs and VAEs are opening new avenues in the visual arts and image generation fields in agriculture, science, production, education, and entertainment [19]. Using these models, AI can generate high-quality, realistic images, even if such images do not yet exist.

- **Applications of image generation:**
  - *Art generation:* Now, AI is still able to reproduce photos in different art styles (abstract, cubism, and realism). Or else, AI models have been used to create original pieces that mimic the styles of famous artists or completely new visual ideas. It can have applications in advertising, fashion, and gaming, where distinctive images are needed.
  - *Style transfer:* We can take one image, merge it with another image, and transfer the appearance of style to another image. You could, for instance, convert a photo to look like a Van Gogh painting or even a landscape photo into a watercolour image. This is one of the most common cases, however, specifically for graphic and textual works like promotional material, social media posts, etc.
  - *Facial recognition and editing:* For example, GANs can generate the most realistic human faces, and some lower-resolution images even exist. These AI faces become increasingly realistic and can be applied in many

domains, including health and education, the initial use case in video games and virtual avatars, and, alas, nefarious uses such as enhancing digital facial recognition systems.

1.4.3   Audio generation

AI has also come a long way when it comes to generating audio, now capable of generating realistic voices, music, and sound effects for uses that span from virtual assistants to entertainment.

- Applications in audio:
  - Speech synthesis: Artificial Intelligence-based speech synthesis has been one of the most influential use cases with generative AI. Text-to-speech systems such as those used in virtual assistants, audiobooks, and accessibility tools rely on AI to generate voices that sound natural. These voices can be further customised in their tone, pitch, and pace to allow users to have more natural interaction.
  - *Music composition:* AI models like OpenAI's MuseNet can create music in many different styles, everything from classical to jazz to pop. These AI systems enable creators to produce background music, jingles, soundtracks, and even entire compositions without requiring much musical expertise. Music production is being reinvented with AI tools, providing new ways for artists to experiment with sound.
  - *Noise cancellation:* Audio processing uses generative AI to suppress background noise and amplify weak or distorted signals. It is especially helpful in uses like voice recognition, where DSP is warranted and important.

1.4.4   Video generation

Generative AI for video generation and editing is a rapidly evolving domain and has begun to produce disruptive results in a variety of subdomains, such as deepfakes, AI-powered video editing tools, and fully AI-generated video.

- Video generation applications:
  - *Deepfakes:* The best-known of generative AI in video are deepfakes. These are videos that use AI-generated faces and voices overlaid on actual video or audio to make it appear as if a person said or did something that they never said or did. Despite the extreme controversy surrounding them, deepfakes are already extensively utilised across commercial pursuits, including entertainment, publicity, and education, to illustrate events or create believable visual responses to verbal prompts.
  - *Artificial intelligence in editing:* Ongoing developments in AI are transforming the way video editing happens; AI-assisted editing reduces laborious processes through automated scene detection, video stabilisation, and colour correction. This allows editors to be creative and automate boring tasks using AI tools. So, if you colour grade your video, then the colour will be changed + match where you want it to be, right down the list.

o *Complete AI-generated video:* The highest-level AI models create entire clips from a single, simple text prompt or script. Including composing the audio, which syncs with the visuals. AI is another area that could allow companies to create all of those explainer videos, commercials, or feature-length animated films for a fraction of the cost and at a much quicker rate.

1.5 Ethical, societal impact of GAI

Creative AI will transform how things are created, but like every other disruptive technology, it is laden with ethical implications. These challenges span the spaces of privacy and disinformation, bias in AI models, and intellectual property. As generative AI systems evolve more rapidly, it is becoming more crucial to address the ethical and societal implications to ensure responsible use of the technology for the overall interest of society.

1.5.1 Misinformation and deepfakes

A notorious area of ethical concern for very generative AI has been the emergence of deepfakes, hyper-realistic videos or images that exist due to AI models, most often GANs, modifying existing content to make it seem as though someone is doing or saying something they did not do or say.

- Deepfakes: Deepfakes can be used to stage political blunders or create videos that claim to show politicians doing or saying unscrupulous things they never actually did or said. These changes could influence the elections, public perception, or create tensions. Deepfakes can impersonate world leaders to wreak havoc on international relations.
- *Fake news and misinformation:* Deepfaking could also be used for the creation of false news stories or assertions. You can create a video of a public figure or a public servant and spout something they totally would not have said to contribute to the avalanche of misinformation. That makes it hard for people to know what the truth is, precisely because it makes it hard to tell this kind of content apart from actual videos.
- Reputation ruin: Scandalous deepfakes can also damage a person's reputation. Imagine, for instance, a photoshopped video of someone engaging in embarrassing behaviour gets issued, and they suffer socially, legally, and on the job because of it, even though the video is simply fabricated. Now it would be easier to create and distribute damaging deepfakes.

Emerging technologies and legislation to fight deepfakes. AI helps find inconsistencies in deepfake images. Already, platforms like YouTube and Facebook are developing systems to detect, flag, and delete deepfake videos.

1.5.2 Bias in AI models

Data is a reflection of the bias in the world, and since AI models, generative AIs included, are trained on these large datasets, the bias is passed on. Whether it is racism, sexism, or something relevant to another culture, the models tend to reproduce this kind of behaviour in the data and content. This is even more reason to worry, considering these AI systems are used to generate content that can have serious impacts on people's lives, be they news articles, advertisements, or social media posts.

- Generative AI model bias:
  - *Biased and offensive material:* Also, if the model is trained on biased data, then it can generate content that can represent a harmful stereotype. If you have biased data to train on AI models, then AI could generate ads or other media filled with a race or gender, filling out stereotypes that are already quite present in society.
  - *Biased in personalisation:* In fact, one of the major issues is that if generative models indeed display any biased behaviour towards minorities, then the outputs from these AI models are likely to be biased as well. Non-white faces will fail for face identifier software, or non-white accents for speech acceptance tools, and such stakeholders will be left in the shackles of a heavyweight AI application.
  - *History replicator:* Many of the AI models are trained on historical data that is essentially grounded in the historical bias against society. For example, say an AI is suggesting who you should hire; the model may be learned using historical hiring information, which could contain male or racial bias.

- Solution and mitigation:
  - In order to avoid bias, a person has to make sure that the data is suitable for every subsection of society. For instance, fairness-auditing algorithms are now being employed by AI practitioners to minimise potential bias. Similarly, the type of performance evaluations facilitated by transparency through regular audits of AI systems can prevent bias from causing harm in the first place.

1.5.3   Intellectual property

That question is made more challenging by the intricacies of IP as applied to genAI. As AI systems are now composing their own music, painting their own pictures, and writing their own books, it remains unclear who owns the copyrights. Who owns a song, for instance, created by an AI in the midst of determining a single human creator amongst the attorneys? Should an AI do damage, however, it gets harder to point fingers. It remains unclear whether responsibility should rest with the AI developer, the entity that trained or deployed the system, or whether accountability cannot be clearly attributed to any single party.

- AI-generated content and copyright
  - *Copyright in the work created by AI:* For better or worse, copyright law has a long history on the issue of ownership of the work vis-a-vis human authorship. There is a third one, to be fair: the work of the AI could have (or not have) an author. An example of this may be an AI-generated painting or story that owns the output (or the blame), the algorithm, the

creator who programmed the algorithm, or the dataset on which the algorithm was trained? This brings legal and ethical challenges regarding ownership ambiguity.

o   *Impact on creators:* AI-generated content is going to disrupt industries in music, writing, and other creative arts, some of which have been with us for centuries. Then art created using more traditional means will be worth nothing if it can be created in seconds by AI that can do the same or better. And it could cause harm to the livelihoods, jobs, and pathways of human creators, especially professional creators for whom increasing levels of automation now threaten their existence.

o   *Copyright and plagiarism:* AI systems can unintentionally infringe upon pre-existing copyrights. So, we can receive an image that could have been seen before because it is certainly generated from AI that had been trained on the work of others, resulting in potential legal claims of copyright infringement.

- Solution and mitigation
  o   But there could also be a solution to these problems in establishing a legal regime whereby AI would be given the IP rights to the inputs beyond their own work. Simultaneously, copyright law must evolve to contend with AI as an original creator or as an agency in human hands.

1.5.4   Challenge related to privacy and security of data

Although generative AI models are now able to create higher-quality content than ever before, there is a flip side to this, as they also present new privacy questions, especially with respect to healthcare, finances, and personal information. This is because, to train any AI model, large sets of data must be publicly and freely available to feed it, with an academic career that often has access to sensitive data and is available to malicious actors [20].

- On generative AI issues on privacy
  o   *Data collection:* Generative AI models need a good amount of data that needs to be prepared by you. This is sensitive personal data; hence, it carries the privacy risk if misused/exposed. In a similar vein, one recent example involves the generation of artificial medical records from healthcare data, representing a significant privacy threat to patients where this data is not effectively secured.
  o   *Data collection and consent:* Data that is the fundamental building block for training AI models should be collected ethically and with the consent of the individuals it is sourced from. This could cause misuse of such content for espionage on a specific group of people and can be a violation of privacy rights if an organisation or individual persists with such content using personal data against them without exposing correct authorisation.
  o   *Private data is leaked by AI models:* There is a chance every time we generate data that the private data is memorised into the AI models during the training and leaks with the output. This becomes more applicable to the AI model as it would not provide any type of information if there were no sensitive or

representational datasets created to train that AI model. This means that the models can generate text that contains information, such as personal data, which can be a leak of information about people and/or private organisations.

- Potential plans to mitigate:
  - *Anonymising and de-anonymising:* one way of safeguarding privacy is to anonymise or de-anonymise the data used to train the generative models. This lowers the risk of exposing your personal data, exposing you during the process of generating the content.
  - *Privacy in private AI:* New methods are coming for federated learning and differential privacy to train AI models collaboratively without requiring centralisation of sensitive data to enable residual training on a digital twin of a sensitive private population while preserving privacy.

- Regulator and monitor
  Governments and regulatory bodies can frame provisions for the ethical use of AI and seek transparency around personal data exchange. This means your consent and measures set up to root out misuse of that sensitive information before it happens.

1.5.5 Social and cultural impact

Generative AI is a hybrid of so many components that may be an important factor in social norms, cultural and human creativity icons and dynamics [6]. While today, generative tools are made available to all, and this is a step towards democratising the business of generating content, it also opens up a can of worms surrounding originality, artistry, and the plight of human creators in art and media alike. This can be illustrated under the following headings:

- Cultural and societal impacts:
  - *The pen and the brush for all:* Now, even normal people and low-end creators do not need access to lengthy professional paragraphs needing special talent. This is where the AI apps come in handy. It has given rise to more voices and has put forth great, quality art, music, and text for everyone. The other side, which opposes the proposal, argues that the proposal only looks at the worth of human-promoted works of art and poses the question of whether AI-generated funds would even qualify as a work of art in the first place and how they are to be valued in relation to human generation, either.
  - *Authorship and the idea of inventors:* The proliferation of content created by artificial intelligence systems challenges traditional notions of authorship. If an AI model creates an image, story, or piece of music, who owns that? Who owns the copyright—the AI developer who built it, the prompt creator, or the AI itself? For both creatives and machines, this becomes a fight for the art world and legalities, with those arguing IP and ownership of works.
  - *Impact on generative jobs:* AI is still in its infancy stage, but when mighty, it will also take a few jobs, but in journalism, design, content

creation, and even some legal jobs as well. Much of routine work can now be automated using generative AI, but what does this mean for creative professions rooted in the making of original work? However, on the other hand, AI can be able to create jobs that never existed before as businesses evolve with this new technology available.

o *AI versus human creativity:* Generative AI as a tool that complements rather than devalues human creativity, or maybe what will work, finally, will be the collaborative model, where humans guide and hone AI, and where specificity is the province of human art, and the AI will do its best large-scale work.

o *The proper societal evolution of ethical AI:* Generative AI should be intentionally developed in line with ethical principles such as fairness, transparency, and inclusivity. That ought to prevent AI from developing into immortalising harmful stereotypes or cultural bias, and it helps human imagination, rather than substituting it.

1.5.6 Future of generative AI

Generative AI will lead to even more innovation and utility in places where you never thought it was possible. Now, if we hopped in a time machine and shot back just a few years from now, we would likely have quite a bit of further development in AI tech, bringing us better generative content, smarter personalisation/heavy investments, and applications in lots of different technology verticals—healthcare, entertainment, education, etc.

• New developments on the horizon:
  o *Multimodal model:* We would love to see future generation models not be unimodal (such as models like GPT-3) but be multimodal, being able to generate multiple modalities of content given a single prompt (e.g., video with sound and text simultaneously). That would create the groundwork for much more, well, integrated content creation across all sorts of media.
  o *Greater control and customisability:* Generative AI systems are going to be significantly more controllable, and the users will be able to steer the creative process with finer-grained intent. They might be custom in style, tone, and emotion in text or prompt sheets. These enhancements will help produce high-quality and even more personal content.
  o *Technology crossover:* A more intelligent AI will get us closer to cross-connecting to any other emerging technology like VR, AR, and Blockchain. The result could be a new generation of realistic AI-driven worlds, experiences, and environments, with the border between the real world and the unreal world once again thinner and flimsier than ever.

1.6 Conclusion

Multimedia content generation is the first step in the development of AI technology to reach out to digitise and convert complex information into an image or motion picture. We consume it differently and see the last mobile hand-held devices; after that, it is just not lucrative—a disc won and lost online. In the future, multimedia content creation will be both ultra-high-quality and so easy to use. Empowering artists, the industry, and businesses to personalise their creations: how they make changes when ordering print runs and what materials are used in wrought iron welding.

This high power of GI inevitably comes with great responsibilities to face the moral, social, and legal issues bound up in its use. In many ways, it is a microcosm of digital transformation that could well determine whether our age stands comparison with earlier periods or not for adventurousness and the number of steps forward made on all fronts. Ecology invites us all to think in global terms, to take responsibility for the world. As the potential of generative AI is further realised, we must support responsible and fair use of generative AI and, in a way that promotes benefits in balance with suitable innovative evolution, help to solve the problems of generative AI. We need to be guided by our principles of privacy, fairness, and accountability—approved by humans, of course, for humans.

In the next few sections, we will take a close look at the architecture in generative AI models, including their types and associated examples, as well as the effects this revolutionary technology has had on specific industries.

References

[1]   Kakaraparthi N. Generative AI in content creation and CMS integration: Transforming digital content management through intelligent automation. *Journal Of Multidisciplinary*. 2025;5(7):303–309.

[2]   Huang ZH, Chen P, and Yan S. Generative AI in multimedia: Challenges and opportunities for academic and industrial impact. In *Proceedings of the 32nd ACM International Conference on Multimedia* 2024 Oct 28 (pp. 11123–11124).

[3]   Jadhav D, Agrawal S, Jagdale S, Salunkhe P, and Salunkhe R. AI-driven text-to-multimedia content generation: Enhancing modern content creation. In *2024 8th International Conference on I-SMAC (IoT in Social, Mobile, Analytics and Cloud) (I-SMAC)* 2024 Oct 3 (pp. 1610–1615). IEEE.

[4]   Kumar S, Musharaf D, Musharaf S, and Sagar AK. A comprehensive review of the latest advancements in large generative AI models. In *International Conference on Advanced Communication and Intelligent Systems* 2023 June 16 (pp. 90–103). Cham: Springer Nature Switzerland.

[5]   Chen Y, Ni C, and Wang H. AdaptiveGenBackend: A scalable architecture for low-latency generative AI video processing in content creation platforms. *Annals of Applied Sciences*. 2024;5(1):1–17.

[6]   Malik A, Onyema EM, Dalal S, Lilhore UK, Anand D, Sharma A, and Simaiya S. Forecasting students' adaptability in online entrepreneurship education using modified ensemble machine learning model. *Array*. 2023; 19:100303.

[7]   Onyejelem TE, and Aondover EM. Digital generative multimedia tool theory (DGMTT): A theoretical postulation in the era of artificial intelligence. *Advances in Machine Learning & Artificial Intelligence*. 2024;5(2):1–9.

[8]   Liu J, Adsumilli B, Yanagawa Y, and Dong H. An innovative industry program in a new era of multimedia with generative AI. In *Proceedings of the 32nd ACM International Conference on Multimedia* 2024 Oct 28 (pp. 11125–11126).

[9]   Chen X, and Wu D. Automatic generation of multimedia teaching materials based on generative AI: Taking Tang poetry as an example. *IEEE transactions on learning technologies.* 2024;17:1327–1340.

[10] Xu M, Niyato D, Kang J, *et al.* Generative AI-enabled mobile tactical multimedia networks: Distribution, generation, and perception. *IEEE Communications Magazine.* 2024;62(10):96–102.

[11] Bhavani K, Vivek N, Kiran Teja K, Rohith K, and Rohitha P. AI verse-a multimodal generative platform. *Journal of Nonlinear Analysis and Optimization.* 2025;16(1):459–469.

[12] El Saddik A, Ahmad J, Khan M, Abouzahir S, and Gueaieb W. Unleashing creativity in the metaverse: Generative AI and multimodal content. *ACM Transactions on Multimedia Computing, Communications and Applications.* 2025;21(7):1–43.

[13] Balkrishna Rasiklal Y. Exploring multimodal generative AI: A comprehensive review of image, text, and audio integration. *Innovative: International Multi-disciplinary Journal of Applied Technology.* 2024;2(10):124–133.

[14] Ramagundam S, and Karne N. The new frontier in media: AI-driven content creation for ad-supported TV using generative adversarial network. In *2024 7th International Conference of Computer and Informatics Engineering (IC2IE)* 2024 Sep 12 (pp. 1–6). IEEE.

[15] Artioli E. Generative AI for HTTP adaptive streaming. In *Proceedings of the 15th ACM Multimedia Systems Conference* 2024 Apr 15 (pp. 516–519).

[16] Liu W, and Kim HG. The visual communication using generative artificial intelligence in the context of new media. *Scientific Reports.* 2025;15(1):11577.

[17] Mehta S, Li XJ, and Dalal S. Convergence of artificial intelligence and internet of things for software-Defined radios. In *Reshaping Intelligent Business and Industry: Convergence of AI and IoT at the Cutting Edge.* 2024 (pp. 475–505). Wiley.

[18] Shetty S, and Dalal S. Bi-directional long short-term memory neural networks for music composition. In *2022 Fourth International Conference on Emerging Research in Electronics, Computer Science and Technology (ICERECT)* 2022 Dec 26 (pp. 1–6). IEEE.

[19] Ramagundam S, and Karne N. Future of entertainment: Integrating generative AI into free ad-supported streaming television using the variational auto-encoder. In *2024 5th International Conference on Electronics and Sustainable Communication Systems (ICESC)* 2024 Aug 7 (pp. 1035–1042). IEEE.

[20] Bhutani M, Dalal S, Alhussein M, Lilhore UK, Aurangzeb K, and Hussain A. SAD-GAN: A novel secure anomaly detection framework for enhancing the resilience of cyber-physical systems. *Cognitive Computation.* 2025;17(4):127.

Chapter 2
Technical foundations of generative AI

Generative AI is anything that can generate new data that is similar to the training data used until point of October 2023 by a machine. Generative AI stands out as it is not just classifying or predicting like most traditional AI models, but instead it learns from existing data to create new, original data. Generative AI is one of the digital trends that could create the largest impact on industries, providing the capability to create realistic multimedia content, including image, video, text, and audio for use cases in entertainment, design, healthcare, security, and more. This chapter discusses the core technical fundamentals of generative AI models through key theories, architecture, and algorithms they are built on, and the phenomenal impact they are having in various fields.

2.1 Introduction

The advent of Generative artificial intelligence (GenAI) has altered the stance of classical AI, even impacting how machines "perceive" the way data is "consumed." While traditional AI systems are often trained to perform specific tasks given the data and then use patterns they detect to decide or predict future outcomes, for them, such patterns may be Election notices or paragraph headings in a piece of legislation. These tasks could include identifying objects in images, detecting items for commercial recommendation or sale, and supporting data-driven research aimed at discovering treatments for various diseases. Meanwhile, GenAI is a new medium that transcends interference and discrimination alike by simply creating an untapped source of new pure material [1].

GenAI TMs' primary role is in the generation of new, as opposed to forecasting or interpreting old, data. This data can be an awful lot of things: text, an app for your cell phone, computer printouts, that can only be heard as being read aloud by speakers' floppy disk with an AI model trained on historic classical music, that writes new melodies that sound like Mozart or Brahms. And GPT-4, trained on a huge corpus of text data, lyricizes human-like song lyrics in response to questions or prose poems. The generative nature of generative AI is the promise of being able to make something new and valuable that looks and feels like something it already knows. Unlike "traditional" AI, where the output is always some derivative or variant of the input data, GenAI could outright make up entirely new content according to its supposition about patterns and how patterns in regularities and patterns in constructions shape the world [2,3].

2.1.1   Significance of training data in generative AI

If the generative AI models have the aspiration of creating meaningful, thematically coherent outputs, then the data they feed on themselves similarly needs to be large and diverse [4,5]. The training data is the inspiring source from which GenAI learns. This data might come in the form of huge amounts of text, images, video, or, if a model serves a different purpose, some other type of information (Figure 2.1). Here are some examples:

- *Text-based generative models:* Models including GPT3 and GPT4 are trained on text data, such as books, articles, websites, and other written forms. The model learns the language itself and then generates text in the language it has learned, and the latter includes even new text that it has never read!
- *Image-based generative models:* These are models that have image datasets as input and include Generative Adversarial Networks (GANs) and Variational Autoencoders (VAEs). In doing so, they learn to identify visual patterns, forms, colors, textures, and spatial relationships to build entirely new, nonetheless experiential images.

While the model does not have a notion of a real instance within the data, it does form a model of the underlying distribution of the data that has properties [6–8]. As long as it sticks to those features, the model can draw new examples from it.

2.1.2   Types of outputs generated by GenAI

The outputs of generative AI can be anything and everything. Some common examples include (Figure 2.2):

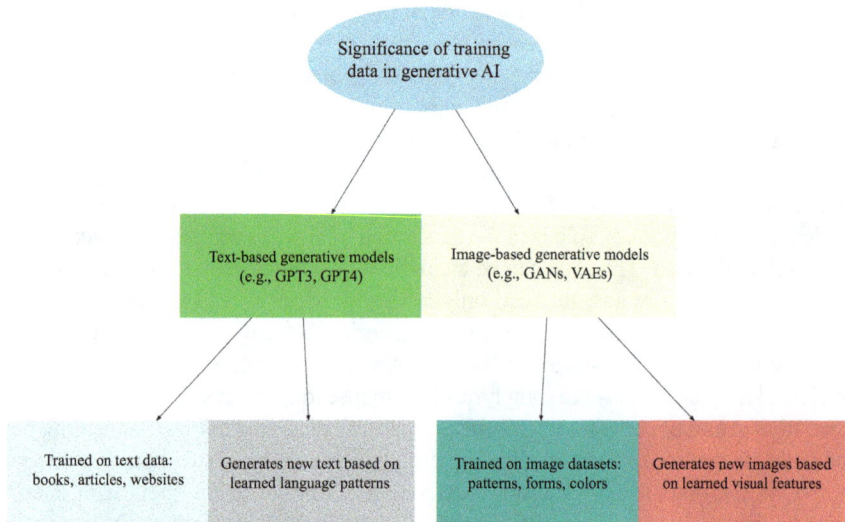

Figure 2.1   Significance of training data in generative AI

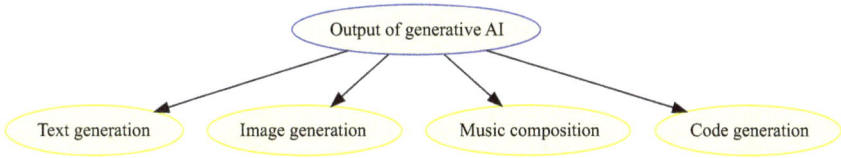

Figure 2.2   Types of outputs generated by GenAI

- *Text generation:* This includes writing articles, generating conversations, creative poetry, code, etc. For instance, GPT-3 is capable of producing text that can fool humans into thinking it was written by another person. Thus, models like this one are useful in chatbots, customer service, etc.
- *Image generation:* High-quality and realistic pictures, GenAI models actually create from nothing. For example, GANs can produce images that look completely natural but are in fact purely the product of a computer, even museum-quality art.
- *Music composition:* From large libraries of musical data, AI models analyze the music's structural traits and produce their own compositions. From classical to contemporary genres, these models can imitate a style rendition that is fitted to the pattern of music that is exposed to data [9].
- *Video generation:* This type of model relates to generating video content, and this has an additional dimension of time. Video generation models create brand new movie scenes and short clips completely from scratch, such as composing a large motion picture in many shorter scenes, generating a scene, or animating movie characters for animation work.
- *Code generation:* GenAI can also create software code, draw databases for existing code, write programs, and provide the code either directly or through suggestions based on input from developers. The productivity of programmers is significantly increased as a result of this [10–12].

2.1.3   Key technical backbones of GenAI

In order to grasp how generative AI works its magic, we need to delve into the mechanics of its structure [13]. There are several key components in the technical framework of GenAI (Figure 2.3):

- *Neural networks and deep learning:* The majority of generative models are deep learning based generative models that leverage neural networks as an architecture. In these networks, there are multiple layers of interconnected "neurons" that sit between the input data and the predicted output target. The richer (i.e., deeper and larger) their connections, the more this model can learn to represent, analyze, and predict new information, in case you feed it a data set.
  - ○ *Generative models:* From the beginning, a large number of generalization models have been developed, for example, GANs, VAEs, and Transformers. All of them vary in strengths or uses, but they all rely on deep learning for generating content.

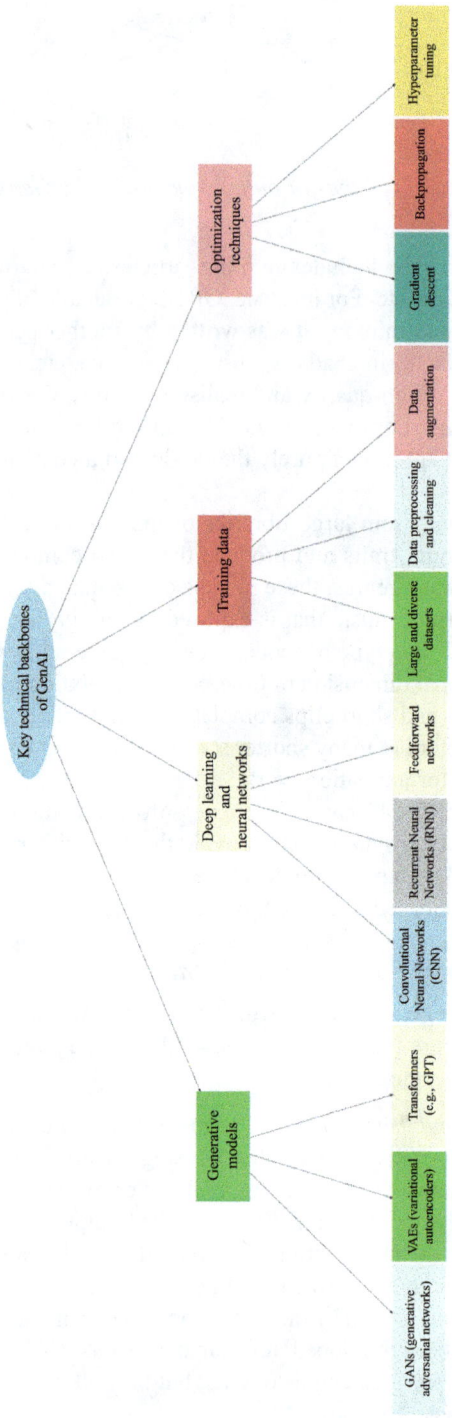

Figure 2.3 Key technical backbones of GenAI

o *Training algorithms:* The training of a generative model involves optimizations such as backpropagation and gradient descent. They tweak the model's parameters to minimize errors in its output and make what comes out better.
o *Mathematical foundation:* These are student-focused models, underpinned by mathematical concepts, such as probability theory, linear algebra, and optimization theory. These principles have a needs-driven development model to allow the model to exploit the patterns in the data to learn from and adapt its output performance [14,15].

2.2   Generative AI's architecture and details

The general structure is formed by a combination of multiple layers that preserve several layers of function. Each of these layers plays a role in order for the model to get trained effectively and to produce the best possible output (see Figure 2.4). The center can be broken down as follows.

- *Data processing layer:* The first half of this layer exports raw data, does some cleaning and conditioning, and drops everything down. We pick up data from Big Data Cloud, Websites, etc., read the data, and pre-process it: we create features, encode Data in a form that our machine learning model can learn from, by filtering out noise and handling missing values. This ensures that the data the models are trained on is of good quality & in a format understandable by machines.
- *Model layer:* The model layer consists of the generative algorithms. These are GANs, VAEs, and Transformers. These models are the crux of GenAI; they all consume data patterns on which to churn out new content in exchange. Every model type has its use case, like GANs are really good at making fake images, and the Transformers are pretty good at gluing words together to make something that is even coherent.
- *Training and optimization layer:* Where training is performed, the generators are trained using optimization methods. Optimization algorithms such a gradient descent update the model's parameters by minimizing the loss function, making predictions from our model increasingly more accurate as time goes on. The training takes a lot of computation time, is computationally quite heavy, and might even require special hardware, such as GPUs.
- *Inference layer:* When a model is trained, the inference layer generally takes over sole responsibility for procedural content generation. This layer is responsible for helping to manage and scale a model efficiently up and out. It accepts input data, feeds it to the trained model, and receives the output we desired (e.g., machine picture or a pronounced text).
- *Feedback/refinement:* Feedback and refinement layer for continuous refinement to the performance of the components, which captures what the user would like to see vs. how the system did. This is all preliminary, of course, and all this makes for a model that, over time, gets fine-tuned to be even more accurate, relevant, and higher-quality generated content based on real-world use.

Generative AI architecture with detailed layers and functions

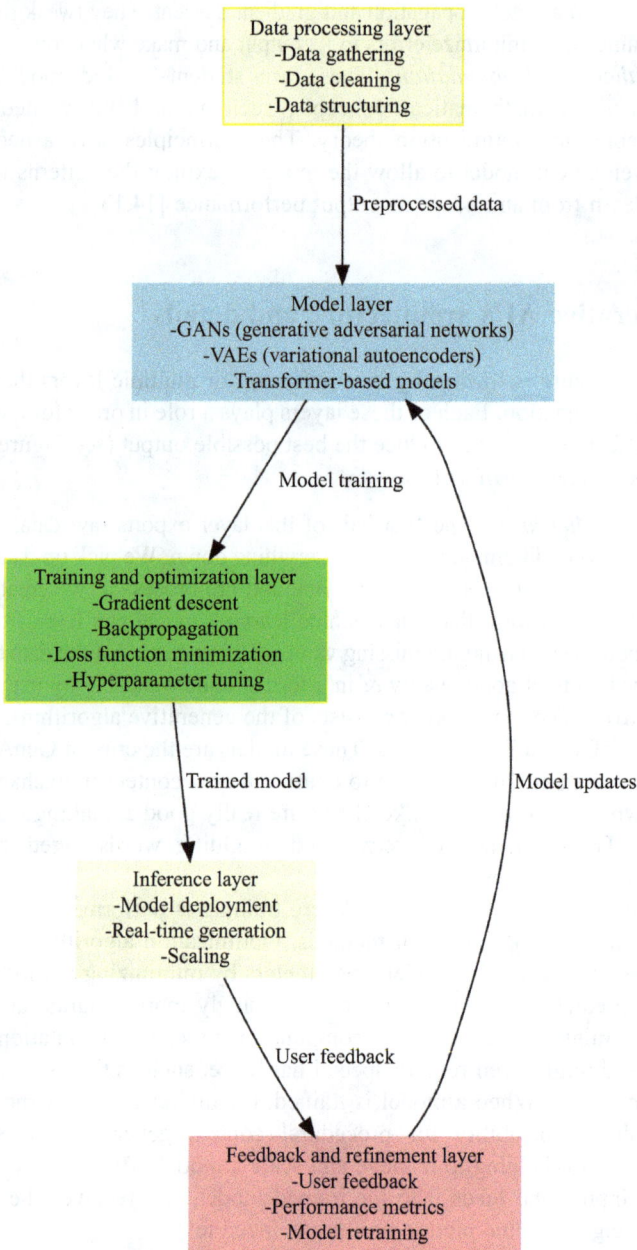

Data processing layer
-Data gathering
-Data cleaning
-Data structuring

Preprocessed data

Model layer
-GANs (generative adversarial networks)
-VAEs (variational autoencoders)
-Transformer-based models

Model training

Training and optimization layer
-Gradient descent
-Backpropagation
-Loss function minimization
-Hyperparameter tuning

Trained model

Model updates

Inference layer
-Model deployment
-Real-time generation
-Scaling

User feedback

Feedback and refinement layer
-User feedback
-Performance metrics
-Model retraining

Figure 2.4   Generative AI architecture with layers and functions

2.3   The functions of technical components

There are several elements in each layer of the GenAI architecture with their own application. They are closely interrelated to assess the system's capability as a whole:

- *Data collection and preprocessing:* The data for any task is sourced from diverse sets of sources and collected using web scraping frameworks, APIs, or data pipelines. Once we have this information in (cleaned up, for example, spam and porn filtered) and transformed into a training model-ready shape, such as CSV files, SQL tables. This is a step toward enhancing the utility of the data for future tasks by setting it to a proper digital form.
- *Model selection and training:* Picking the right model architecture for the content you are creating is important. For instance, if you want to generate images, then you would tend to use GANs... on the other hand, if you want to generate text, then something like a Text Transformer (GPT, GPT3, BERT) will be a good fit! After the model is chosen, you have to train it with lots of data and computer power.
- *Optimization techniques:* Methods like Stochastic Gradient Descent, Adaptive Learning Rate Schedules, and other forms of regularizations, fine-tune the model during its entire training time. In this way, it avoids overfitting, guarantees convergence, and even guarantees that when the model is presented to unseen data, it generalizes well.
- *Deployment and scaling:* Once a model is trained, it should be deployed such that we can scale up or down resources for real-time inferences. In this article, we assume that cloud platforms, such as Amazon Web Services (AWS), Google Cloud, Microsoft Azure, and other comparable cloud services, offer the abstractions needed to host and scale models without issue. Moreover, containerization technologies such as Docker and Kubernetes provide convenient support to deploy models to production.
- *Monitoring and maintenance:* By constantly monitoring the running models, we can be sure that they are working. Measures like response time, accuracy, or error could be measured across development. Additionally, models should be updated regularly with new data and maintained to ensure they are still performing adequately!

The key high-level technical ingredients constituting the GenAI architecture are summarized in Table 2.1. Once the raw data is collected in the data collection and preprocessing step, it will also have been intricately organized and ready for flawless training. Model selection and training cover selecting an appropriate generative model (such as GANs, VAEs, or Transformers) and subsequently training on enormous amounts of data. Model parameters are optimized by optimization techniques that enhance performance and avoid overfitting issues. After training, Deployment and Scaling ensure that the model can be used for real-time content generation. Afterward, with on-time monitoring and maintenance, they are continuously checking how the model is performing, but also taking user feedback to evolve it to be up-to-date.

Table 2.1 Technical components of the generative AI (GenAI) architecture

Component	Function	Tools/techniques/methods
Data collection and preprocessing	The first stage is to collect raw data from different places and change it into an organized, useful format for training. This means getting rid of noise and dealing with missing data.	<ul><li>Web scraping frameworks (e.g., BeautifulSoup, Scrapy)</li><li>APIs for data access (e.g., REST, GraphQL)</li><li>Data pipelines (e.g., Apache Kafka, Apache Airflow)</li><li>Data cleaning (e.g., handling missing values, normalization)</li><li>Feature extraction and transformation (e.g., scaling, encoding categorical variables)</li></ul>
Model selection and training	Picking the right model based on the problem and the type of data. This step is about leveraging big datasets and a lot of computing power to train the model.	<ul><li>GANs (for image generation)</li><li>VAEs (for generating variations and reconstruction)</li><li>Transformers (e.g., GPT, BERT for text generation)</li><li>Recurrent Neural Networks (RNNs) (for sequence generation like text and music)</li><li>Training frameworks (e.g., TensorFlow, PyTorch)</li><li>Large datasets for training (e.g., ImageNet for images, Common Crawl for text)</li><li>High-performance computing (e.g., GPUs, TPUs)</li></ul>
Optimization techniques	Methods for making the model work better and stop it from overfitting. By adjusting the model's weights to minimize the loss function, optimization helps the model generalize better.	<ul><li>Gradient Descent (e.g., Stochastic Gradient Descent, Adam optimizer)</li><li>Adaptive learning rates (e.g., learning rate schedules like exponential decay or cyclical learning rate)</li><li>Regularization (e.g., L2 regularization, dropout)</li><li>Early stopping to prevent overfitting</li><li>Data augmentation to improve generalization (especially for images)</li></ul>

(Continues)

Deployment and scaling	Make sure that the trained model can make data in real time and handle a lot of requests and settings at once.	<ul><li>Cloud platforms (e.g., AWS, Google Cloud, Microsoft Azure)</li><li>Containerization (e.g., Docker, Kubernetes)</li><li>Model serving frameworks (e.g., TensorFlow Serving, TorchServe)</li><li>Scalability (e.g., serverless architecture, load balancing)</li><li>APIs for real-time inference (e.g., FastAPI, Flask)</li><li>CI/CD pipelines for continuous deployment (e.g., GitHub Actions, Jenkins)</li></ul>
Monitoring and maintenance	Keeping an eye on how well the model works after it has been deployed to make sure it still meets expectations and can handle fresh data.	<ul><li>Model monitoring tools (e.g., Prometheus, Grafana, New Relic)</li><li>Real-time metrics (e.g., latency, throughput, accuracy, error rate)</li><li>A/B testing for model comparison and improvements</li><li>Automated retraining pipelines based on new data (e.g., Model Drift monitoring)</li><li>Data collection for model retraining (e.g., feedback loops, active learning)</li></ul>

2.4   The key mathematical foundations of GAI

The exact reasons behind the success of generative AI, however, are largely shaped by a set of theoretical principles that underpin how models learn and produce content. These include:

- *Probability and statistics:* Models like VAEs are based on probabilistic representations of data distribution. This allows the model to create new data values that are of the same nature as the relationships in the aggregated training data but do not look like them.
- *Linear algebra:* Middle-level operations such as matrix multiplication and eigenvalue decomposition are the core operations required for the neural networks to operate. Linear algebra is also utilized at different stages of a neural network, with particular relevance to dimension reduction and model structure.
- *Optimization theory:* Techniques like gradient ascent are crucial for the training of generative models. The model subsequently iterates to optimize its weight, trying to align itself to higher-quality content by kicking down the loss function.
- *Information theory:* Concepts like entropy, mutual information, and Kullback–Leibler divergence are used to understand and measure how much information is preserved or lost with the progression of training. These theories improve the efficiency of the model.

2.5   Types of generative models

There are numerous types of generative models because different jobs need different ones. Here are some of the most common ones (Figure 2.5):

2.5.1   GAN

A GAN has two networks: a generator and a discriminator. The generator makes fake data, and the discriminator decides if it is real or not. Because of this, these networks are trained at the same time in a competitive way: the generator tries to trick the discriminator, while the discriminator tries to differentiate good data from poor. Over time, this kind of oppositional behavior allows this model to create incredibly realistic sights, sounds, and videos (Figure 2.6). Table 2.2 presents the essential elements, purposes, and difficulties of GANs.

2.5.2   Autoencoders with variations

VAEs are a type of probabilistic model that finds a good way to represent data in a space with fewer dimensions, called the latent space. It takes input data, encodes it into this latent space, and then decodes it. VAEs can be used for many things, including removing noise from images, finding anomalies, and making realistic image samples from noisy data. Table 2.3 and Figure 2.7 present the VAEs key components, functions, and applications.

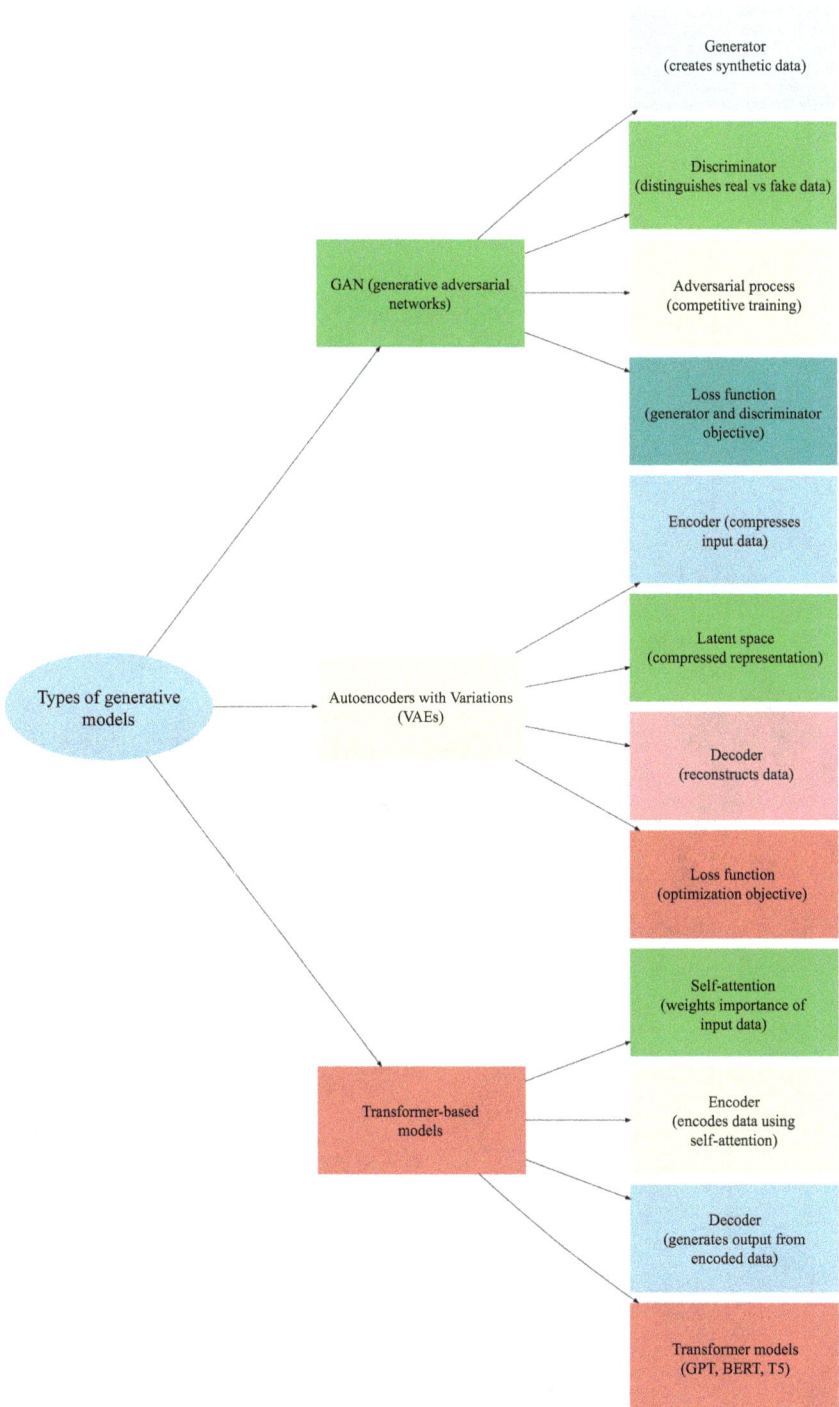

Figure 2.5   Types of generative models

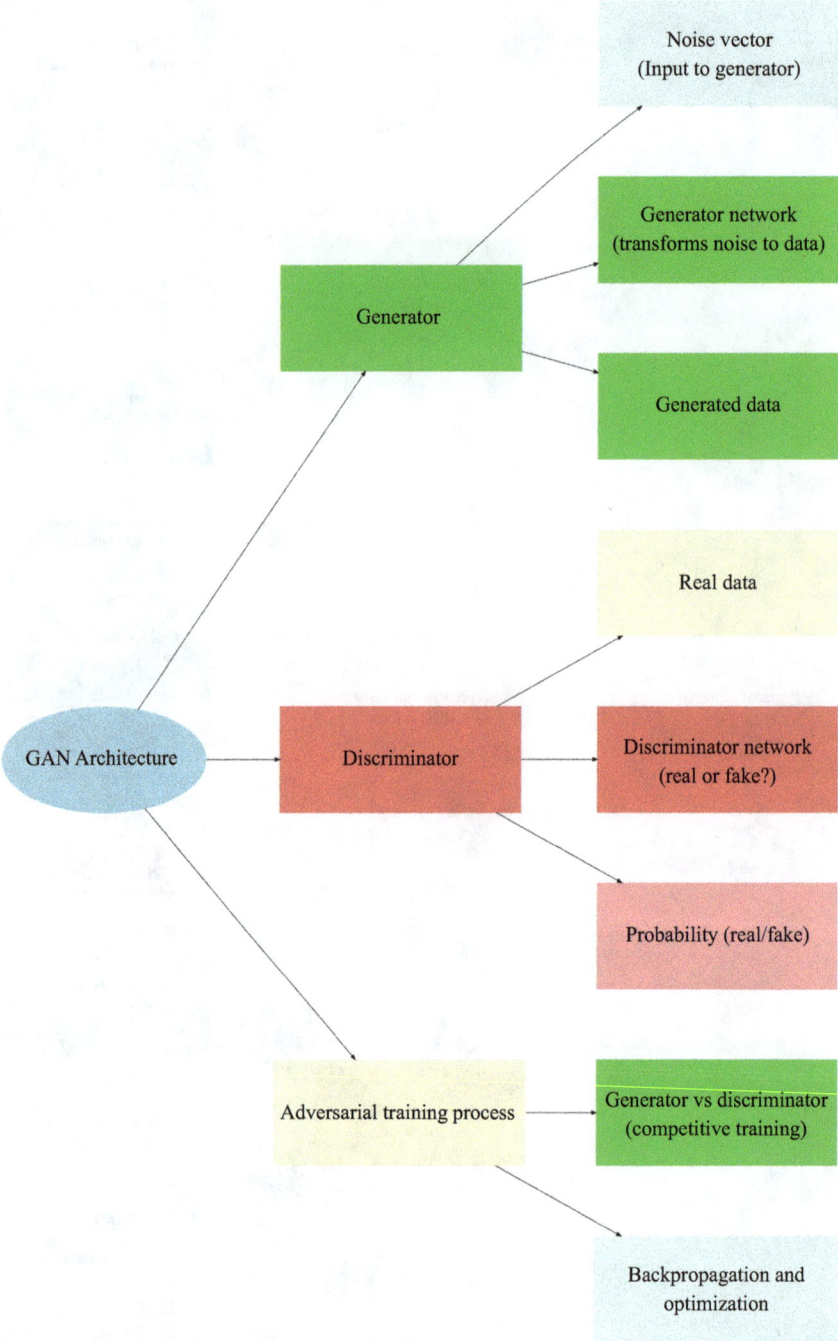

Figure 2.6   GAN architecture

Table 2.2   GAN essential elements, purposes, and difficulties

Component	Description	Function	Challenges
Generator	A neural network that generates synthetic data (e.g., images, audio) intended to mimic real data.	• Creates new, realistic data based on input noise.	• Can suffer from Mode Collapse, producing limited types of outputs.
Discriminator	A neural network that distinguishes between real and fake data generated by the Generator.	• Evaluates the authenticity of data (real or fake).	• Requires careful balancing during training to prevent instability.
Adversarial Process	The process in which the Generator and Discriminator are trained simultaneously, competing with each other.	• Generator improves by attempting to fool the Discriminator.	• Training can be unstable, requiring fine-tuning of hyperparameters.
Loss Function	The objective function that both networks use to evaluate and adjust their performance.	• Generator: Minimize the difference between real and generated data. • Discriminator: Maximize accuracy in distinguishing real from fake data.	• Difficult to achieve equilibrium between the two networks.
Applications	GANs are used in various fields like image generation, data augmentation, and artistic creation.	• Image synthesis, art generation, data augmentation, and style transfer.	• Requires substantial computational resources and large datasets.

Table 2.3   VAEs key components, functions, and applications

Component	Description	Function	Applications
Encoder	A neural network that compresses input data into a lower-dimensional representation in the latent space.	• Maps high-dimensional input data to the latent space.	• Image denoising, data compression.
Latent Space	The lower-dimensional space where the model encodes data, representing key features in a compact form.	• Captures the essential structure of the data in fewer dimensions.	• Anomaly detection, latent space exploration.
Decoder	A neural network that reconstructs the original data from the latent space representation.	• Reconstructs the input data from its compressed representation.	• Image generation from noise, reconstructing missing data.
Loss Function	Measures the difference between the original input and the reconstructed output, guiding the optimization.	• Ensures the reconstructed data closely matches the original data.	• Used in training to optimize the encoder and decoder.

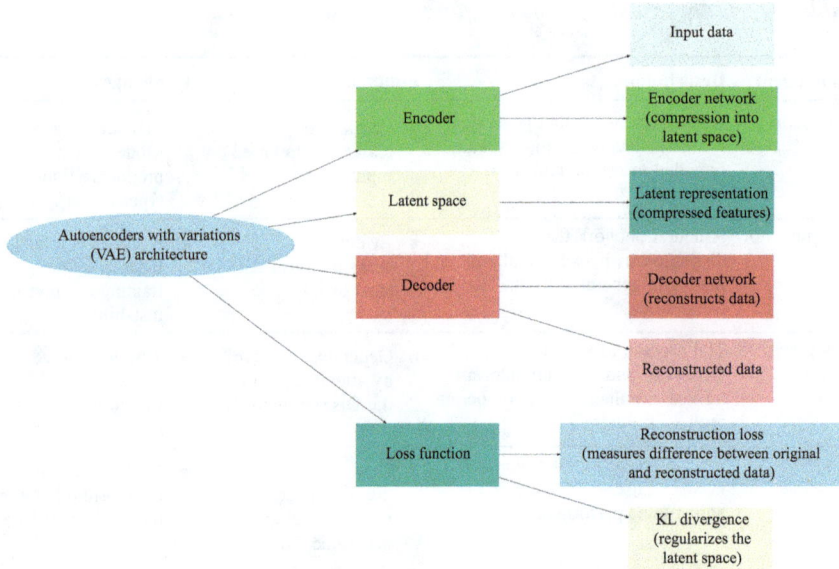

Figure 2.7　Autoencoders with variations

Table 2.4　Key components and applications of transformer-based models

Component	Description	Function	Applications
Self-Attention	Mechanism that assigns different importance to various parts of the input sequence.	• Efficiently processes long-range dependencies in data.	• Text generation, summarization, translation.
Encoder	Encodes input data into embeddings using self-attention layers.	• Captures contextual relationships in input data.	• Language modeling, text classification.
Decoder	Generates output by attending to encoded input.	• Produces text or predictions based on the encoded input.	• Text generation, question answering.
Transformer models	Models like GPT, BERT, and T5 utilize multiple attention layers for diverse NLP tasks.	• Handles large input sequences efficiently.	• Text generation, summarization, translation, sentiment analysis.

2.5.3　Models based on transformers

Transformers have changed the field of natural language processing (NLP). These models, which use self-attention mechanisms, can analyze many data streams at once, making them very efficient. GPT, BERT, and T5 are all transformer-based models that can do things like generate text, summarize it, and translate it. Table 2.4 and Figure 2.8 present the key components and applications of transformer-based models.

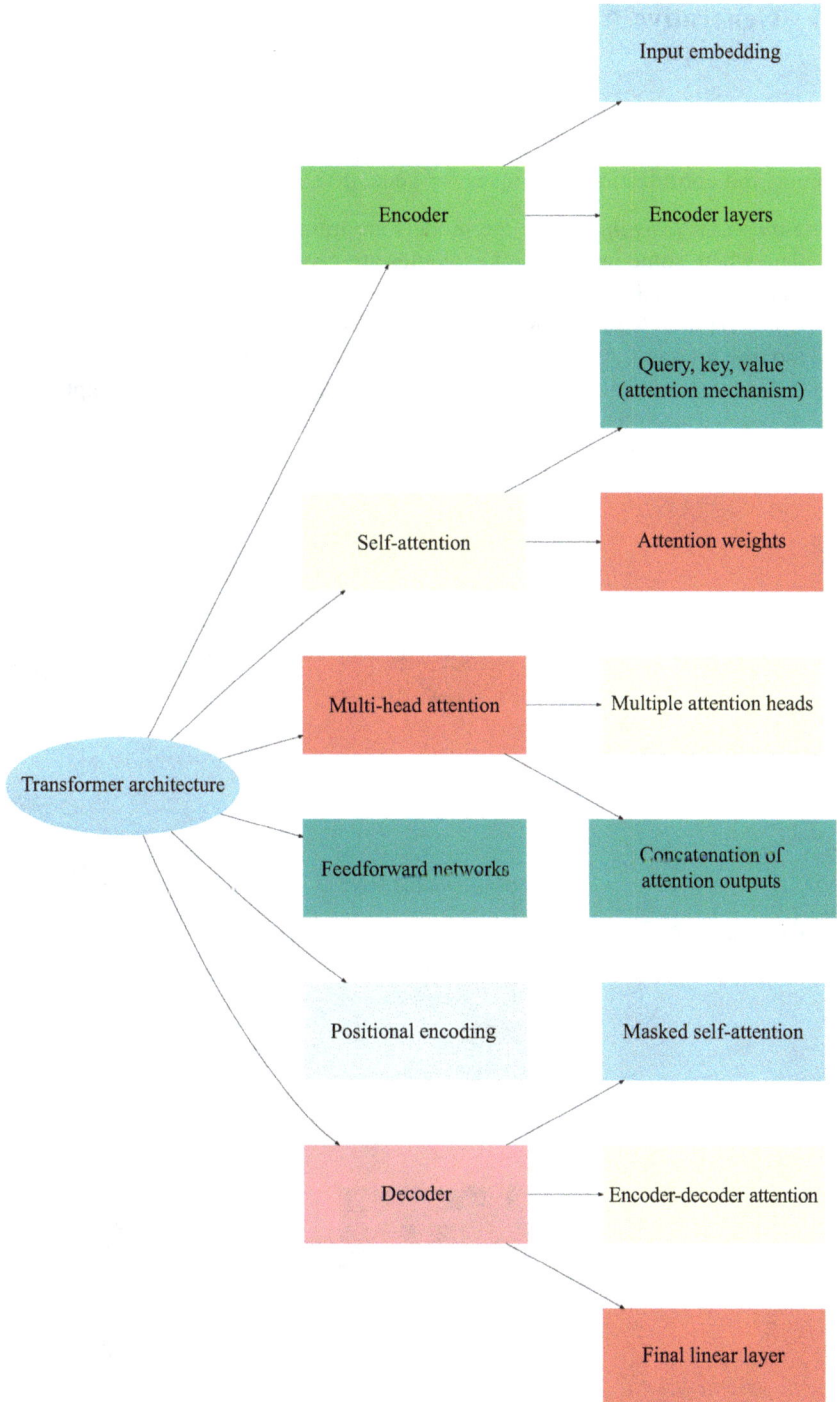

Figure 2.8   Transformer architecture

2.6   Generative AI models training and optimization techniques

There are a few important techniques used in training GenAI models, which are all crucial for the model's ability to learn and generalize. Figure 2.9 presents the training and optimization techniques for generative AI models.

- *Supervised learning:* Here, the models are trained or "supervised" on labeled data where some input-output examples are given to be learned. These models find widespread use in tasks involving text generation and image recognition.
- *Unsupervised learning:* Models are trained on unlabeled data here and go looking for yang. A secret pattern or structure within the material around them. Divination, anomaly detection, and dimensionality reduction are applications of unsupervised learning.

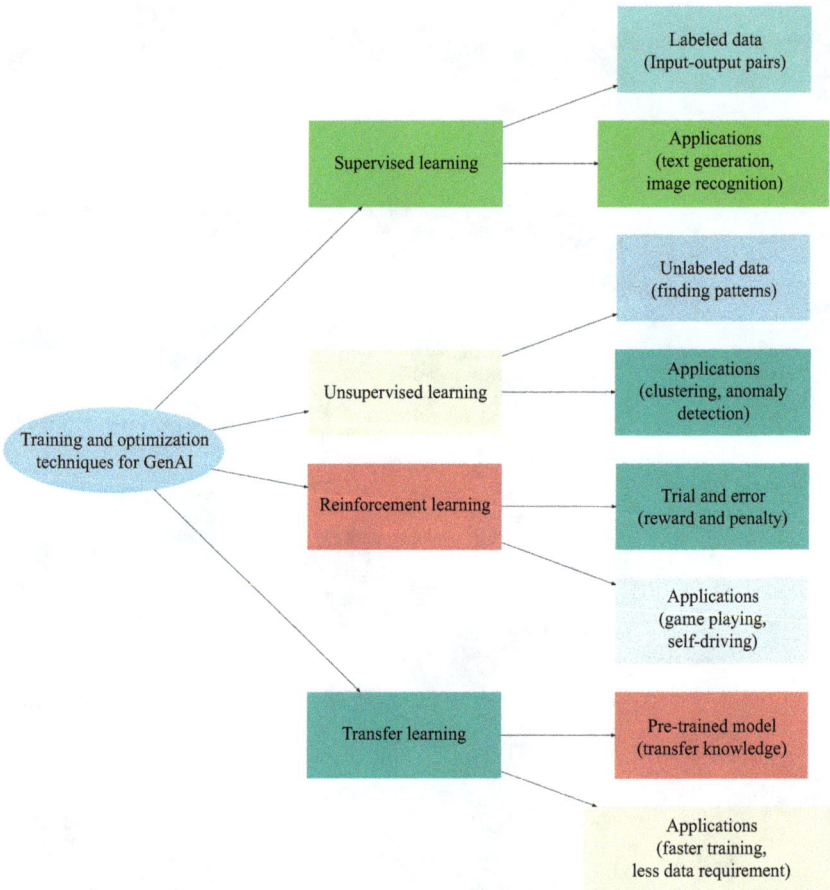

Figure 2.9   Training and optimization techniques for generative AI models

- *Reinforcement learning:* This models how to act based on trial and error, finding the best actions to take. They are rewarded or penalized for doing this. Importance of the technique: There are application scenarios such as game playing and self-driving.
- Transfer learning: It is possible to train a model with a pre-trained model, which has been trained with a large data set, and apply it to specific tasks. This could lower the voracious appetite for massive amounts of data and speed up training.
- Optimization methods include:
  - o *Learning rate schedules*: We can use different learning rates at different steps of training, resulting in efficiency. This avoids a locally minimal solution by the model.
  - o *Regularization:* Techniques like dropout, L2 regularization, and early stopping help to mitigate overfitting by controlling the model complexity.
  - o *Batch normalization:* At training, this makes him nudge the number of activated particles toward an integer. When it accelerates the training and improves the stability in papers.

2.7 Generative AI models deployment and inference

Once GenAI models need to be deployed, there will be a need for a market or network of infrastructure and optimization strategies. The idea is to make it possible for promotions, especially of full-scale content, to be available "in real time" and on demand, in a manner that is large-scale, "cheap to the creator" and extremely cheap to the consumer in whose face it is shoved, as an ad or a product recommendation (Table 2.5 and Figure 2.10). The core aspects of this process are as follows.

- *Cloud providers:* The likes of AWS, Google Cloud Platform, and Microsoft Azure, which bring the scale required for deploying GenAI models at scale, as High-Performance Computer resources (GPUs and TPUs) and storage options necessary to run large models well are part of the package [16–18]. They also tend to offer easy-to-integrate tools, secure data storage, and monitoring, so

Table 2.5   GenAI model deployment key infrastructure components

Component	Description	Benefits
Cloud Providers	AWS, Google Cloud, and Microsoft Azure offer scalable computing resources, storage, and easy integration tools for deploying GenAI models at scale. These platforms provide GPUs and TPUs for high-performance computing.	• Scalable and flexible resource allocation • Easy integration and secure data storage
Containerization	Uses tools like Docker and Kubernetes to encapsulate GenAI models and their dependencies in portable containers that can run consistently across different environments (cloud, on-premise).	• Fast and simple in use

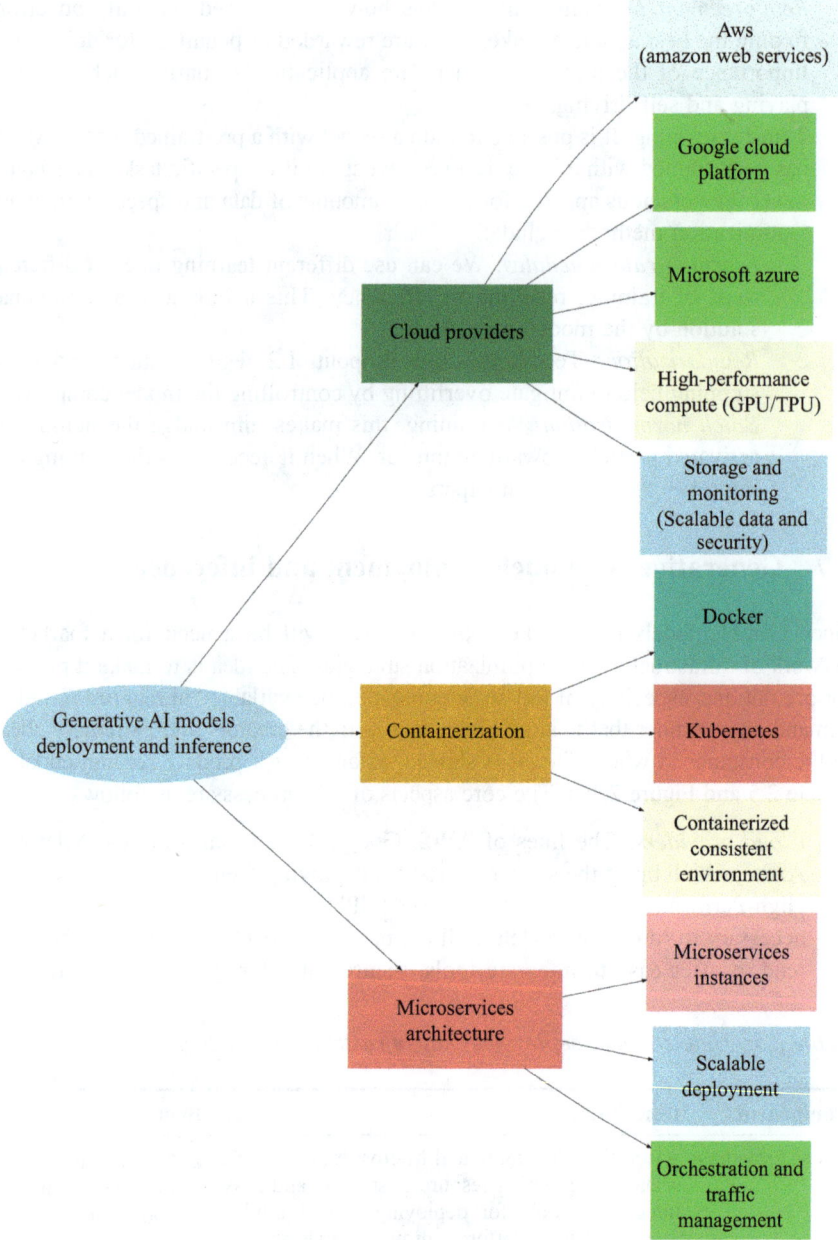

Figure 2.10   Generative AI models deployment and inference

companies can focus on building their AI apps and not maintaining their own hardware. Cloud platforms mean scalability [18]. So GenAI models can develop to suit data in different challenge levels and user demand all over the world [19].

- *Containerization:* Containerization approaches such as Docker and Kubernetes are usually employed to encapsulate GenAI models and their dependencies, running as a portable container and running consistently across different environments (e.g., clouds, on-premises servers, etc.)

  o *Docker:* Create the same environment your model will run in when development, QC, and production will reduce load variances.

  o Kubernetes: can manage these containers with Kubernetes; it can be used to deploy them automagically and can also handle scaling of resources, orchestration of traffic between different containers, and monitoring health between each & every pair at low and mid-level. Do that regularly, a job no human could do efficiently.

  o *Microservices architecture*: GenAI models can be implemented as microservices, which can scale in terms of instances/not instances and maintenance as well.

- *Edge computing:* Current edge applications with small scans – such as unmanned vehicles, real-time recommendations, and terminal-side GenAI applications – are in urgent demand. Edge computing places the model closer to the data source, reducing dependence on cloud infrastructure and minimizing the latency associated with sending and receiving requests. It was very recently pointed out to me how completely essential this can be in fast decision-making or even in areas where internet connection doesn't exist or is as hard as rocks.

  o *Low latency:* The data is processed at the edge, resulting in a faster response time.

  o *Less reliant on clouds:* Bandwidth, transmission data, and when to transmit become much less of a factor.

  o *Real-time processing:* Anywhere applications, such as AR/VR, IoT, or autonomous systems, can make real-time decisions now.

- Inference

  The single step of simulating our pre-tuned GenAI model to produce real-time forecasts or new data points (e.g., new text sequences). We assume the generated text sequences are a visible representation of the unobservable event of interest. Furthermore, the potential size and complexity of these models show just how important it is to minimize time to inference to ensure the model can actually be used (Table 2.6).

  o *Quantization:* Method to lower computational precision of model parameters (e.g., 32-bit floating to 8-bit integers), reducing model size and accelerating inference (while typically incurring a minimal loss in accuracy).

  o *Pruning:* It is a technique that removes unnecessary weights or connections from the model (those that do not influence the output greatly). This decreases the size of the model and its computational costs, and the latter enables making the inference faster.

Table 2.6   Inference and optimization techniques for GenAI models

Technique	Description	Benefits
Inference	The process of using a pre-trained GenAI model to generate real-time outputs or predictions (e.g., text sequences).	• Real-time predictions • Allow models to be used for various applications, such as text generation
Quantization	Reduces the precision of model parameters (e.g., from 32-bit floating to 8-bit integers), reducing model size and accelerating inference with minimal accuracy loss.	• Faster inference • Reduced model size • Lower computational cost
Pruning	Removes unnecessary weights or connections in the model that do not significantly impact the output, reducing model size and computational costs.	• Improved efficiency • Faster processing • Reduced resource usage

Put another way, to ensure GenAI models work as effectively as possible and can be scaled, one needs solid infrastructure, optimization strategies, and decisions about cloud, containerization, and edge computing.

2.8   Generative AI system feedback loops and model refinement

If we are to have GenAI systems, that is, systems that keep getting better over time and above their current level, they will require continuous adjustments, the very things that make up a well-crafted feedback loop. Feedback loops allow the model to learn from users' experiences with it, its own performance metrics, and new data. We can define the main constituents of a feedback loop, as presented by Table 2.7, as follows.

- *User feedback:* User feedback is a valuable resource to help better the GenAI models. Real-time feedback from users once a model is deployed on whether the output is wrong, garbled, or biased, or limited in various ways will indicate the points of failure for developers. There will be feedback in various guides: from real users, small statistics, and studies based on actual observation. For example, if the signal tells us that you believe AI-generated text "is not coherent or relevant," that type of feedback acts as a signpost for where the model currently needs improvement to continue.
  - *Instant feedback:* Users can provide ratings or comments for generated content.
  - *Implicit feedback:* Analyze users' behaviors on the content produced, including click-through rates and time spent reading.
- Performance metrics: Performance metrics are critical drivers for the measurement of how the GenAI model performs in the field. When it comes to

Table 2.7   GenAI model: important constituents of feedback loops

Component	Description	Type	Example
User feedback	Real-time feedback from users about model outputs, including their quality, relevance, and coherence. This feedback highlights model failures and areas for improvement.	• Instant feedback • Implicit feedback	• Instant: User ratings or comments on generated content. • Implicit: Analyzing behaviors like click-through rates or time spent on content.
Performance metrics	Quantitative indicators that measure the model's effectiveness, guiding improvements based on predefined metrics like accuracy and recall.	• Accuracy • Precision and Recall • F1 Score • BLEU Score	• Accuracy: Model's prediction vs actual result. • BLEU: Evaluates the quality of text generated compared to human references.
Model retraining	The process of updating the model with new data or feedback to ensure its continued relevance and effectiveness.	• More learning • Active learning • Ongoing learning	• More learning: Adding new data to update the model. • Active learning: Selecting useful data for retraining to reduce large datasets.

testing the quality of model output, we must keep track of metrics such as accuracy, precision, recall-F1 scores, and BLEU scores for text. Scrutinizers of these metrics yield a numerical compass for improving models.

o   *Accuracy:* Describes how well the model's prediction matches with actual result.

o   *Precision and recall:* "Precision" is the fraction of generated interesting records that are relevant, and "Recall" is the fraction of relevant interesting records that were retrieved.

o   *F1 score:* It is the harmonic mean of precision and recall.

o   *BLEU score:* This is used in language models to evaluate the quality of a generated text in relation to the human quality given, with respect to references.

• *Model retraining:* GenAI systems require the continual feed of new data and feedback to remain operational. Model retraining learns new (user) feedback with new data for a model. This subsequently reduces the risk of systems breaking and becoming obsolete and allows redesigned models to be still able to satisfy present-day needs and, to a degree, keep up with technology. The retraining can be full retraining (from scratch) or more learning (from fine-tuning a pre-trained model with new data). Furthermore, active learning techniques could be employed for ranking and labeling the most useful data for retraining.

Table 2.8   Model refinement and improvement techniques for GenAI

Technique	Description	Benefit	Example
Feedback integration	Incorporating user feedback and performance metrics into the model for ongoing improvement.	• Helps identify areas of failure and improvement.	• Feedback from users about model coherence and relevance.
Model retraining	Regularly updating the model with new data and feedback to prevent obsolescence and ensure the model meets current needs.	• Ensures the model stays updated and relevant over time.	• Fine-tuning a model with new data to adapt to user needs and trends.
Optimization	Using active learning to prioritize the most valuable data for retraining the model, reducing the need for large datasets.	• Reduces the resource and time requirement for retraining.	• Using active learning to select critical examples for training, reducing data labeling efforts.
Continuous Monitoring	Monitoring model performance consistently to spot changes in user behavior or content quality that might require adjustments.	• Allows for proactive model adjustments.	• Regular performance tracking and quick model refinements based on emerging user needs.

- ○ *More learning:* Incorporate new data to refresh the model without restarting from the beginning.
- ○ *Active learning:* Choose the most helpful examples for retraining, reducing the necessity of large labeled datasets.
- ○ *Ongoing learning:* Feeding your model with new data when it is coming to you, making the whole process automatic.

With effective user feedback, ongoing monitoring of performance measures, and occasional retraining in response to new data, the GenAI system would keep on evolving and produce improved outputs and effectively serve user interests. Table 2.8 presents the model refinement and improvement techniques for GenAI.

2.9   Conclusion

Generative AI technical elements: In general, all these elements of generative AI technical elements science can be thought to form interdependent parts: data processing model, architecture, teaching routines, and deployment strategy. These are its organizing principles. With all of these combined, it is a genuine mechanism that can lead to the ability to bring about new forms of realistic and inspired, even entirely original, content in text, image, music, and code, rather than having to continue to reprocess more of the same past on into eternity.

At a more fundamental level, data processing ensures that the raw data is translated into something literal you can run with, while model architecture is also what's educating AIs and teaching them to generate totally brand-new data. Models like GANs, VAEs, and Transformers are available to generalize these patterns on covariate-rich context-sensitive high-quality sampling outputs. Training technologies (optimization algorithms, regularization techniques) adjust the model for the shadow of model performance. This is what enables it to generalize and generate content gracefully that humans have come to expect as well. But once these models are trained, deployment patterns can guarantee these models are big and efficient when they need to be and return outputs in real time as well. That can happen in the cloud now, thx, and future people (all people, in fact) will never again allow themselves to be sheep to the carriers.

The next chapter in GenAI's evolution will see models that are faster, smarter, and better at multitasking. Simultaneously, increasingly there will be a focus on erasing the ethical shadows hanging over AI development – to ensure these systems are used responsibly, transparently. This handwringing requires that we will have to struggle with bias, fairness, privacy, and consequences for society more broadly that arise as AI comes into common use. Therefore, generative AI has a glorious future, with many breakthroughs to be expected, in both industry and art applications. Here, what is required is full foresight, but also, with the coming down the pike forbearance to prepare for what is soon to come; it must be taken as seasoned patience that yields golden fruits for all.

References

[1]   Rashid SF, Duong-Trung N, and Pinkwart N. Generative AI in education: Technical foundations, applications, and challenges. In *Artificial Intelligence and Education-Shaping the Future of Learning*. 2024. IntechOpen. doi:10. 5772/intechopen.1005402.

[2]   Huang K, Wang Y, and Zhang X. Foundations of generative AI. In *Generative AI Security: Theories and Practices* 2024 (pp. 3–30). Cham: Springer Nature Switzerland.

[3]   Corchado JM, López S, Garcia R, and Chamoso P. Generative artificial intelligence: Fundamentals. *ADCAIJ: Advances in Distributed Computing and Artificial Intelligence Journal*. 2023;12:e31704.

[4]   Narapareddy VS. Generative AI and foundation models. *Universal Library of Innovative Research and Studies*. 2025;2(2):7–21.

[5]   Ardi N. Generative AI: A comprehensive review of foundational models and emerging methods. *Applied Systems and Technologies Journal (ASTJ)*. 2025; 1(1):1–6.

[6]   Babu T, and Nair RR. Foundations of generative AI. In *The Pioneering Applications of Generative AI* 2024 (pp. 136–166). IGI Global.

[7]   Banh L, and Strobel G. Generative artificial intelligence. *Electronic Markets*. 2023;33(1):63.

[8]   Hacker P, Engel A, Hammer S, and Mittelstadt B. Introduction to the foundations and regulation of generative AI. Available at SSRN. 2025 Feb 14.

[9]   Mitra R, and Zualkernan I. Music generation using deep learning and generative AI: A systematic review. *IEEE Access*. 2025;13:18079–18106.

[10] Fruehauf E, Beman-Cavallaro A, and Schmidt L. Developing a foundation for the informational needs of generative AI users through the means of established interdisciplinary relationships. *The Journal of Academic Librarianship*. 2024;50(3):102876.

[11] Manganelli A. Foundation models and generative AI applications: What competitive concerns? Available at SSRN 5242028. 2025.

[12] Hacker P, Engel A, and Mauer M. Regulating ChatGPT and other large generative AI models. In *Proceedings of the 2023 ACM Conference on Fairness, Accountability, and Transparency* 2023 (pp. 1112–1123).

[13] Chen XA, Burke J, Du R, *et al.* Next steps for human-centered generative AI: A technical perspective. *arXiv* preprint arXiv:2306.15774. 2023.

[14] Salloum SA, Al-Marzouqi A, Gaber T, Masa'deh RE, and Shaalan K. Foundations and frontiers: The evolution and impact of generative AI technologies. In *Generative AI in Creative Industries* 2025 (pp. 3–12). Cham: Springer Nature Switzerland.

[15] Trigka M, and Dritsas E. The evolution of generative AI: Trends and applications. *IEEE Access*. 2025;13:98504–98529.

[16] Seth B, Dalal S, Jaglan V, Le DN, Mohan S, and Srivastava G. Integrating encryption techniques for secure data storage in the cloud. *Transactions on Emerging Telecommunications Technologies*. 2022;33(4):e4108.

[17] Lilhore UK, Simaiya S, Dalal S, Alshuhail A, and Almusharraf A. A post-quantum hybrid encryption framework for securing biometric data in consumer electronics. *IEEE Transactions on Consumer Electronics*. 2025; 71(3):8289–8297.

[18] Onyema EM, Dalal S, Romero CA, Seth B, Young P, and Wajid MA. Design of intrusion detection system based on cyborg intelligence for security of cloud network traffic of smart cities. *Journal of Cloud Computing*. 2022; 11(1):26.

[19] Dalal S, Manoharan P, Lilhore UK, *et al.* Extremely boosted neural network for more accurate multi-stage Cyber attack prediction in cloud computing environment. *Journal of Cloud Computing*. 2023;12(1):1–22.

Chapter 3

Generative AI for image and video processing

Artificial intelligence is interwoven into our daily lives, often operating behind the scenes to shape our interactions with technology [1]. Generative AI, a subset of artificial intelligence, is rapidly evolving and demonstrating impressive capabilities across various domains, including image and video processing [2,3]. Generative AI possesses the remarkable ability to produce high-quality artistic media, encompassing visual arts, concept art, music, fiction, literature, video, and animation [4]. This technology excels at creating novel data samples that closely resemble the examples it was trained in. This capability has profound implications for how we create, manipulate, and interact with visual content [5]. Generative AI models use advanced deep learning, transfer learning algorithms, and machine learning techniques to discern patterns and relationships from existing data to generate new content that mirrors the style, tone, or structure of the original [6]. Generative AI's ability to learn from diverse datasets and produce a broad spectrum of multimedia outputs offers significant potential for automating content creation, personalizing user experiences, and unlocking new creative avenues for businesses and individuals [7,8]. Generative AI is poised to reshape industries from entertainment and marketing to healthcare and education, as well as virtual reality (Figure 3.1) [9].

Generative AI is redefining the creative process, becoming a new tool for media professionals focused on visual content creation. In the worlds of image and video processing, it has become a font of innovation – letting machines not only analyze or interpret visual data, but also generate fresh, often photorealistic content from scratch or with very little human input. Through models such as [9] GANs, VAEs, transformer-based models, and diffusion models, generative AI can create human faces that never existed, animate photos, edit videos, and create a full movie scene from a single text prompt [10].

The creation of images and videos was historically a resource-intensive endeavor, one that involved studios, their lights and actors, and costly hardware. Generative AI is challenging this status quo by providing tools for creators to produce such effects using code and computation [11]. Such a democratization of content production revolutionizes across the industry field, be it film, game, journalism, or education.

This study will give an in-depth overview of the theoretical frameworks of this technology and its architecture and show the actual changes occurring now in the field of image and video processing [12,13]. Generative AI was more recently

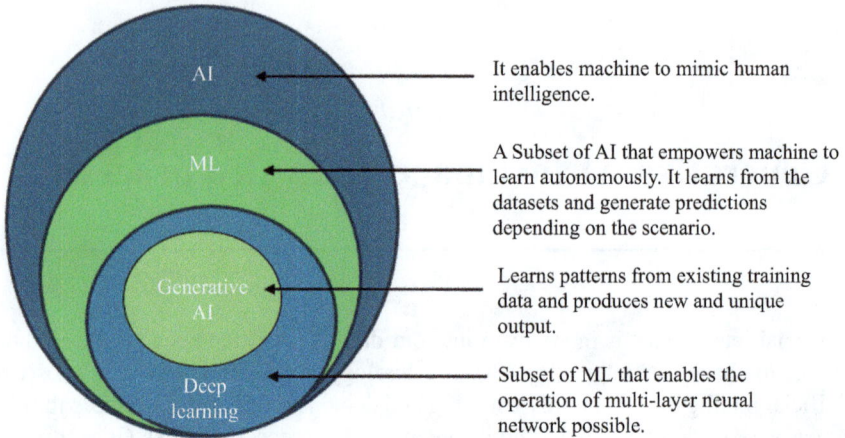

Figure 3.1   Generative AI's relationship with AI

leveraged to transform how brands engage with their potential clients, creating new types of advertising strategies and media. Compared to other advertising formats, AI-driven image and video processing is examined with respect to its technical advancements and the broader implications of generative AI. This chapter addresses the complexities of video synthesis and manipulation while highlighting recent innovations in the creation of realistic video content.

In this chapter, the evolution and the paradigm shift of the generative AI is explored. It also highlights the technological changes and leaps that have spurred the creation of the image and the video content based on reality. As we get into the effects and synthesization of the video and alteration of the same, we can realize that the functionalities of the generative AI go beyond the existing usage of the generative AI. There are multiple methods that are actually being used in AI usage, such as frame interpolation, neural video synthesis, and motion transfer, all of which play a role in the smooth generation of realistic video clips and manipulation of existing video content.

Frame interpolation enables the generation of intermediate frames between existing frames, resulting in smoother motion and reduced temporal artifacts, while neural video synthesis employs deep learning models to generate entirely new video content from learned data representations. Motion transfer is a method that allows the transfer of one object's movement to the other, resulting in the original animations that raises the question of our perception of authentic visual media [15]. Navigating all these developments is really an important source so that we can confront the wider implications of generative AI for society, such as ethical dimensions to content authenticity and potential misuse in the production of deepfakes. The development of these themes encourages the technical visuality of the generative AI and also highlights the role of the creators and the developers in building a future where such high-powered technologies are employed ethically and constructively [16].

This further study works on the objective to give an all-around view of the state-of-the-art of generative AI applied to image and video processing, both highlighting its revolutionary potential and the challenges, considering the impact which is directly on society. As AI continues to evolve as a dynamic and ongoing process, it presents both significant opportunities and challenges for developing reality-based content. For example, the application of generative models in video streaming has the potential to transform viewer experiences by enabling dynamic, real-time adaptations in response to audience demand. But the innovation also creates important questions regarding the authenticity of the live material and the possibility of manipulation, especially in the applications, and such developments require a complete framework to have a secured functionality. The continuous evolution of generative AI not only extends the branches and the limitations of creativity but also forces us to redefine visual trustworthiness in an era where technology is capable of being so close to reality.

3.1 Generative AI: an overview

Generative AI refers to algorithms and models that can generate new content based on the prompt and the data for which the algorithm is trained for. In the traditional AI model, it majorly focuses on the classification and the prediction tasks; generative models actually create new data instances that collate the training data. Generative AI is able to create fully loaded charts and also images and videos as prompt demands, whereas traditional AI is only trained to show the data in the form of text. Generative AI is able to create new data inferences that resemble the training data. High-quality images and video generations are only possible with the help of technological advancements and advancements in algorithms and neural network architectures, which overall support content creation abilities in different types of media.

In addition, these advances have important ethical and social implications that require serious consideration of their effect on employment and privacy [13]. With the advancement of generative AI, it is important to meet the challenges it brings, especially in terms of privacy rights and the prospect of bias in created materials. The stakeholders will have to initiate open conversations to see that the technology is produced and used ethically and responsibly to help create a reliable environment that blends innovation with social values [18]. It will become pertinent to resolve these issues for the sustainable development of generative AI technology across sectors.

3.1.1 Key technologies in generative AI

Generative AI is the advanced technology that completely relies on advanced neural network models and designs to produce various kinds of updated content. This technology is evolving and making changes in many fields, including IT operations and Natural Language Processing (NLP). It enables the creation of text, images, and code, showing its innovative role in all the theoretical and practical implications. The ongoing development is actually reshaping the future of the industry with the evolution of the solutions and the improvisation in productivity across all sectors. As it is progressing, generative AI is also having certain challenges as it is disrupting the traditional creative practices, such as providing new ways for artists, musicians, manufacturers, designers, and authors to expand their boundaries of expression. This paradigm shift challenges the old considerations of the authorship and creativity, which have raised questions about the future of human creativity and how technology applies to art.

The intersection between technology and creativity has highlighted the need for security and ethical considerations to use generative AI and its advances in art and culture. To overcome the issues of the ethical challenges, which is necessary to ensure that all human creativity is being replaced by the content that is produced with the generative AI tool. The basis of generative AI in image and video processing rests on a number of fundamental technologies.

3.1.2   Generative adversarial networks (GANs)

Introduced by Ian Goodfellow in 2014, GANs are a breakthrough in generative modeling. The GAN model consists of two neural networks – the generator and the discriminator – that engage in a game-theoretic setting and try to improve in a competitive manner.

(a) *Generator:* Accepts random noise as input and attempts to generate realistic images.
(b) *Discriminator:* Attempts to distinguish between real images (actual images from the training data) and fake images (images generated by the generator).

Developed by Ian Goodfellow and co-workers in 2014 [16], GANs are two neural networks – a generator and a discriminator – racing against each other. The generator produces synthetic data, while the discriminator assesses its reality. This adversarial process results in generating highly realistic images and videos. Applications: Deepfakes, Style transfer, and synthetic training data. Famous models: StyleGAN2, StyleGAN3, CycleGAN

3.1.3   Variational autoencoders (VAEs)

VAEs are another type of generative models that learn to map input data into a lower-dimensional representation and then reverse-map it back to the original space. This method is specifically used to generate new points that are similar to the training set. VAEs are a type of probabilistic generative model that learns a latent space from input data to generate new data points similar to the training data. They consist of:

• Encoder: Transforms input to a latent space representation
• Decoder: reconstructs input from the latent representation
• Applications
• Image editing
• Denoising
• Semi-supervised learning

Diffusion models: Diffusion models have emerged in the past year to a lot of popularity for their capacity to create high-quality images by building up from random noise to coherent visual information incrementally through a sequence of iterative steps. Diffusion models are one of the most promising developments in generative AI. They learn to reverse a process of gradually adding noise to data. At inference, they progressively denoise a random signal back to reconstruct intricate structures. Examples: Stable Diffusion, DALL·E 2, Imagen.

3.2 Applications of generative AI in image and video processing

Generative AI is a subset of AI technologies that allows machines to work according to the prompt given to the tool to create and display the content that is desired by the user by learning the patterns of the data from the already existing data. Generative AI simplifies the data and also displays the data in categories. It has an advantage that it creates the content which has already been reassembled from what it was trained on.

The complete research says that the data generated by generative AI is totally for the use of text applications, due to which the industry is actually adopting this. Also, there are certain tools that actually produce the authentic data which can be used for further processing and being implemented in the adoption by various categories of the industry. There are multiple applications that are used for the advancements in creating content in the formats of texts, audio, video, and also visuals (Figure 3.2).

- *Audio applications:* AI can generate music and content in human-like speech, which works on the content which is based on the authentic audio creation

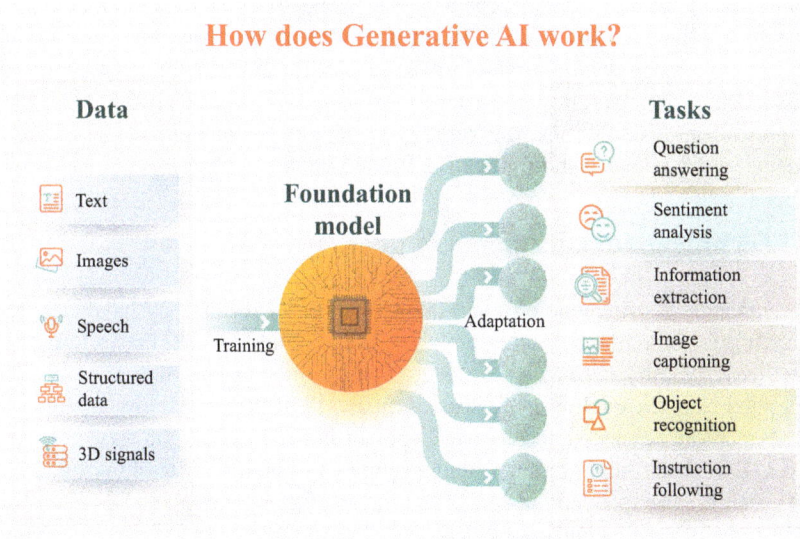

Figure 3.2 Applications of Gen AI

based on the demand of the user, and also it is a tool which is reading the algorithm and implements the use of various function in ways beyond the thoughts of the user.

- *Text applications:* The text content creation application is creating the research and work more rigorously as the content that is shared and used in a vast way, also, it helps the user to work efficiently to use the work in the best ways where the new approach of the work is used and followed.

- *Conversational applications:* All the content in these types of applications is actually based on the conversational formats, where the content is based on the applications that are either used for better conversation, so that the relevant content can be shared and used for any conversation in a professional way, as expected by certain users.

- *Data augmentation:* This model is really relevant where the relevant content is scarce, which will definitely change or augment the techniques, and the models are actually more trained to display the relevant content that is expected for the use of various users.

- *Video/visual application:* These are applications which are expected to display the visualization of the data and need to be matched with the expectation of the users so that they can be easily mapped and used for the expected reality of the future in terms of the visual effects and also as per the quality of the content displayed in the video which is much higher than what a user can create. The model is well trained so that the output is not at all affected by any other keywords, and also the quality of the output should not be tampered.

- *Application to create images:* the realistic images, which are actually a conversion of a text to an image with the help of the prompt given for displaying the drawings and the images in a better and more significant manner. The unique models like the GANs models are used to fill the gaps between the text and visual outputs, which broadens the scope of creative applications, also these applications are crucial to ensure human and machine contributions, which are recognized and also protected. All these technologies are vital for addressing the changing landscape of intellectual property rights. Also, these applications must ensure the right goal of addressing unique challenges to develop the relevant and innovative frameworks.

3.3   Technical advancements in generative AI

The advancements in technology and the growth in AI technology have advanced the capabilities of generating high-quality of images and videos. This section of the chapter majorly emphasizes the key developments of the technology. Therefore, the paradigm shift in the evolution has shaped the future of the industry by enabling the creation of more advanced and relevant content in the fields of the arts, functions, pictures, flowcharts, and graphical representations of any work to showcase.

This shift has expanded the creative horizons of the industry and has also raised the questions of content authenticity and the role of a user in creativity. The growth has integrated the future endeavors pretest both for the challenges and also the opportunities, making it essential to examine its influence on the traditional practices. The change in the relationship between technology and creativity is purely working in the hands of the quality of art, but also prompts are evaluation of authorship and ownership in the digital realm [20]. With the change in the landscape of the creative output, it is very critical to create the functionalities and also the result based on the requirements. There are certain protocols and architectures that have resulted in the relevant outputs based on the functionalist, which is given below.

3.3.1   Enhanced model architectures

The creation of Generative Adversarial Networks (GANs) and Variational Autoencoders (VAEs), which have heavily reinforced the generative capabilities of AI in multiple sectors., with the advancements in the developments this model is able to work on a more realistic image creation with better augmented functionalities and also the usage is applied in the novel approach in areas of gaming and medicine which has demonstrated the change in the potential of generative AI. In addition, the combination of GANs and VAEs has given rise to hybrid models that draw on the advantages of each strategy, again raising the bar for the quality and diversity of produced outputs. Additionally, building explainable AI (XAI) frameworks will be critical to inform about how their information affects AI-based decisions in their treatment and the associated risks.

3.3.1.1   Progressive growing of GANs

This technology works with the advancements in the result, where the training methodology of GANs starts from the very low images, which progressively increase the resolution by adding loads of layers in the network, which will finally enhance the resolution and will produce the image in the proper way. This enhances the technology to move from the large-scale structure of the image distribution and shifts the attention to the increasingly finer scale detail. There is a use of progressive training, which has loads of uses and functionalities as well. With the use of this technology healthcare can also be used in the advanced sector that requires precision and ethical consideration.

3.3.1.2   Self-attention mechanisms

The implementation of self-attention mechanisms in GANs and VAEs has enhanced the models' capacity to capture long-range dependencies in images, resulting in more coherent and contextually relevant outputs. The use of self-attention mechanisms in GANs and VAEs has enhanced the capacity of the models to learn long-range dependencies in images, resulting in more coherent and contextually meaningful outputs [17]. These mechanisms actually enable the high-quality images that are highly important for medical use, and with the incorporation of the self-attention mechanism, it improves the medical imaging. Self-attention in GANs has many benefits, which have improvised the sector of health with the use of improved generation quality, long-range dependencies, and state-of-the-art results.

3.3.2   Unsupervised learning

Since models can learn from large amounts of data without the need for human annotation, methods that use unlabeled data for training have grown in popularity. Especially in high-quality output-based applications like image production and data augmentation, these techniques are essential for enhancing generative model performance. They have also been successful in mitigating some of the drawbacks of the traditional supervised learning paradigm. Researchers can use generative modeling techniques to find novel ways to synthesize data with varied distributions. Furthermore, these difficulties have been substantially mitigated by the creation of models like GANs and VAEs, which have improved the variety and caliber of outputs produced. Along with improving the quality of the data produced, these advancements expand the use of generative models in a variety of fields, such as image.

Additionally, the development of models such as VAEs and GANs has greatly helped to circumvent these challenges, improving the diversity and quality of outputs generated. These improvements not only enhance the quality of generated data but also broaden the scope of generative models in numerous applications, including image classification and video generation. These advancements highlight the revolutionary ability of generative models, especially GANs, to generate high-fidelity outputs and tackle inherent issues like mode collapse and training instability.

3.4   Real-time processing capabilities

Real-time image and video processing demands have led to innovations in hardware and software optimizations [12]. Acceleration through Graphics Processing Units (GPUs) and AI-specific accelerators has made it possible to have lower training and inference times, which is manageable for deploying generative models in real-time applications like video games and live streaming. In order to maximize effectiveness and decision-making across applications, they are all crucial. These real-time computing capabilities might be further improved by fusing AI with edge computing, which would ensure low latency in critical decision-making scenarios [9]. In addition to increasing operational effectiveness, the integration of these technologies makes it possible to develop personalized healthcare solutions that are suited to each patient's needs. By combining AI and edge computing, a more robust healthcare environment is produced, allowing for the prompt implementation of focused interventions to address individual patient circumstances. This responsiveness is essential because, particularly in emergency care settings where time is of the basic terms, successful interventions can lead to better patient outcomes [12].

3.5   Broader implications of generative AI

The disruptions related to AI are not only limited to the functionalities but also go beyond its technical innovations, which are affecting multiple domains and bringing the relevant questions to the front. They are efficient for improving the decision-making across many applications such as health care and autonomous systems. All these have the ability to make it possible to quickly analyze data, creating timely responses that can dramatically enhance patient care and operational efficiency in healthcare environments. Adding to this, the use of AI with edge computing can further streamline the real-time processing functions to ensure the limitations of latency in critical decision-making applications. With the combination of these technologies, it not only improves the operational efficiency but also leads to working on personalized solutions to the various individual requirements.

With the extension of this, the implementation of AI-based analytics can evolve the way various health care departments are working and also where the patients can also be demanding as per their requirements, and this act not only takes care of the need but also the outcomes. The use of AI in healthcare not only improves operational effectiveness but also requires strong training plans to prepare professionals with the ability to handle these new technologies effectively [18]. The broader implications of generative AI across multiple sectors, including economic, ethical, and societal dimensions, are summarized in Table 3.1.

3.5.1 Finance and marketing

Generative AI is making a few changes as they are updating the risks along with the security and also enhancing the fraud detection techniques along with the aspects of the resolution [16]. In the marketing aspects where the AI tool provides specialized content based on the demand and the requirement. The personalized touch is the key to using this application.

3.5.2 Media and entertainment

In media and entertainment, they are providing the content based on the customers' demand and create a realistic situation which helps the user to work on the content based on the use and the adaptability [19].

3.5.3 Education and training

The advancements in the model for adoption in the education sector, with generative AI playing a role, where the use is to update and adapt the functionalities based on learning and applying. Usage of AR and VR has also given an edge to the education area, which has not only targeted the students but also the generation of any age bracket [20].

3.5.4 Fashion and manufacturing

Using these models, manufacturing can also be useful as it has created designs that are unique and also enhances the model to find the quality and apply the aspects based on the future trends and demands.

Table 3.1   Broader implications of generative AI

Dimension	Implication	Opportunities	Risks/ Challenges	Examples	Stakeholders affected
Economic impact	Reshapes industries, automates workflows, and creates new markets	Increased productivity, cost savings, and new business models	Job displacement, monopolization by big tech	AI-driven content creation, automated design, and customer support chatbots	Businesses, employees, entrepreneurs
Social implications	Influences creativity, communication, and cultural practices	Democratization of creativity, personalized experiences	Deepfakes, misinformation, and social manipulation	AI-generated art, personalized media feeds, synthetic influencers	Society, communities, media consumers
Ethical concerns	Raises fairness, transparency, and accountability issues	Bias detection tools, ethical AI frameworks	Bias reinforcement, unfair outcomes, copyright misuse	Generative AI in recruitment, biased training datasets	Policymakers, ethicists, and AI developers
Legal and regulatory	Requires new laws for intellectual property, liability, and data governance	Clearer accountability, protection of IP rights	Ambiguity of AI authorship, cross-border compliance	AI-authored books, disputes over ownership of generated content	Governments, courts, and legal institutions
Education and learning	Redefines teaching, learning, and assessment practices	AI tutors, personalized education, adaptive learning	Plagiarism, reduced critical thinking, and academic integrity	ChatGPT in classrooms, automated essay writing, skill-gap risks	Students, teachers, and universities
Healthcare and science	Advances in discovery, diagnostics, and medical simulations	AI-designed drugs, synthetic datasets, faster research	Ethical use of synthetic data, reliability of models	Protein folding predictions, generative drug design	Doctors, patients, pharma companies
Culture and creativity	Expands artistic possibilities and content production	New genres of art, film pre-visualization, and co-creation	Undermining originality, the devaluation of human art	AI-composed music, film scripts, digital storytelling	Artists, musicians, cultural institutions
Security and privacy	Introduces risks of malicious exploitation and identity misuse	Advanced fraud detection, anomaly monitoring	Cybercrime, phishing, voice cloning, and synthetic IDs	Deepfake scams, AI-driven cyberattacks, fake identities	Cybersecurity agencies, individuals

3.6   Video synthesis and manipulation challenges

The advances in video editing and synthesis from AI have both immense potential and serious challenges, primarily in ensuring realism and temporal coherence. To overcome these challenges, studies still attempt to improve texture details and the limitations of current generative models using novel architectures and loss functions that optimize fidelity in generated material and minimize artifacts. More research into such approaches will be crucial to developing more robust AI systems with the capacity to produce high-quality synthetic videos capable of meeting the demands of a variety of applications. It is critical and majorly crucial to know the ethical implications of producing the synthetic video as technology becomes more relevant and applicable for the users to work [20]. As video synthesis continues to advance, growth is much associated with an ethical framework for use and social accountability (Figure 3.3).

The framework needs to address many new challenges and the dangers of misinformation and privacy violations while ensuring the benefits of AI-generated content that are realized without compromising ethical privacy and integrity. To establish guidelines in using AI with certain protocols always balances the innovations and also ensures that the video synthesis brings improvements that do not aggravate the existing problems.

With the assurance of establishing media literacy among citizens can also equip the popularity to critically analyze synthetic content, thereby enhancing the resilience against disinformation and integrity of digitally advanced communication. The multi-layer approach not only solves the negative concerns but also fosters the content that needs to be updated and informed, which is more engaging to the public. Specifically, if we are considering the video data, we introduce the motion vector from the compressed form of video, which is explicitly based on the control signals to provide guidance regarding the temporal dynamics. Extensive results on using the generative AI suggest that the video composers are able to control certain issues of the spatial and temporal patterns simultaneously within a synthesized video in different forms, like text descriptions, sketch sequence, reference video, or even simply many hand-crafted options.

3.6.1 Temporal consistency

The consistency between the frames is the biggest concern, where the images are static and do not require any motion or continuity, whereas the videos are dynamic and need motion and continuity.

3.6.2 Realism and fidelity

To attain realism in the video is not only for the extremely high-quality motion dynamics but also for the visually based quality output where the model is demanded to create the aspects of lighting, shadows, and object interactions to produce convincing video content. Improved levels of physics-based rendering and motion modelling have helped raise the realism of generated videos [10].

3.6.3 Ethical considerations in video manipulation

Manipulations of the videos have raised issues of content and authenticity. With generative AI technologies, the ethical concerns are the prime measures that have a high chance of tampering with the contents and also misusing the data.

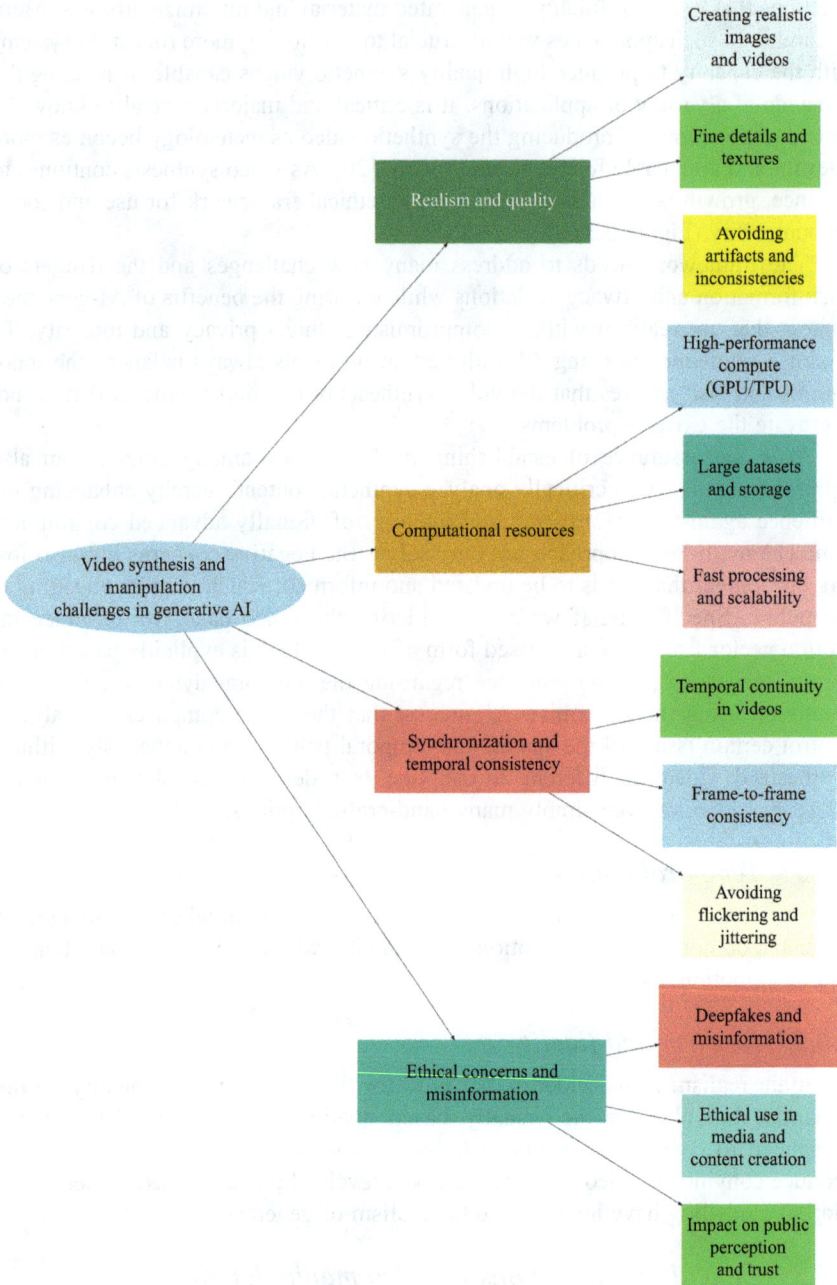

Figure 3.3   Video synthesis and manipulation challenges in generative AI

3.7   Development of producing realistic video material

The search for making realistic video content has spurred significant advances in generative AI techniques. This section discusses some of the most significant advances in this area (Figure 3.4). Integration of generative AI is revolutionizing video content creation, enhancing workflows, and enabling production of highly realistic and engaging multimedia experiences [15].

This shift not only simplifies the process of content production but also provides new opportunities for storytelling and audience interaction through immersive media. The ability of generative AI to produce customized and interactive multimedia content is revolutionizing how content is produced and consumed across disciplines [12]. As generative, these models allow educators to produce content-rich stories, making learning more interactive and effective through the use of advanced AI technologies. The ongoing evolution of generative AI not only enhances video quality but also facilitates interactive learning spaces, ultimately transforming teaching practice and the learning experience [12]. Such innovation represents a milestone in education where technology and creativity come together to improve learning and build more links with content. As generative AI evolves, it is crucial to explore its potential for multimedia storytelling, particularly in the learning setting, where it can increase learner engagement and understanding significantly.

The study of generative AI's impact on educational video content production showcases its ability to not only improve visual quality but also drive individualized learning experiences that cater to specific students' needs. This two-pronged concern with visual quality enhancement and individualized learning experience personalization renders generative AI a revolutionary force in modern education, which is transforming the method of knowledge transmission and understanding.

3.7.1   Frame interpolation

This is used to create the missing frames in a video, producing smoother motion and better frame rates. By using the optical flow estimation and all deep learning models, the researchers and the users have actually achieved seamless transitions with visual quality enhancements.

3.7.2   Motion transfer

This method has enabled the transfer of motion patterns from one video to another, emphasizing the dynamic content generation without the basic requirements of manual animation. The completely new video can be created with the help of the use of the characters or the objects, which would have increased the realism of the generated video.

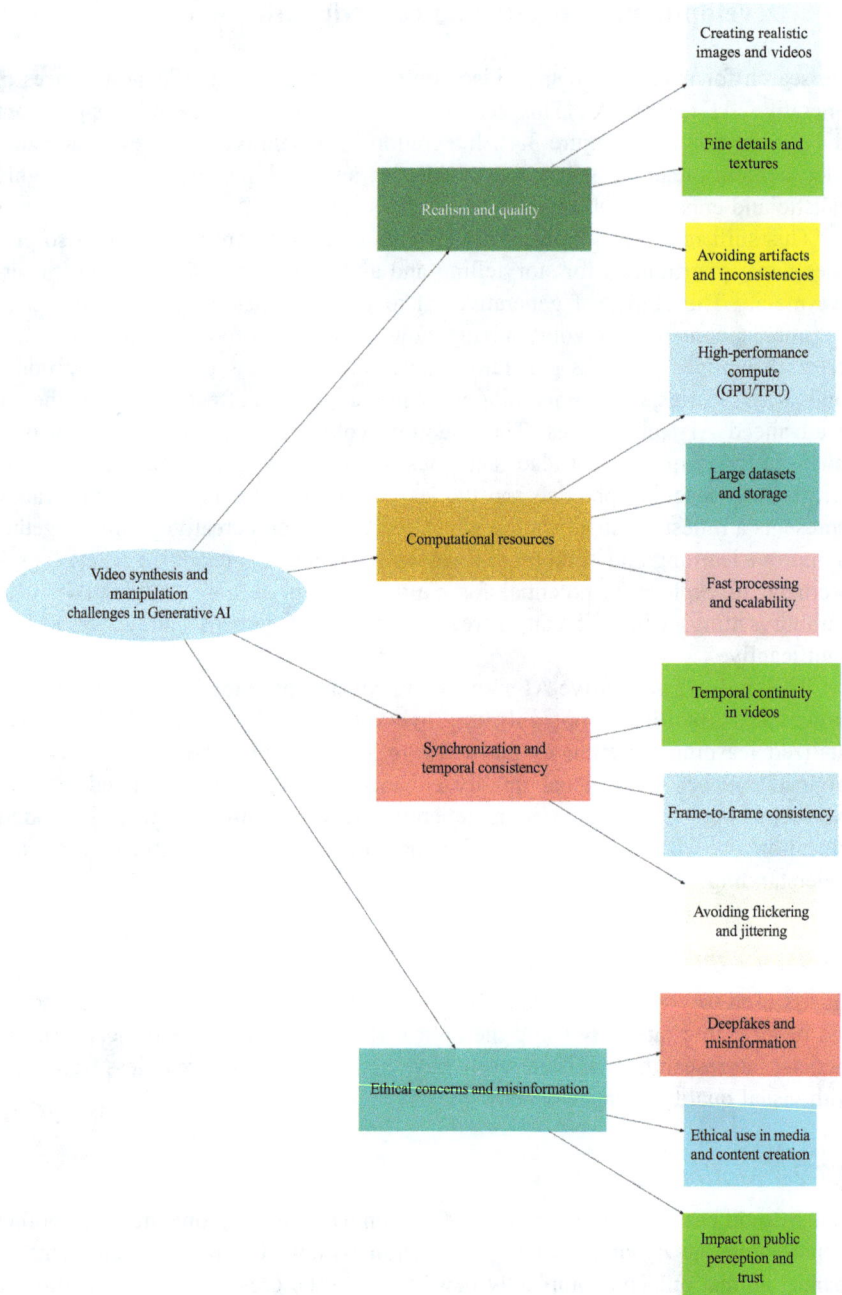

Creating realistic
images and videos

Fine details and
textures

Avoiding artifacts
and inconsistencies

Realism and quality

High-performance
compute
(GPU/TPU)

Large datasets
and storage

Fast processing
and scalability

Computational resources

Video synthesis and
manipulation
challenges in Generative AI

Temporal continuity
in videos

Frame-to-frame consistency

Synchronization and
temporal consistency

Avoiding flickering
and jittering

Deepfakes and
misinformation

Ethical use in media
and content creation

Ethical concerns and misinformation

Impact on public
perception and
trust

Figure 3.4   Development of producing realistic video material

3.8   Seamless video sequence techniques

Certain methods have been seen to produce continuous, natural video sequences and manipulate content previously recorded. are being researched more and more, particularly toward enhancing the end-user experience and efficiency (Figure 3.5).

These technologies not only simplify the production process but also allow for more interactive and customized content delivery, showcasing AI's potential to revolutionize the world of video production. With advancing AI, its use in video production processes is going to redefine creative workflows and enhance the quality of visual storytelling further [12]. The study of the AI functionality emphasizes the way in which AI is able to automate the functions and credibility of the response. The seamless transitions and smooth model functionality interpolate the new frames to maintain temporal consistency [11]. Diffusion models are the most useful formats of which have become leading methods for high-quality video synthesis by learning to

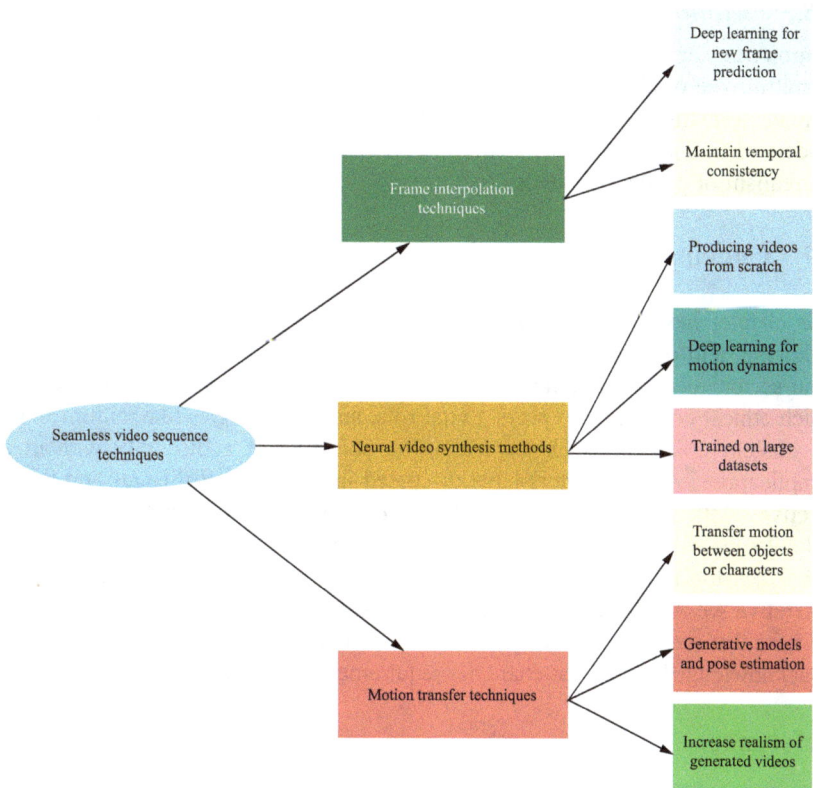

Figure 3.5   Seamless video sequence techniques

gradually reverse a process to add noise to the video. The techniques are majorly based on the datasets of the large video to produce. There are certain autoregressive models that have each frame generated based on the frames that come before it, the application has a strong impact which requires a strong narrative flow. Some of the most prominent methods are explained in this section.

3.8.1   Frame interpolation techniques

This technique uses deep learning to predict the new frames from the already existing ones. Through the analysis of the motion patterns and pixel data, all these models are able to modify and ensure that the frames are consistent.

3.8.2   Neural video synthesis methods

Neural video synthesis methods employ deep learning architecture to produce videos from scratch or under predefined conditions. Trained on large datasets, models can acquire intricate motion dynamics and produce realistic video sequences according to the desired properties.

3.8.3   Motion transfer techniques

Motion transfer methods allow the transfer of motion from one location to another, permitting the production of dynamic content without the necessity for long-lasting manual animation [14]. Researchers have used pose estimation and generative models to find ways to transfer motion between objects or characters, increasing the realism of produced videos.

3.9   Conclusion

This chapter has completely defined the challenges to the traditional concepts of authorship and originality of using generative AI in many areas like the entertainment sector, media, marketing, and manufacturing. These are the various sectors in which ethical consideration plays a vital role, and technologies like multimedia and the content creation, which have a prime objective of authenticity without any complications. As the authors have discussed in depth the challenges and the perspective of the complete AI tool, which has ensured the cooperative effort of the technologies, artists, and various creators in the marketing of other innovative sectors to balance the innovations and also the ethical considerations while the usage of generative AI. All these approaches and aspects have actually assisted in minimizing the risks that are related to AI-generated content and that can create content that can be acknowledged in the fast-changing requirements and needs of the user.

References

[1]   Othman I. AI video editor: A conceptual review in generative arts. In *Proceedings of the 3rd International Conference on Creative Multimedia* 2023 Nov 14 (p. 16).

[2] Chen Y, Ni C, and Wang H. AdaptiveGenBackend A scalable architecture for low-latency generative AI video processing in content creation platforms. *Annals of Applied Sciences*. 2024;5(1):1–17.

[3] Akhlaq A, and Liu TA. Text-to-video generation—A cutting-edge generative AI application. *JAMA Ophthalmology*. 2025;143(8):632–633.

[4] Aldausari N, Sowmya A, Marcus N, and Mohammadi G. Video generative adversarial networks: A review. *ACM Computing Surveys (CSUR)*. 2022; 55(2):1–25.

[5] Vijay K, Berna E, and Samuel P. Generative AI in visual media for image, video, and animation generation. In *Fusion of Multimodal Generative AI and Blockchain Technology in Digital Media* 2026 (pp. 181–208). IGI Global Scientific Publishing.

[6] Bansal G, Nawal A, Chamola V, and Herencsar N. Revolutionizing visuals: The role of generative AI in modern image generation. *ACM Transactions on Multimedia Computing, Communications and Applications*. 2024;20(11): 1–22.

[7] Sharma A, Jindal N, and Rana PS. Potential of generative adversarial net algorithms in image and video processing applications–a survey. *Multimedia Tools and Applications*. 2020;79(37):27407–27437.

[8] Husac F, and Simian D. Enhancing live performances with AI-driven visuals: A machine learning and generative AI approach. In *International Conference on Modelling and Development of Intelligent Systems* 2024 (pp. 105–122). Cham: Springer Nature Switzerland.

[9] Kumar S, Musharaf D, Musharaf S, and Sagar AK. A comprehensive review of the latest advancements in large generative AI models. In *International Conference on Advanced Communication and Intelligent Systems* 2023 (pp. 90–103). Cham: Springer Nature Switzerland.

[10] Gozalo-Brizuela R, and Garrido-Merchán EC. A survey of generative AI applications. *arXiv* preprint arXiv:2306.02781. 2023 June 5.

[11] Du Y. Utilization of generative artificial intelligence in visual effects. In *2024 2nd World Conference on Communication & Computing (WCONF)* 2024 July 12 (pp. 1–7). IEEE.

[12] Zhou P, Wang L, Liu Z, Hao Y, Hui P, Tarkoma S, and Kangasharju J. A survey on generative AI and LLM for video generation, understanding, and streaming. *arXiv* preprint arXiv:2404.16038. 2024.

[13] Hannouni S, and El Filali S. Generative AI for education: A study of text-to-video generation for personalized learning. In *2025 International Conference on Circuit, Systems and Communication (ICCSC)* 2025 (pp. 1–6). IEEE.

[14] Liu MY, Huang X, Yu J, Wang TC, and Mallya A. Generative adversarial networks for image and video synthesis: Algorithms and applications. *Proceedings of the IEEE*. 2021;109(5):839–862.

[15] Rabowsky B. Applications of generative AI to media. *SMPTE Motion Imaging Journal*. 2023;132(8):53–57.

[16] Dalal S, Seth B, Radulescu M, Secara C, and Tolea C. Predicting fraud in financial payment services through optimized hyper-parameter-tuned XGBoost model. *Mathematics*. 2022;10(24):4679.

[17] Lilhore UK, Simaiya S, Dalal S, Alshuhail A, and Almusharraf A. A post-quantum hybrid encryption framework for securing biometric data in consumer electronics. *IEEE Transactions on Consumer Electronics*. 2025; 71(3):8289–8297.

[18] Dalal S, Lilhore UK, Radulescu M, Simaiya S, Jaglan V, and Sharma A. A hybrid LBP-CNN with YOLO-v5-based fire and smoke detection model in various environmental conditions for environmental sustainability in smart city. *Environmental Science and Pollution Research*. 2024:1–24.

[19] Dalal S. The smart analysis of Poisson distribution pattern based industrial automation in industry 4.0. In *2023 International Conference on Distributed Computing and Electrical Circuits and Electronics (ICDCECE)* 2023 (pp. 1–6). IEEE.

[20] Malik A, Onyema EM, Dalal S, *et al*. Forecasting students' adaptability in online entrepreneurship education using modified ensemble machine learning model. *Array*. 2023;19:100303.

Chapter 4

Generative AI for audio and speech processing

Generative AI is performing in the way that we are interacting with the advancements in technology, and also how we consume the content. We are not only improving the creation and working with the content but also improving the synthesis quality of the content for the output. Large-based applications where there is use of audio and speech usability are various chatbots and AI assistants used by Google or YouTube to speak for the queries or to resolve what needs to be responded. AI-powered technology is also changing the facts of how the industry is seamlessly working with this innovation adaptation. Speech-to-text models or the model for text-to-speech can be used effectively so that users can easily use the different voices to correspond to the different problems. These advancements are not only changing the adaptability of the use of these tools, but the use has also given positive and negative impacts.

There are various areas where these tools can easily fit in for better performance, and the creators are also taking advantage of these tools to create novel content. Therefore, the users are fascinated to use the idea of building intelligent systems that can learn, play, and adapt the audio and speech process for many of the usages. With the adoption of deep learning and data-driven models, the generative AI has come up with a game-changing force in the area of audio and speech processing. This change has not only improved the quality of the audio effects but also raised the question of authenticity. The innovation has given the new upcomers to get a platform where, with a few keywords, they can go to high levels using the technology.

When we talk over chatbots, we are really unable to be recognized on the basis of the responses, that is, whether it is the user on the other side responding or the questions are being answered by the bots. They also give us the solution in the speech recognized form, whenever we need to know the pronunciation of the text written, or there are tools that actually read our text loudly are also the tools which are also working on the technology of the speech processing techniques. All the innovations have a negative impact as well.

There are scenarios where these tools are responding in a positive manner; there can be situations where these tools can be used to digitally arrest the users by altering the voice of the family members and misusing it. Therefore, with the advancements, it is always advised to address the ethical implications of the applications for creativity and the proprietorship. All these applications or tools can be used for creating music, snippets, generating audio-video effects, small GIF files with sound and audio content, and synthesizing speech. The complete work is done on the pretrained models of the AI tools, where the data is already being trained with the previous data, using the sequence-to-sequence model, tasks like ASR, where the input of the audio text can be given in response to the text output, using components like the long-term short memory to record the temporal dependencies.

4.1 Foundations of audio signal processing

The development of AI-based algorithms in the context of audio processing highlights challenges related to selection-based taxonomy, particularly in choosing appropriate learning paradigms and model architectures. In the previous chapter, the authors have discussed about the data-driven approach using the supervised or unsupervised learnings adjusting to the parameters of the various functions revolving around the deep neural networks where the examples are purely working around the noise reductions in the speech recordings where the signals pairs of the noisy data inputs and being trained based on the pairs of the noisy signals so that the clean output can be expected. The key concept is the learning of AI and ML to learn the resolution of the problem statements and get the output data based on the input data.

The complete data-driven concept is based on the input data. On the basis of Figure 4.1, the input data is being trained on the supervised model, where the model is working on the already installed and used/stored data, which has certain refer- ences for the expected data that are based on the conditions of the responses, and along with this, the approach of using the difference between the referenced data and the condition-based resulted data is the lost data. A similar approach and model examination are followed in audio signal processing, where the model understands the audio data as per the recorded trained data already being used in the model, and then it is synthesized to get the expected result, which is more organized and easily adaptable for the users. This process involves the removal of irrelevant or non- informative components from the audio signal, thereby improving the quality and usefulness of the resulting output.

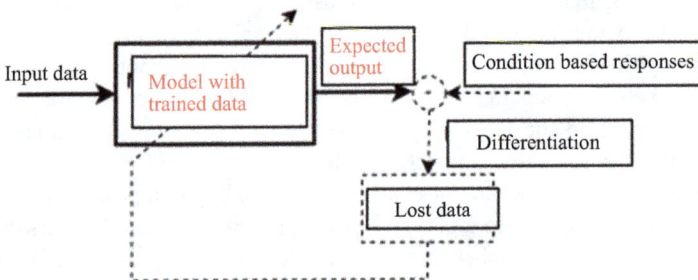

Figure 4.1 Block diagram of the supervised learning

4.2 Basics of audio signals

Audio signals in generative AI are the simple or loud sound waves which are used for the input or output of the data for various AI models, which are trained and learned to synthesize and generate novel sound (audio) as the output for the given data. There are algorithms like GANs and diffusion models that are being implemented to get the new and real based output based on the learned patterns of the data already inserted in the model.

The advancements in data processing through neural networks are done through predefined models, where the data is pretrained with the help of stored and AI-processed data. Then, it is being labeled and processed, and using the text descriptions, it is being generated with the help of the mixtures using the algorithm, i.e., Digital Signal Processing (DSP).

These advancements not only enhance sound but also increase the possibilities of applying audio technology in various domains like virtual reality and tele-communication. When audio technology continues to advance, its use in virtual reality systems and telecommunication will revolutionize user interactions, bringing an immersive experience by merging sound and surroundings in a perfect blend. With the integration of machine learning algorithms in the audio input data, the DL enables tremendous progress, where the audio source works on separation, and the network learns to segregate the audio source from the mixtures, as shown in Figure 4.2, and with the combination of the ML methods along with the DSP components using the latency components. The authentic data that is being generated after the usage of fundamental concepts of AI, ML, and audio signal processing is being used and processed by the users with high fidelity. Few characteristics define the use of generative AI audio processing.

4.2.1 Analog

Analog signals are wave signals that are used to speak and record the audio text in the AI tool or the application, and also that are being generated as the audio responses are also in the form of the wave (sound) that can clearly audible by the users. All the users who are actually using AI assistance in the various applications

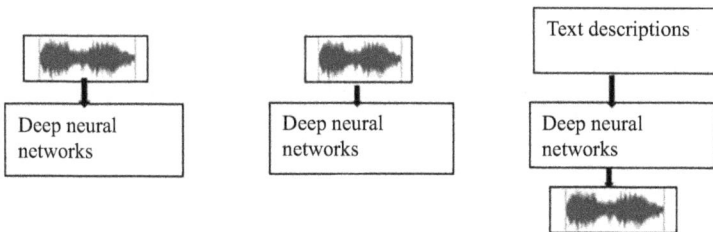

Figure 4.2 Process of generation of signals using the labeling the processing and generation of signals

or AI tools for any kind of response are actually using the analog data to send the input to the tools and the applications, and they also get the results in audio formats.

The ongoing advancements of such algorithms will pave the way for more efficient solutions to issues encountered in audio signal processing, eventually enhancing the overall user experience on different platforms [1]. The incorporation of deep learning approaches plays a vital role in overcoming the shortcomings of traditional algorithms in audio signal processing. With advancements in such technologies, they hold the potential to offer better accuracy and efficiency to applications such as automatic speech recognition and audio synthesis. The future of audio signal processing is bound to be shaped by continued advances as researchers delve into new deep learning models and continue to improve current methods to a level of unprecedented accuracy and efficiency in audio applications.

4.2.2   Digital signal processing

The foundation of any work is the DSP, which provides algorithms and techniques to manipulate and analyze the digital wave signals, such as audio and sensor data. It processes the raw data to extract the meaningful information, lower down and synchronize the sound. DSP not only enables the AI tool to process raw data but also extract meaningful futures, simultaneously reducing the unwanted noise and enhancing new methods to understand and transform the complex methods. These are mainly used in the autonomous signals for better responses and results.

4.2.3   Machine learning in audio signal processing

This emphasis on adaptive algorithms is especially important in active noise control systems, where real-time adaptation can greatly enhance noise reduction performance and user satisfaction [2]. It is a tool and an algorithm that is being used in generative AI to process, enhance, and generate complex data signals such as images, audio, and sensor signal data, which direct the application-enabling process like synthetic data creation, signal restoration, and extraction of the exact data, which processes results based on the inputs (Figure 4.3).

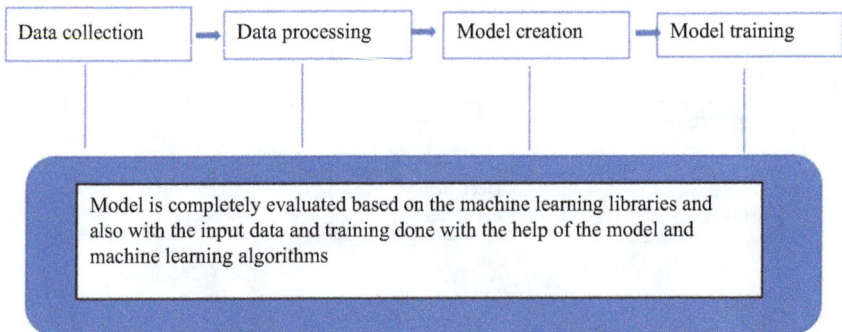

Figure 4.3   Data processing – audio format

4.2.4 Audio signal analysis

This ability enables better and more efficient processing of audio signals, opening the doors for innovation in applications such as music genre classification and speech recognition. The feature of analyzing audio signals is upgraded by machine learning, enabling better performance of tasks like music genre classification and automatic speech recognition, hence innovation in the area (Figures 4.4 and 4.5).

The incorporation of machine learning methods into audio signal processing not only improves existing applications but also drives innovation in new areas such as adaptive digital audio effects and artificial reverberation. With further development, these technologies have the potential to recast user experiences and enhance system performance in many audio applications [3].

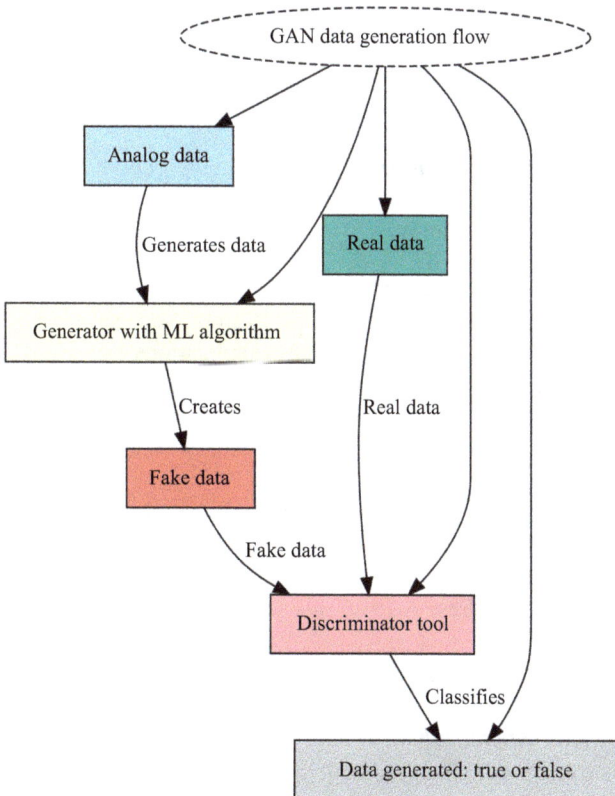

Figure 4.4 Transformation of audio signals into real data formation

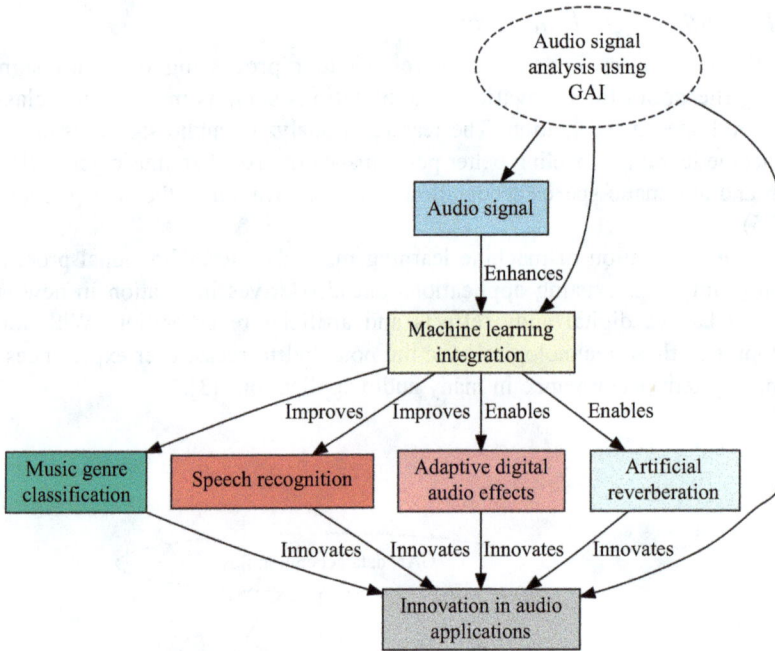

Figure 4.5   Audio signal analysis using generative AI

4.2.5   Creation of audio content

These innovations become ever more crucial as they allow for more efficient and precise analysis of audio signals, which in turn improves user experiences in various domains. As the need for advanced audio applications expands, learning about these deep learning methods becomes essential for researchers and developers. Knowledge about the underlying principles of the methods will enable researchers to develop better audio processing solutions, which will tackle the emerging challenges in the field [4].

This ever-changing environment requires constant interaction between industry practitioners and researchers to ensure that deep learning developments are translated into tangible, real-world applications. The interaction will bring about systems that not only address existing needs but also future challenges in audio processing technologies.

The joint initiatives between industry and academia will play a pivotal role in propelling the evolution of the next generation of audio processing solutions, which in turn will benefit various industries at large. This collaboration will augment the performance of audio processing systems so that they are always leading in terms of technologies and keeping pace with evolving needs in numerous applications.

The prospect of real-time audio analysis and adaptive soundscapes highlights the need for continued research in deep learning applications, especially in improving user experience and satisfaction in various fields. With researchers continuing to discover the potential of deep learning in audio processing, the emphasis is more likely to be on creating more efficient algorithms that would run smoothly on resource-limited devices. This development will be critical to increasing the availability and usability of these technologies in day-to-day situations. This move toward efficiency will enable deep learning models to be used on consumer hardware, ensuring that advanced audio processing becomes available in different real-world use cases. The discovery of effective algorithms for resource-scarce devices is pivotal because it makes deep learning models deployable in consumer electronics to upgrade audio processing without degrading performance. This emphasis on efficiency will not only expand the scope of applications for deep learning in audio processing but also enable its inclusion in real-time consumer devices to improve user experiences tremendously (Figure 4.6) [5].

Seeking better deep learning algorithms is necessary for improving audio processing operations on resource-limited devices to provide accessibility and enhanced user experiences across applications [5]. Optimization is necessary for facilitating the mainstream adoption of next-generation audio processing technologies in common consumer devices, eventually revolutionizing user interactions and experiences. The current challenge is to reconcile model complexity with the constrained computational resources of consumer devices, calling for innovative solutions for efficient deployment in real-world applications [6].

Lightweight deep learning models designed specifically for audio processing tasks are essential for overcoming the constraints of resource-limited devices. Ongoing research into deepening deep learning models for audio processing will play a significant role in ensuring the technologies remain effective and relevant to addressing the needs of users in practical applications [7].

The investigation of novel model compression methods, including quantization, will be pivotal in improving the performance and efficiency of deep learning-based audio processing on constrained devices. The combination of these cutting-edge methods is expected to bring about advancements in real-time audio analysis and adaptive acoustic environments, further improving user experience and engagement across different applications [8].

4.2.6   Spectrogram analysis

The transformation of an audio signal into a visual display of its frequency spectrum enables detailed analysis of time–frequency characteristics, which is essential for tasks such as speech recognition, music analysis, and audio classification The merging of these state-of-the-art deep learning methods not only enhances performance in audio recognition but also creates opportunities for new research and application across various fields [9]. Deep learning models are capable of learning patterns from spectrograms, allowing for more accurate manipulation and creation of sound.

4.2.7   Time-frequency representations

This feature is important for music transcription and emotion detection tasks, where knowing the frequency spectrum is key to achieving correct results. Machine

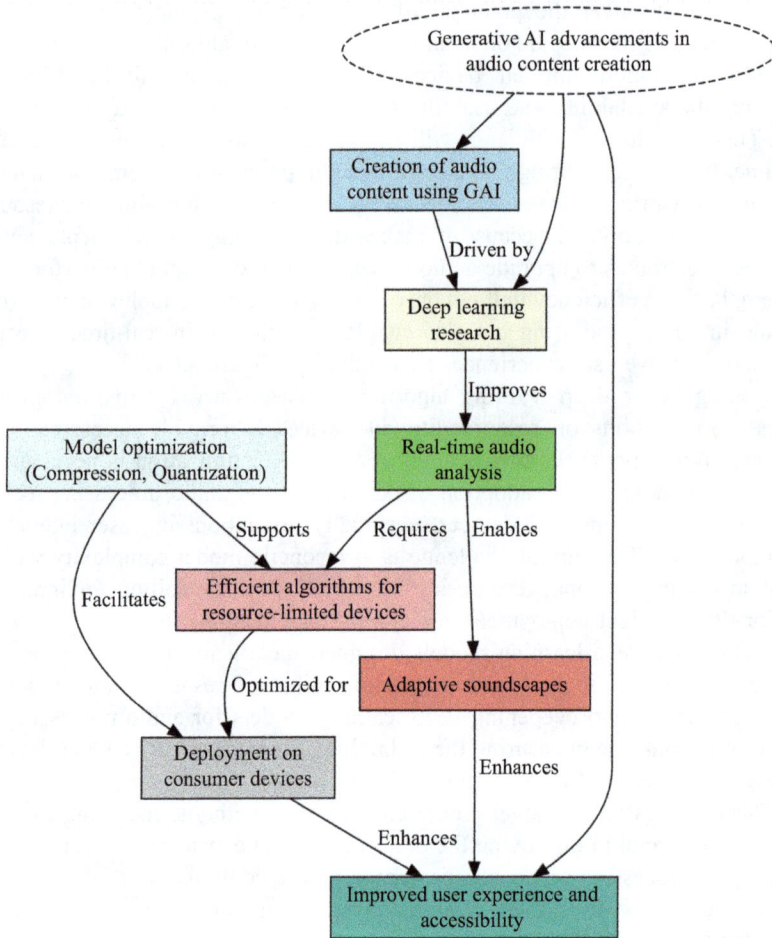

Figure 4.6   Audio content creation with GAI

learning can generate time–frequency representations that support audio and speech enhancement tasks, improve voice clarity across different languages, and advance the overall capabilities of modern audio processing systems. The emotional function in the speech-enabling tool is one of the areas using the machine learning signals and time-frequency representations, which has a stronger purpose in the medical human-signaling area. AI is enhancing time-frequency based on the denoising, extraction and representation features, automated labeling, signal generation, and enhancements.

- Autoencoders
  These are the deep learning models that use the encoder and decoder structures to learn compression and probabilistic representation of data, which enables to generate new and realistic data that is similar to the training set. They work

differently, where instead of the single unit distribution, a continuous latent space is considered. Such unsupervised algorithms, which are being trained in the model, are used to compress the audio signals into lower-dimensional representations, which are very well integrated with applications like audio compression and denoising. The real-time usage of these is being used in the emotion recognition systems, which enhances the engagement and the satisfaction across the platforms. The role of the various emotional recognition systems is used to promote engagements and satisfaction which are related to education and various therapy-related applications. Also, these are the various areas which are being used for the model to work as per the utility and the needs of the users. The responses are generally for the satisfaction of what the user has asked for. The model is also getting more trained with the help of the previous data and the data relevant to the research.

- Speech synthesis
  This is the feature in which the complete speech data is converted into human language speech using high-end deep learning models to convert the speech response from the text. The most useful applications are the Google translators, which convert the text language into different languages and not only give the response in text but also give a result in speech format for the user to learn or understand the language being defined or converted. There are multiple applications that are being used under this process, where it is not only converting but also giving the response in conversations using speech, in addition to the data expected. These applications are useful for educational purposes and also in the adaptability of the automated data response where the chatbots are being used.

- Concatenative TTS
  This model is being used as a base technology for this algorithm, which utilizes pre-recorded speech data from a large storage of database. This is the algorithm that is being used to develop the human voice quality response based on the previously recorded data, which is refined using TTS and is labor-intensive and less flexible than neural approaches. This approach works on the following:

  (a) Database to the speech units: The speech is first recorded and segmented into units, which are then processed and stored in a database for later retrieval and synthesis.
  (b) Text analytics: The text is being analyzed and used to determine the required results.
  (c) Unit usability: Algorithm is designed to pick the desired and expected units that are appropriate in the result variants.
  (d) Concatenation: The selected data/units are combined to complete the spoken output.
  (e) Quality intensive responses: The responses are quality defined and related to the expected results, which are used by the users.
  (f) Less flexible: The algorithm is less flexible in making transformations easily, as it is majorly more labor-intensive because it uses the real recorded data for the enhancements.

- Parametric text-to-speech (TTS)

With advancing technologies, it is necessary to keep the focus on user-centric design to prevent them from failing to meet the varied needs of the users while contributing to an inclusive environment for every person, particularly one with a communication barrier. This user-centered design commitment is essential to the goal of facilitating not only enhanced communication through speech synthesis technologies but also enabling people with disabilities to fully engage in society [10]. Continuing partnership between developers and users is vital for developing effective assistive technologies that improve communication and promote independence among people with disabilities. By promoting a joint methodology in designing speech synthesis technologies, we are able to create ones that not only work efficiently but also empower people with disabilities, leading to an improvement in their communication capacity [11]. Enabling people with disabilities through user-centered design in assistive technology is important for maximizing their communication capabilities and overall quality of life. It enables the users' needs and desires to be addressed first, thus leading to better and more meaningful communications [12].

4.3   Voice cloning and personalization voice cloning

These developments enable the production of personalized voice profiles that respond to personal tastes, adding to the quality of interaction in voice-based systems. These personalized voice profiles can be realized through the use of synthesis parameters that are adapted based on individual enrollment data of speakers, promoting a more natural interaction experience [13]. Not only does this technology improve the naturalness of synthesized speech, but it also encourages richer emotional interactions between voice-enabled systems and users, eventually changing the way users interact. Additionally, the incorporation of voice technology on e-commerce websites is a demonstration of its capability to deliver tailored shopping experiences, thus increasing customer satisfaction and interaction. This integration is a demonstration of how personalized voice interactions can lead to customer loyalty and greater satisfaction in the competitive e-commerce environment. Additionally, voice technology utilization in e-commerce can ease the process of shopping and make it more convenient and accessible to consumers, further enhancing customer loyalty and retention.

4.3.1   Methods of voice cloning

Voce cloning involves the extraction of key features that are the voice samples that are considered to be the data for the new speech that mimics the original speech. It uses sparse data, neural networks, and deep learning models, which have the capabilities to define well learning speaker properties and generate the best quality synthesized speech even with small data. This is mainly used in translator applications, along with education and chatbots, where complete data is recorded and also used for the quality training purposes [14]. Methods include:

- Speaker adaptation: This is one of the methods that is used to adapt more speakers' voices and produce a more accurate and effective voice that is more synthesized and user-friendly. This method is mostly used in digital assistance, which is more appealing and impressive to the customers. There are multiple e-commerce platforms that are using this method for personalization and building customer relationships. Voice cloning is also being used in e-commerce and m-commerce platforms for assistance and giving a better response to the user's requirements based on their searches and keywords [10].

- Speaker encoding: This is the use of the speaker's identity, which is being embedded with the networks within the vector identification space. This evolution has not only defined the need and requirements but also redefined the customer's response based on their demand and inputs of the data in a continuous process. There are multiple platforms that are adapting the advancements of the technology in using this method to store and format the data, which is given, and then format it the way it has to be identified and collated for better and more organized results.

- Few-shot and zero-shot learning: This is the method where the learning is possible only with a single, short sample of the target voice. This helps in creating the framework where the complete data is refined properly and trained based on the few integrations of the system itself.

4.3.1.1 Ethical and technical challenges

These advancements and adaptability give major consideration to the technical and ethical challenges, which are major concerns for privacy and also the improper functionalities of the user's content for usage. If there are multiple platforms that are using voice cloning functionalities can change the content for the users with someone else's voice and can affect the credibility of the users' basic roles and responsibilities toward the content creation. But the security ethics and the protocols being deployed by various platforms always give an assurance that the data on these platforms is always safe to be used and uploaded [15].

- **Privacy issues:** The paradigm shift in the industry, be it social media or the shopping applications, the privacy is the biggest concern as the complete information of the users profile is there in the application along with the details of the last and upcoming products that are being ordered and also the content that is been loaded in the application for any assistance or usage. The privacy of the users' details is purely in the hands of the application admin servers, which are being regularly monitored and trained for any kind of assistance.

- **Bias and representation:** Overcoming these ethical dilemmas will be important for brands looking to establish consumer trust and create a better shopping experience in the fast-changing market of voice commerce. While brands work to overcome these ethical and technical concerns, establishing open practices will become important to gain consumer trust and promote the right use of voice cloning technology in e-commerce. The moral consequences of voice cloning technology need to be carefully regulated in order to avoid its misuse and ensure consumer trust within e-commerce settings, particularly in relation to privacy and representation matters. Further, resolving these ethical problems will not just safeguard consumer trust but also maximize the overall efficiency of voice cloning technology within e-commerce, eventually contributing to a better user experience. Voice cloning technologies require constant cooperation between regulators and industry players to develop successful guidelines that safeguard consumers while supporting innovation. As the technologies evolve, the necessity for strong regulatory interventions becomes ever more imperative to curb risks linked with misuse and promote ethical principles in the market. [16].

- **Regulation:** Legal frameworks continue to evolve to tackle deepfake audio. The success of voice cloning technology being incorporated into e-commerce depends upon tackling these ethical dilemmas while maintaining consumer protection and trust at all stages of the shopping process.
- **Audio applications of generative AI:** The ability of generative AI to aid musicians in the creative process emphasizes the need to learn about its use and shortcomings in promoting artistic work [17].
- **Assistive technologies:** As the technology evolves, it is critical to critically evaluate how generative AI can enrich musicians as well as tackle the ethical dimensions of its application in creative industries and ensure that the technology is used as an enhancement tool and not a substitute for human creativity. Screen readers are key assistive tools that allow visually impaired musicians to access music composition, promoting inclusiveness and availability of creative resources in the field. The creation of generative AI software has to focus on accessibility so that every musician, no matter their ability, can utilize these technologies to freely develop their creativity. By providing an inclusive framework, generative AI will be able to empower different musicians to pursue their creativity, enriching the musical world and the extent of artistic expression eventually. Implementing these guidelines will involve continued collaboration between technologists, musicians, and ethicists to ensure responsible and effective use of generative AI within the creative process. Prioritizing ethical guidelines will allow the music industry to leverage the innovative potential of generative AI to drive innovation while protecting human artistry's integrity. The continuous development of generative AI in music requires a harmonious approach that balances innovation with ethical considerations to ultimately ensure that technology is used to facilitate human creativity, not replace it [18].
- **Voice enhancement:** Using generative AI in voice improvement technologies has the potential to enhance the quality and clarity of audio signals, facilitating communication for speech-impaired users [19]. The continuous innovation in voice-enhancing technologies via generative AI not only enhances communication among users with speech disorders but also provokes ethical issues involving authenticity and representation in sound production. The inquiry into voice enhancement technologies brings to the fore the need to ensure that these

technologies prioritize user agency and ethical issues in sound representation and communication. The application of generative AI in voice improvement technologies emphasizes the need to balance innovation with ethics, that innovations benefit users in a way that empowers them without sacrificing their authenticity.

- **Low-bandwidth speech synthesis:** It is crucial to maintain the assurance that generative AI technologies enhance accessibility and inclusivity for everyone, especially people with disabilities [12]. In order to implement an inclusive environment in Telecommunications, it is important to place the needs of people with disabilities foremost so that generative AI technologies support greater accessibility and user experience for everyone. Securing that the needs of users with disabilities take precedence when it comes to generative AI technologies is key to developing a fully inclusive telecom environment. This pledge is part of the larger vision to promote an equal society where technological innovations serve to empower all people, especially those with disabilities, in accessing communication devices.

4.4 Conclusion

In this chapter, the authors have majorly discussed the use of generative AI for the purpose of speech and voice; there are certain areas where speech recognition and use are highly effective. Search engine tools, various e-commerce applications, and social media also use speech to be converted into text, and the text message is then converted into voice. There are certain areas where languages are also considered to be barriers; there this machine learning approach is being followed. Using generative AI, it not only converts the voice and speech text but also adds certain added information that is true for the results based on what is expected by the users in their prompts. There are various tools which are working based on the results, and their working is based on the functionalities of how AI is integrated with other results so that the responses can be easily defined for the audio and speech functionalities using the tools and other applications for their smooth responses. These also give authenticated results, and a few of the data points are dropped, which are affected and validated. All the output generated have certain drawbacks, which are majorly based on the authentication and also the validity of the relevant and real data. Further study will revolve around the negative effects of the usage of generative AI tools for clear and unaltered data.

References

[1]   Parmanand SL, Chandankhede PH, and Deshmukh AR. Use of generative AI for audio speech recognition: Methods and selection criteria. In *2025 6th International Conference on Mobile Computing and Sustainable Informatics (ICMCSI)* 2025 Jan 7 (pp. 1113–1120). IEEE.

[2]   He Y, Seng KP, and Ang LM. Generative adversarial networks (GANs) for audio-visual speech recognition in artificial intelligence IoT. *Information.* 2023;14(10):575.

[3]   Zhang Z. AI-powered intelligent speech processing: Evolution, applications and future directions. *International Journal of Advanced Computer Science & Applications.* 2025;16(2):918–928.

[4]   Assudani PJ, Balakrishnan P, Leema AA, and Nasare RK. Generative AI-powered framework for audio analysis and conversational exploration. *Metallurgical and Materials Engineering.* 2025;31(4):206–211.

[5]   Yehia E. Developments on generative AI. In *AI and Emerging Technologies* 2024 (pp. 139–160). CRC Press.

[6]   Saini H, Singh G, Dalal S, Lilhore UK, Simaiya S, and Dalal S. Enhancing cloud network security with a trust-based service mechanism using k-anonymity and statistical machine learning approach. *Peer-to-Peer Networking and Applications.* 2024;17(6):4084–4109.

[7]   Regondi S, Pugliese R, and Mahroo A. Towards a predictive model of speech signatures: Insights from spectral analysis and generative AI models. In 2024 *IEEE International Conference on Metrology for eXtended Reality, Artificial Intelligence and Neural Engineering (MetroXRAINE)* 2024 Oct 21 (pp. 782–786). IEEE.

[8]   Kim M, and Skoglund J. Neural speech and audio coding: Modern AI technology meets traditional codecs [Special Issue On Model-Based and Data-Driven Audio Signal Processing]. *IEEE Signal Processing Magazine.* 2025; 41(6):85–93.

[9]   Dasgupta D, Venugopal D, and Gupta KD. A review of generative AI from historical perspectives. *TechRxiv.* 2023:1–12. doi:10.36227/techrxiv.22097942.

[10] Latif S, Shahid A, and Qadir J. Generative emotional AI for speech emotion recognition: The case for synthetic emotional speech augmentation. *Applied Acoustics.* 2023;210:109425.

[11] Anibal J, Landa A, Nguyen H, *et al.* Generative AI and unstructured audio data for precision public health. *NPJ Health Systems.* 2025;2(1):19.

[12] Battini P, Chung K, Dontuboyina N, Ozkaya S, and Rentachintala K. Bridging the gap in generative AI for audio generation. 2023;10(9);1–15.

[13] Rouf M, and Jadon JS. Generative AI for text to speech and sign language translation. In *2025 3rd International Conference on Disruptive Technologies (ICDT)* 2025 Mar 7 (pp. 1124–1129). IEEE.

[14] Julio C. Evaluation of speech recognition, text-to-speech, and generative text artificial intelligence for English as foreign language learning speaking practices PhD Thesis. 2024:1–119.

[15] Iorliam A, and Ingio JA. A comparative analysis of generative artificial intelligence tools for natural language processing. *Journal of Computing Theories and Applications.* 2024;1(3):311–325.

[16] Lilhore UK, Simaiya S, Dalal S, Alshuhail A, and Almusharraf A. A post-quantum hybrid encryption framework for securing biometric data in consumer electronics. *IEEE Transactions on Consumer Electronics.* 2025.

[17] Kawakami R, and Venkatagiri S. The impact of generative AI on artists. In *Proceedings of the 16th Conference on Creativity & Cognition* 2024 June 23 (pp. 79–82).

[18] Dalal S, Rani U, Lilhore UK, *et al.* Optimized XGBoost model with whale optimization algorithm for detecting anomalies in manufacturing. *Journal of Computational and Cognitive Engineering.* 2024.

[19] Parmanand SL, Chandankhede PH, and Deshmukh AR. Use of generative AI for audio speech recognition: Methods and selection criteria. In *2025 6th International Conference on Mobile Computing and Sustainable Informatics (ICMCSI)* 2025 Jan 7 (pp. 1113–1120). IEEE.

Chapter 5

Ethical and regulatory perspectives of generative AI

In this chapter, ethical and regulatory dimensions of generative AI with their societal implications will be discussed. First, the exploration of the ethical implications of GenAI will be explained, followed by examining the moral responsibilities of developers and users. Consequently, highlighting key issues, such as bias, privacy, misinformation, and the potential for misuse, this chapter will transition to the regulatory landscape of using AI, delineating the current compliance requirements for AI technologies across various domains. Additionally, an overview of noteworthy regulatory frameworks, such as the European Union's AI Act, the General Data Protection Regulation (GDPR), and the United States' emerging AI policies, is also discussed.

5.1 Introduction

The potentials of machine learning technologies took a transformative leap in the form of generative AI, portraying extraordinary prospects for innovation and advancement across several fields, including education, media, entertainment, healthcare, and finance [1]. Although fundamentally, GenAI algorithms are capable of creating data similar to the data (but not identical) they are trained on, thus generating new and original content ranging from images and text to synthetic data sets as represented in Figure 5.1. This content is not identical (or copied) but trained on the existing knowledge.

Similar to conventional AI, this new generative AI also raises risks and ethical concerns related to data privacy, security, political impact, energy consumption, and the workforce. There is a tendency in GenAI to bring some new business risks, such as copyright infringement, plagiarism, misinformation and hallucinations, and harmful content. Furthermore, the lack of explainability and transparency, and the potential for worker displacement are crucial concerns [2].

The regulatory models for GenAI are presently fragmented all over the globe, indicating a lack of coordinated international standards due to this sudden shift in the market. For striking a balance between promoting technological innovation and safeguarding public interests, many countries and regions are approaching AI regulations and governance through varying lenses. The regulatory and compliance

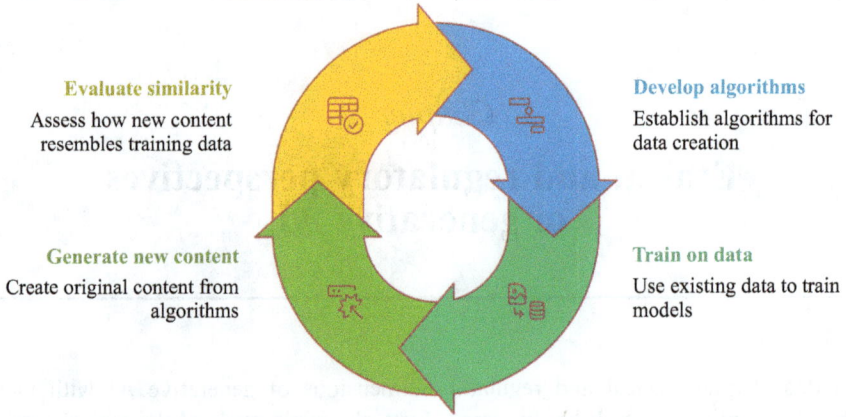

Figure 5.1   Generative AI cycle

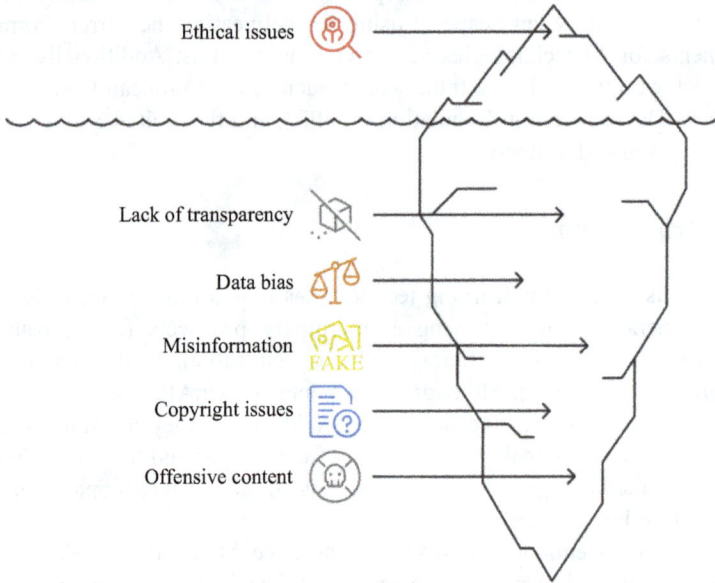

Figure 5.2   Deep-rooted ethical issues of GenAI

patchwork results in inconsistencies that further complicate compliance for developers and users. Another issue lies in resolving the need for flexibility in AI development with demands for transparency, ethical accountability, and risk mitigation [3]. With the increased number of GenAI applications, ranging from automated content creation to synthetic media generation, an increased rate of concerns about potential harms such as misinformation, bias, and privacy violations is raised (as depicted in Figure 5.2). Therefore, there is an upward momentum to design regulatory frameworks that can support responsible innovation with the least societal risks [4].

5.2   Ethical implications of generative AI

The use of GenAI would amplify a cluster of ethical concerns (including privacy, fairness, bias, accountability, transparency, and misuse; projected as dominant topics in Table 5.1). The nontransparency, often referred to as the 'black box' nature of GenAI, makes it difficult to understand the underlying decision-making processes This lack of transparency makes it hard to understand the decision process and thus raises concerns about responsible use, input independence, but also bias in output, especially when 65% of organizations are using AI systems. And the majority of those organizations operate without sufficient explainability mechanisms. The organizations should emphasize the need for transparency and explainability in the ethical principles of AI systems (Table 5.1). Recent generative AI frameworks increasingly integrate ethical safeguards and contextual awareness to support responsible deployment across real-world applications [5].

5.2.1   Privacy and consent

One of the most significant ethical issues around GAI is privacy-invasive and a lack of consent in content generation. GAI systems are being trained on huge datasets, usually including personal data, and can be used with unlawful methods to misuse private information. For instance, deepfake technologies can produce believable-looking videos impersonating actual individuals, making it possible to misuse the likeness of a person without their permission. This matter is particularly influential when GAI generates malevolent content to spread fake news, revenge porn, etc.

Table 5.1   Description of ethical concerns

Ethical issue	Description	Example
Privacy and consent	GAI systems are trained on huge datasets, often including personal data, leading to privacy invasion and lack of consent.	Deepfake technology used to create fake videos of celebrities or politicians without their consent, harming their reputation.
Bias and discrimination	If GAI systems are trained on biased data, they propagate stereotypes and discrimination, especially in multimedia applications.	Facial verification systems or avatar generation in VR that reflect biased representations of certain demographics.
Authenticity and misinformation	Generative AI can create highly realistic fake content, leading to misinformation and trust issues in the media.	Deepfakes used in political campaigns to spread misleading content and manipulate public sentiment.
Intellectual property and ownership	Generative AI raises questions about ownership of content produced by AI, especially in areas like music, film, and art.	In 2018, an AI-created artwork sold for $400,000, raising questions about AI's role as an artist and who owns the copyright.

- **Example:** A deepfake of a celebrity making a statement the celebrity never made in reality can do great harm to that person's reputation, and he or she might not have granted permission for his or her image or voice to be used that way.

5.2.2   Bias and discrimination

Like any form of generative AI, these models are only as good as the data they train on. And if it is biased to begin with, you are just going to propagate that bias forward. This is particularly a problem in multimedia applications, such as facial verification and automatic event summarization. If one is to train GAI on data that is under-representative of some demographic or weighted by certain cultural norms, then the GAI might perpetuate stereotypes or score content in ways detrimental to groups with particular representation or undertones.

- **For example:** a GAI system to generate avatars in VR games might close in and develop characters based on certain skin tones, body looks, or facial features, which kind of disregards the full diversity of how we show up. This could carry dangerous biases and put underrepresented groups at a fatal disadvantage.

5.2.3   Authenticity and misinformation

Generative AI can already generate incredibly realistic fake content, which does not bode well for the true authenticity of media today. Deepfakes, news articles written by AI, and fake imagery can easily trick the audience into buying misinformation. This presents a danger to media public trust and can be leveraged to interfere with political hum, distribute false or misleading information, and mold public sentiment.

- **For example:** In political campaigns, fake videos of the candidates can be made using deepfakes to trick voters with convincing content that will not immediately ring false.

5.2.4   Intellectual property and ownership

Generative AI also raises thorny issues around IP. Who owns the content produced by AI? If a GAI system creates music or art, who owns the copyright to it? Is it the person who made the algorithm, supplied and/or taught the dataset inputs, or described how to choose them, or is it the end user of their AI performing service? These questions are becoming more pressing as AI product-created content rises in use, especially within music, film, and advertising.

- **Example:** In 2018, a piece of art created by an artificial intelligence was purchased at auction for more than $400,000–raising questions about whether AIs can be artists and who gets the copyright.

5.2.5   GenAI ethical failures

The ethical failures in generative AI stem from previously mentioned issues such as biased data, privacy lapses, and misuse. In this section, some of the relevant examples of these issues are listed to help us understand the gravity of such issues.

Algorithm bias: A widely used U.S. healthcare risk-prediction algorithm favored white patients over Black patients because it used historical healthcare spending as a proxy for medical need. This faulty metric led to underestimating the care required by Black patients. Similarly, Twitter's AI image-cropping algorithm favored white faces over Black faces when generating thumbnails, reinforcing racial bias [6–8]. The problem was due to training data choices prioritizing "salient" features that inadvertently led to biased outcomes. Twitter removed the automatic cropping feature following widespread criticism. Another example of cultural bias occurred when generative AI used to create Barbie dolls from different countries produced racially and culturally inappropriate images, such as a German Barbie in a Nazi uniform and a South Sudan Barbie with a gun, revealing embedded cultural stereotypes. The algorithm was found accountable for gender bias as well. Amazon discontinued an AI hiring tool after it was found to discriminate against women because it was trained on historical recruitment data mostly reflecting male candidates.

Misinformation and deepfakes: Generative AI-driven deepfakes and fake news generation have fueled misinformation challenges, thus eroding public trust in media and, in many cases, exacerbating political polarization. Lessons need to be learned to enhance the GenAI in a responsible and transparent way (discussed in Table 5.2).

Table 5.2   Lessons learned and strategies formation for ethical concerns

Ethical concern	Strategy to combat	Lesson learned
Algorithm bias	Testing for biased data	AI models must be rigorously tested for bias with diverse data sets to avoid reinforcing harmful stereotypes. Transparency about training data and ongoing bias audits is critical to prevent discrimination.
	Use of proxy variables	Using proxy variables correlated with sensitive attributes like race can perpetuate inequality. Careful selection and evaluation of training data and performance metrics are crucial to ensure fairness in critical domains like healthcare.
	Fairness in systems	AI trained on biased historical data will replicate those biases. It is essential to design AI systems with fairness objectives, remove discriminatory data patterns, and continuously monitor outcomes.

(Continues)

Table 5.2   (Continued)

Ethical concern	Strategy to combat	Lesson learned
Misinformation and deepfakes	Detection tools and enforcement of accountability	Technology developers, policymakers, and users must collaborate to develop detection tools, improve media literacy, and enforce accountability to mitigate misinformation risks.
Privacy Breaches	Transparent data handling	Enterprises must establish strict data governance policies and restrict the use of generative AI platforms for sensitive data. Developers need robust privacy controls and transparency in data handling practices.

Privacy breaches from GenAI use: Samsung employees accidentally leaked sensitive internal data, such as source code and confidential notes, by inputting them into ChatGPT. OpenAI also suffered a data exposure incident where user chat histories and payment data were briefly accessible to others.

These case studies reveal the severity of ethical and ethical concerns, which can lead to severe consequences and require comprehensive, proactive approaches involving governance, transparency, regulation, and continuous ethical oversight.

5.3   Moral responsibilities of developers and users

Ethical AI guidelines and principles are being established to enforce responsible usage and development, considering transparency, fairness, and accountability. The raised ethical concerns (as discussed in Section 5.2) of GenAI prompted questions about the moral duties of its users and, most significantly, its developers. These extensive ethical issues surrounding generative AI necessitate a nuanced understanding of the ethical responsibilities of developers and users. The comparative moral responsibilities of both groups need to be analyzed by drawing insights from the literature. Thus, a thorough understanding of their roles and obligations can be provided.

5.3.1   Moral responsibilities of developers

The ethical landscape of Gen AI cannot be shaped without the responsible intentions of the developers. The responsibilities of a developer consist of ethical considerations along with the technical aspects. Thus, to guarantee Alignment of AI systems with societal values.

- *Ethical design and development:* Ethical principles need to be embedded by the developers during the design and development of AI systems. These ethical principles are the fuel to make an AI system fair, transparent, and neutral.

Recent work has demonstrated how the demographic and moral preferences of developers can significantly influence the output of an IA system. Hence, potentially exacerbating socio-economic discrimination and inequalities [9]. Therefore, developers should enthusiastically work to tackle these disparities and strive for diversity in developing teams to mitigate such risks.

• *Accountability for AI outputs:* Developers are also answerable for the outputs produced by their AI systems. This accountability extends to safeguarding AI systems from the dissemination of misinformation and damaging or destructive biases. For instance, generative AI provides an easy way to produce and proliferate realistic deepfakes or spread emotionally resonant misinformation, and the developers must implement their system to prevent such misuse [10–12]. A solution can be proactive testing of the AI system by the developers for these ethical issues and updating models iteratively to address the misuse of AI and emerging ethical concerns.

• *Transparency and explainability:* Explainability is necessary for ensuring the transparency of the decisions made by AI systems. Thus, transparency and explainability emerge as one of the critical ethical considerations for developers. Stakeholders and users need a thorough understanding of the reasoning behind the decisions taken by an AI system, and whether it aligns with ethical standards. Henceforth, developers need to prioritize explainable AI techniques for enhancing trust and accountability [13–15]. This is principally critical in high-risk fields where the consequences of AI decisions can be profound, such as healthcare and law enforcement.

5.3.2 Moral responsibilities of users

As the developers are significantly responsible for the development of ethical design of AI systems, likewise, a user should also be morally obligated while interacting with these systems. These moral obligations range from critical evaluation of AI output to awareness of ethical use of AI, as discussed below:

• *Ethical usage and decision-making: The responsible use of GenAI systems must be ensured by the user, thereby* not exploiting these tools for harmful purposes. For example, using AI to produce and proliferate realistic deepfakes or spread emotionally resonant misinformation is unethical and can have widespread societal impacts and damages [16]. Thus, users should be conscious of the potential risks associated with GenAI and make informed decisions about how they utilize these technologies.

• *Critical evaluation of AI outputs:* In addition to the ethical use of AI, users also have an obligation to critically assess the outputs of GenAI systems. Though AI offers valuable insights and support, it is not infallible, and these limitations must be recognized by the users to avoid potential biases of these systems. For instance, users ought not to instinctively rely on AI recommendations without considering the context and looking for potential errors [17].

• *Advocacy for ethical AI:* Users play a significant role in advocating for ethical AI practices. Users influence the GenAI development by providing feedback on bias, transparency, and engaging in discussions about the ethical implications of generative AI. This includes holding the developers accountable when the ethical standards are ignored, or supporting developers who prioritize ethical considerations.

5.3.3   Shared accountability and collaboration

The ethical implications of generative AI are not merely the responsibility of users or developers; rather, they require a collaborative and collective effort between all stakeholders. Table 5.2 highlights the key moral responsibilities of developers and users, emphasizing their respective roles in ensuring the ethical development and use of generative AI.

- *Distributed moral responsibility:* The view of distributed moral responsibility implies that all the stakeholders (including developers and users) have a shared accountability for the ethical implications of GenAI systems. This approach recognizes that the development and deployment of AI systems are complex procedures involving numerous actors, each contributing to the overall ethical landscape [18].
- *Ethical frameworks and governance: For responsible development and use of AI systems,* governance structures and ethical frameworks must be enforced. These ethical frameworks and governance structures must clearly state the roles and responsibilities of both developers and users, thereby providing guidelines for accountability and ethical decision-making. For instance, frameworks that emphasize transparency, fairness, and beneficence can help align the development and use of AI with societal values [19, 20].

Table 5.3   Comparative analysis of moral responsibilities in generative AI

Aspect	Developers	Users
Ethical design	Responsible for embedding ethical principles into AI systems to ensure fairness and transparency.	Must use AI responsibly and avoid exploiting it for harmful purposes.
Accountability	Accountable for AI outputs and must implement safeguards against misuse	Should critically evaluate AI outputs and recognize limitations.
Transparency	Prioritize explainable AI to enhance trust and understanding	Advocate for transparent AI systems and hold developers accountable.
Bias and Fairness	Must address biases in AI systems to prevent discrimination	Be vigilant in identifying and mitigating biases in AI outputs.
Education and Awareness	Educate users about ethical considerations and AI limitations	Take the initiative to understand AI ethics and the implications of their actions.

- *Addressing bias and misinformation:* One of the most compelling ethical challenges is the potential for generative AI to perpetuate misinformation and bias. Developers must prioritise fairness and neutrality in their models, while users must be alert in identifying and mitigating these issues [21].

- *Education and awareness:* Education and awareness are critical components of shared accountability. Developers must educate users about the ethical considerations of generative AI, while users must take the initiative to understand the implications of their actions. This mutual understanding can foster a culture of responsibility and ethical AI usage.

- *Ensuring accountability and transparency:* As discussed in Section 5.2, accountability and transparency are keystone principles for ethical use of AI. Developers must be held accountable for the outputs of their AI systems, and users must demand transparency in the working and operation of these AI systems. This comprises encouraging explainable AI and robust oversight mechanisms.

- *Fostering collaboration and education:* As mentioned before, for addressing the ethical implications of generative AI, the collaboration among all the stakeholders (including developers and users) is indispensable. This collaboration can be established by the promotion of open dialogue, sharing knowledge, and endorsing education about AI ethics. Stakeholders can only ensure that generative AI development and use align with ethical principles and societal values if they work together collectively.

- To summarize, the ethical implications of generative AI are compound and multifaceted, necessitating a comprehensive and complete approach that contemplates the moral obligations of both developers and users highlighted in Table 5.3. Where developers must prioritise ethical design, accountability, and transparency, users should engage in responsible usage and advocacy for ethical AI practices. Through this shared accountability and mutual collaboration, all stakeholders can move toward the ethical compliance of generative AI. Hence, the benefits of society can be ensured by using and developing these powerful technologies, not otherwise.

5.4   Regulatory landscape for generative AI

The current regulatory landscape for generative AI is fragmented and evolving, with various countries and regions adopting different approaches to governance. This fragmentation stems from divergent national priorities, levels of technological development, and legal traditions. While some jurisdictions have taken a precautionary approach, emphasizing control and risk mitigation (e.g., the EU), others have prioritized flexibility and innovation (e.g., the U.S.) or the development, content, and ethics (e.g., China and the African Union).

A key challenge in this landscape is balancing innovation with accountability. Generative AI technologies offer unprecedented opportunities for creativity, productivity, and economic growth, but they also raise serious concerns about privacy, misinformation, bias, copyright infringement, and the erosion of trust in digital content. Effective regulation should aim to promote responsible innovation supporting AI development while protecting fundamental rights and societal values. These frameworks and governance structures are vital for ensuring that generative AI is developed and used responsibly. They should define the roles and responsibilities of developers and users, offering guidelines for ethical decision-making and accountability (Figure 5.3). For example, frameworks that stress transparency, fairness, and beneficence can help align AI development and use with societal values.

5.4.1   Significant regulatory frameworks

- European Union's AI Act
  For tailored governance of AI and GenAI systems in the region of European Union, this act is a revolutionary regulatory framework for the safe use of AI. The main aim of the European Union Act is to embed safety measures during the designing, developing, and deploying process of AI to ensure transparency and accountability. A risk-based classification is used. It adopts a risk-based approach, categorizing AI applications into different risk levels, each with specific regulatory requirements. This framework is particularly relevant for GenAI, which has raised concerns due to its potential ethical implications and misuse. The Act's provisions for GenAI focus on transparency, data protection, and compliance with EU copyright laws, aiming to balance innovation with the protection of rights.

  o   **Risk-based classification:** The AI Act classifies AI systems into three risk categories: unacceptable risk, high risk, and low or no risk, with corresponding regulatory measures for each category. GenAI models, often considered general-purpose AI, are subject to specific transparency obligations, including the requirement to disclose technical documentation and the data used for training.

  o   **Transparency and compliance:** The Act mandates transparency obligations for GenAI, ensuring that AI developers provide clear information about the AI systems' functioning and the data used. Compliance with EU copyright laws is emphasized, requiring GenAI systems to respect intellectual property rights while fostering innovation.

  o   **Innovation and safety:** The AI Act aims to promote responsible innovation by establishing a legal framework that mitigates risks while encouraging the development of AI technologies. The Act's focus on safety and adherence to fundamental rights is intended to build trust in AI technologies, facilitating their adoption within the EU market.

While the AI Act sets a comprehensive framework for regulating GenAI, it also faces challenges in balancing innovation with regulation. The ongoing technical negotiations and the evolving nature of AI technologies mean that the Act must remain adaptable to address new developments and potential risks effectively. This adaptability is crucial for maintaining the EU's competitiveness in the global AI landscape while safeguarding fundamental rights (Figure 5.4).

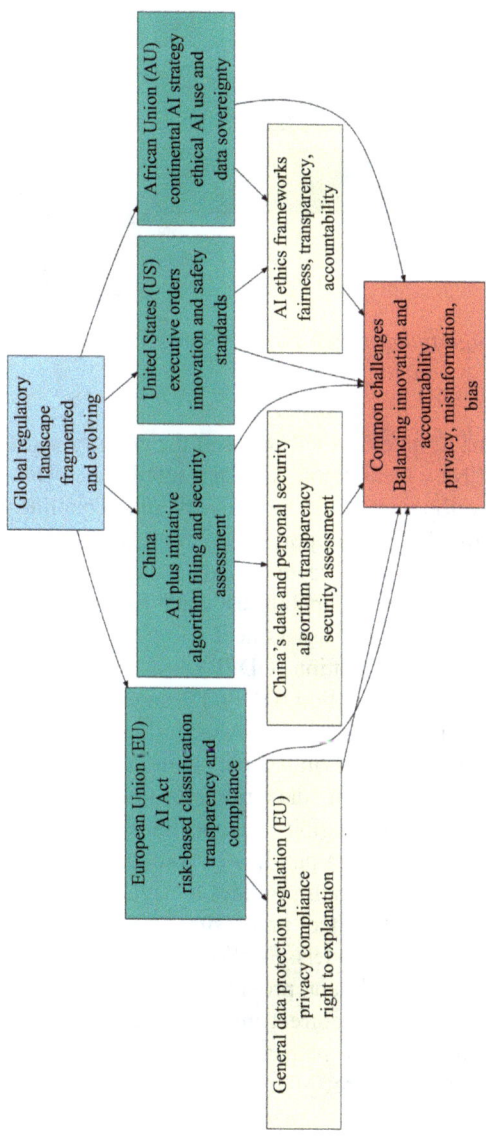

Figure 5.3   Regulatory landscape for generative AI

Global regulatory landscape
fragmented and evolving

European Union (EU)
AI Act
risk-based classification
transparency and
compliance

China
AI plus initiative
algorithm filing and security
assessment

United States (US)
executive orders
innovation and safety
standards

African Union (AU)
continental AI strategy
ethical AI use and
data sovereignty

General data protection regulation (EU)
privacy compliance
right to explanation

China's data and personal security
algorithm transparency
security assessment

AI ethics frameworks
fairness, transparency,
accountability

Common challenges
Balancing innovation and
accountability
privacy, misinformation,
bias

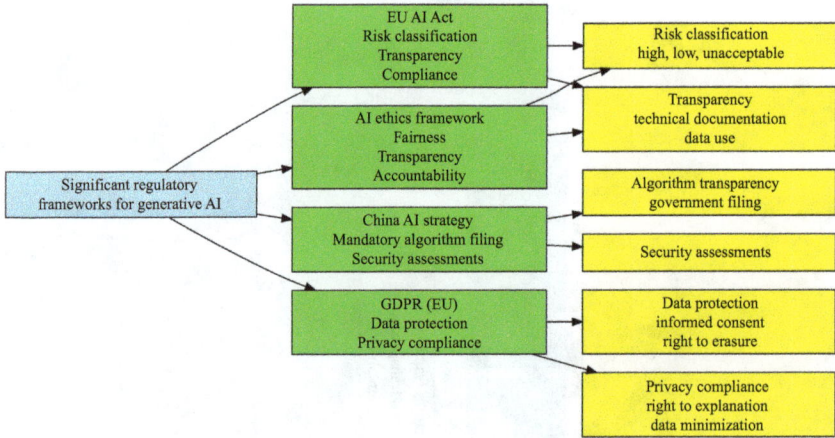

Figure 5.4   Significant regulatory frameworks for generative AI

- China's approach
  In July 2017, China's State Council released the country's strategy for developing AI entitled "New Generation Artificial Intelligence Development Plan" to promote the development of AI for security and economic growth by providing incentives and funding support. Also, implementing the frameworks for data and personal information security. Also, the AI services with "public opinion or social mobilization capabilities" must file their algorithms with the government and pass a security assessment.
- General Data Protection Regulation (GDPR)
  General Data Protection Regulation (GDPR) is an existing framework for data regulation on a wider scale that is not AI-specific; however, it substantially impacts the safer development and deployment of GenAI systems as well. Nevertheless, informed consent, data minimization, and purpose limitation principles of GDPR are challenging to reconcile with GenAI models as they are trained on data scraped from public web sources.

  Article 22 of the GDPR, which provides a "right to explanation" for decisions made solely by automated processing, poses additional compliance challenges for black box AI models. Furthermore, GenAI systems must ensure lawful processing of personal data, provide users with access to their data and offer mechanisms to delete or correct information, a complex task in AI systems that absorb and replicate patterns from countless inputs. Thus, GDPR remains a critical benchmark for privacy-compliant GenAI deployment in the European context (Figure 5.4).
- African Union (AU) continental AI strategy
  The African Union (AU) adopted a continental AI strategy in 2024, built on data sovereignty and responsible use. The strategy aims to use AI to address Africa's most pressing challenges in sectors like healthcare, agriculture, and education, aligning with the UN Sustainable Development Goals and the AU's Agenda

2063. This policy encourages investments in education, digital infrastructures, and training to foster a vibrant AI ecosystem and close the digital divide between Africa and more developed regions. Rule of Law, Human Rights, Ethical principles, and responsible uses are the core of its governance framework. It also states and addresses the concerns of a lack of diversity and bias in algorithms.

- Emerging AI policies in the United States
  In contrast, the United States has not yet enacted a federal AI-specific regulatory framework. However, several policy instruments and state-level initiatives signal a shift toward greater oversight. Notably, the White House released the Blueprint for an AI Bill of Rights, which outlines five guiding principles: safe and effective systems, protection from algorithmic discrimination, data privacy, notice and explanation, and human alternatives to AI systems. While non-binding, the blueprint sets a normative foundation for future regulation. Federal agencies such as the Federal Trade Commission (FTC) have also issued guidance on AI use, emphasizing consumer protection and prohibiting deceptive practices involving AI-generated content. At the state level, laws such as the Illinois Biometric Information Privacy Act and California Consumer Privacy Act offer more specific safeguards. Despite this patchwork, the U.S. appears poised to take a more cohesive regulatory stance in response to growing public concern over deepfakes, data misuse, and AI ethics. The most recent 2025 executive order titled "Removing Barriers to American Leadership in AI" aims to foster innovation and reduce restrictive regulations. The "Winning the Race: America's AI Action Plan" outlines federal policy actions focusing on innovation, AI infrastructure, diplomacy, and security. Legislation like the National Artificial Intelligence Initiative Act and various state laws also shape the governance of AI use. Overall, US policies balance AI leadership promotion with emerging regulatory frameworks

In summary, the regulatory landscape for generative AI is evolving rapidly but unevenly. While the EU leads with comprehensive, legally binding legislation, other regions are still exploring principle-based approaches or reactive policies shown in Table 5.4. As GenAI becomes more integrated into critical sectors, there

Table 5.4   A summary of global AI governance and regulatory approaches

Region	Key policies and initiatives	Description
European Union (EU)	EU AI Act	A legal framework that regulates AI systems based on a risk-based approach, from unacceptable to minimal risk.
China	"AI Plus" Initiative	A national strategy to integrate AI across sectors and an iterative approach with specific regulations like mandatory AI labeling and an algorithm registry.
United States (US)	Executive orders	Evolving policies that prioritize either safety standards or promoting US technological leadership and competitiveness.

is a pressing need for global regulatory convergence that supports ethical, inclusive, and accountable AI innovation.

5.5 Societal implications

The societal implications of generative AI are profound, particularly in the context of existing ethical and regulatory gaps. In the absence of robust, harmonized regulations, generative AI systems risk perpetuating systemic biases, violating individual privacy, and undermining public trust in digital content. The "black box" nature of many generative models exacerbates concerns around explainability and accountability, leaving individuals and communities vulnerable to algorithmic harms without clear avenues for redress. This regulatory void creates asymmetries in power and knowledge between developers, corporations, and the public, contributing to what scholars have termed a "governance vacuum" in AI ethics. Without strong oversight, marginalized groups may be disproportionately affected by AI-generated misinformation, surveillance, or content manipulation, thereby reinforcing existing social inequities.

Addressing these challenges requires cross-sector collaboration among governments, technology companies, civil society, academia, and impacted communities. No single actor can regulate generative AI in isolation, given the technology's global reach and rapid evolution. Governments must provide clear legal frameworks, while organizations have a responsibility to implement ethical design and deployment practices. Meanwhile, stakeholders such as educators, ethicists, and community leaders play a crucial role in ensuring that GenAI applications align with human values, cultural sensitivities, and public interest. Initiatives like the EU's AI Act and the U.S. AI Bill of Rights indicate a growing awareness of this need, but further cooperation is essential to establish inclusive and enforceable standards.

It is anticipated that numerous future scenarios for ethical and regulatory harmony are possible. Optimistically, critical AI principles, such as transparency, fairness, and human oversight, can be enforced through binding agreements or global governance frameworks with international cooperation and efforts. Such principles would protect rights and promote technological innovation. Conversely, continued fragmentation in regulations would bring compliance issues, inconsistent regulations, and widen the digital divide. Achieving harmony will depend not only on legal mechanisms but also on fostering a global ethical culture of responsible AI development. Ultimately, the goal is to ensure that generative AI technologies serve as tools for societal good, enhancing inclusion, agency, and well-being across all communities.

5.6 Ethical and regulatory challenges on generative AI: case studies

Generative AI (GAI) technologies, including deep learning, Generative Adversarial Networks (GANs), and other machine learning models, are already fast adopted in the domain of the multimedia industry, generating new value but also causing serious ethical and regulatory concerns. This section presents case studies that critically examine the implications of these technologies in different fields such as politics, art, privacy, and intellectual property. Each case describes the ethical quandaries, societal effects, and the policy responses currently under consideration or implemented to resolve them.

5.6.1   Political manipulation with deepfake videos

- *Case study overview:* When talking about political meddling, between the 2018 U.S. Midterm Election and the subsequent surge in deepfake videos, we do not have to look very far to imagine how generative AIs can be weaponized. Deepfakes are ultra-realistic videos or audio recordings produced by AI algorithms that manipulate or create fake media. These are technologies that can cause people to appear as if they did or said things they never did and have profound implications for election integrity and public trust.
- *Ethical issues:*
  - *Misinformation:* AI-generated deepfake videos can create misleading content that affects voter perceptions and interferes with democratic processes
  - *No consent:* Politicians, celebrities, people in the news, and everyday citizens can experience a violation of their rights and privacy when their face or voice is used without consent. The person whose likeness is used in a deepfake video has no say over their picture, voice, or character.
  - *Political manipulation:* In a political environment, deepfakes can become tools of malicious actors who fabricate videos for use as political propaganda, discrediting candidates through fake footage. This application of AI-generated content can create societal division and be used to shape public opinion.
- *Regulatory Response*: In the United States Congress, bills such as the Malicious Deep Fake Prohibition Act (2020) criminalize deepfakes with malicious intent in mind for certain purposes (political). The EU has adopted suggested rules through the Artificial Intelligence Act to oversee and limit the usage of high-risk uses of AI, including deepfake technology. In the EU, for example, makers of deepfakes might have to clearly label their synthetic media in order not to deceive consumers.
- *Outcome:* Awareness of the dangers of deepfakes has led social media companies, including Facebook and Twitter, to roll out tools that identify and mark manipulated content. But these are early days, and with technology only getting better, the platforms will have to keep updating their policies as threats develop.

5.6.2   AI-generated music in commercial advertising

The aesthetic use of AI as an artifact for artistic (if not institutional) productions is also close to another aesthetic-ethics relation in the realm of sound: gadgetry and productivism, the creation of gadgets and products with a novel kind. The International Journal of Transmedia Literacy (IJTL).

- *Case study overview:* But in 2019, OpenAI's AI system Jukedeck generated music called The Million Dollar Song, a full-length track written completely by the computer and subsequently picked up for use in an advertisement. It was a new chapter in the industry that saw artificial intelligence having dominion over creative disciplines like music, visual art, and design.

- *Ethical issues:*
  - *Intellectual property:* Ownership of content, and who creates content, is also a big question when we are talking about AI-generated work. Who owns the rights to music made by artificial intelligence? Is it the business that built the AI, is it the user who gave instructions, or is it even the AI? Because these laws are designed with humans in mind, they have a hard time accommodating nonhuman author.
  - *Attribution:* Who gets the credit when a song generated by an AI is sold or used in a commercial? The AI-generated content also lacks a clear attribution to the algorithm and/or the developers, which brings in questions of ethics, viz., how will you credit or pay its authors?
- *Regulatory response:* IP laws are now catching up with AI and content creation. For now, in many parts of the world, AI-written music is currently regarded as property either owned by the company or person who generated the AI, or possibly even belonging to whoever created and provided the dataset with which to train that algorithm. Some copyright offices have begun to examine whether an AI can be the author of a work. For instance, in 2020, the U.S. Copyright Office held that AI developed for web scraping is not a "human author" and therefore its works may not be copyrighted. This decision has left a hole in how traditional copyright principles are supposed to apply to AI-generated works.
- *Outcome:* The case has ramped up the discussion around AI and intellectual property in particular and has indicated that clearer regulations and potentially new laws are required to deal with questions such as AIs as authors. As generative AI becomes more mainstream within the creative fields, safeguards and new models will need to be established around creators' rights as well as fostering of innovation.

5.6.3   AI-generated content and fake news in journalism

- *Case study overview:* In 2019, the Zambia election scandal saw a deepfake video spread widely in which a political leader was shown saying negative things against their rival. The video became a viral sensation, going on to make an impact on public sentiment in the election campaign. This case illustrates how AI-generated content can contribute to misinformation and erosion of trust in the media.
- *Ethical issues:* Fake News: The easy accessibility of AI-generated fake news, be that in videos, audio, or articles, represents such a huge threat to the integrity of journalism. The public might find it hard to tell real and fake apart, eroding trust in media outlets.
- *Shaping public opinion:* Bad actors can produce phony content that shapes public perception, leading to impacts on elections, the stock market, and social trends. Making convincing false stories makes it harder to have a fair and informed public conversation.

- *Regulatory response:* Due to the threat of fake news, legislation is being proposed at regulatory organizations worldwide that requires disclosure of synthetic content. For example, the European Commission has been advancing proposals to mitigate disinformation, with measures including that companies like Facebook and Google label AI-produced content. The United States has passed into law the Honest Ads Act, which seeks to improve the transparency of online political ads and could potentially encompass deepfakes.
- *Outcome:* While some media companies and platforms have created tools to detect fake content, it is still in development. AI-driven fact-checking tools are in development but still need to be strengthened as generative AI becomes more sophisticated.

5.6.4 AI-generated art and copyright concerns

- *Case study overview:* In 2018, an AI-generated work called "Portrait of Edmond de Belamy" was sold at Christie's for more than $400,000. A Paris-based collective called Obvious developed the artwork with a GAN. This sale was "groundbreaking" for the art community as it is a step into AI being considered as an actual creator.
- *Ethical issues:* Copyright and ownership: The central ethical issue is that issues are more about ownership. How do you assert ownership of AI-generated art? Whom do you blame: the creator of the AI system, the teacher of the AI or actually automate/program itself?
- *Authors in art:* The real or fictitious human history behind a piece of art and its attribution, as opposed to the human use of computers and mechanical information processing tools. The art world and legal experts are torn over whether a painting made by AI should be treated as if it were made by humans.
- *Regulatory response:* Many countries (including the United States and UK) have a specific legal prohibition on AI holding copyright. Instead, the inventor or user of the AI often owns the work. There is a global movement underway to recalibrate copyright laws to reflect the fundamental differences between AI and humans when it comes to creators. The World Intellectual Property Organization (WIPO) has issued papers on AI and intellectual property rights, and further regulation is expected down the line.
- *Outcome:* The sale of AI-created art has ignited debate over what constitutes art and who is a creator. It has also triggered calls to overhaul copyright laws to take into account the contribution of AI in creativity. As generative technologies advance, AI and copyright overlap is expected to remain a relevant field of both legal and ethical concern.

5.6.5 Synthetic media and privacy invasions

- *Case study overview:* Nonconsensual pornographic content, also known as revenge porn, is a common application for deepfake technology. This can include generating fake photos or videos that show people in compromising positions – often without their permission. The privacy infringements can be deeply upsetting and destructive to those shown in these videos.

- Ethical issues: Privacy and Consent: The production and sharing of deepfakes generated without consent are a serious infringement on personal privacy and dignity. Sufferers can have their faces used in a manner to which they never agreed, leading to emotional upset and reputational harm.
- *Emotional, psychological damage:* In situations like revenge porn, victims are left to deal not just with the trauma of their image being exploited but also a return to an unforgiving society that judges and stigmatizes them. It is also the inability to have control over their image in these situations that compounds the emotional and mental anguish.
- *Regulatory response:* In deepfake persevere countries have begun to enact laws regarding deepfake pornography. In the U.S., California's Senate Bill 2018 makes it a crime to create deepfakes with the specific aim of defaming someone, and several other states are adopting similar laws. We have seen platforms like Reddit and Twitter adopt policies to take down nonconsensual deepfakes, as well as offer a way for victims to report.
- *Outcome:* Ongoing legal fights and policy responses prove that people's privacy should be better protected in the digital era. Further advancements in deepfake detection and policy enforcement will be important to stem this malicious activity.

5.6.6   Conclusion

The use-case scenarios outlined in this chapter illustrate the wide range of ethical and regulatory issues related to generative AI for multimedia. From the massive amounts of deepfake content created to sway public opinion, to intellectual property issues around AI-generated art, we know new challenges emerge from deploying AI technology and that it requires a new framework for ethical oversight (Table 5.5).

While AI techniques are poised to advance, policymakers, technologists, and ethicists will need to work in concert to design strong regulatory approaches and ethical frameworks for ensuring the responsible governance of these powerful technologies. Transparency, accountability, and fair attribution will be the guiding principles for exploring the ethical terrain in generative AI for multimedia to ensure that it benefits public interest while respecting individual rights and freedoms.

5.7   Conclusion

Though GenAI brings transformational opportunities and a certain pace in scientific advancement, it also brings ethical and social challenges. These challenges and concerns range from bias and intellectual property infringement to deepfakes and misinformation spread, projecting the proactive action from developers for their accountability and transparency. As developers have the moral obligation to integrate fairness, transparency, and accountability, users are also obligated to critically evaluate AI output, avoid its misuse, and engage in only the ethical use of AI.

Table 5.5 Comparison of ethical and regulatory issues in generative AI in multimedia

Case study	Ethical issues	Regulatory response	Outcome	Key challenges
Deepfake videos in political manipulation	• Misinformation • Lack of consent • Political manipulation	• U.S. Malicious Deep Fake Prohibition Act (2020) • EU AI Act proposals • Social media flagging tools	• Increased awareness of deepfake risks • Social media platforms developing detection tools	• Detecting and preventing deepfakes • Keeping up with AI advancements
AI-generated music in commercial advertising	• Intellectual property • Attribution and ownership	• Evolving copyright laws for AI • AI-generated music is typically considered property of creators or owners	• Debate around AI and copyright • AI music gaining commercial use	• Defining ownership in AI-generated art • Establishing fair compensation models
Fake news and AI-generated content in journalism	• Fake news • Manipulation of public opinion	• EU's Digital Services Act • U.S. Honest Ads Act • Platforms required to flag deepfakes	• Media companies developing AI-based fact-checking tools • Ongoing regulation on disinformation	• Detecting AI-generated fake news • Global consistency in regulation
AI-generated art and copyright issues	• Intellectual property • Artistic authorship • Ownership of AI creations	• WIPO exploring AI and intellectual property • U.S. and UK laws do not grant copyright to AI-generated work	• Growing market for AI-generated art • Ongoing debates about AI as an artist	• Defining authorship in AI • Updating copyright laws to address AI works
Synthetic media and privacy violations	• Privacy violations • Consent issues • Psychological harm	• California SB 2018: Criminalizes deepfake porn • Social media platforms enforcing content bans	• Legal cases leading to stronger privacy protections • Growing awareness of harm caused by deepfakes	• Detecting and removing harmful content • Protecting individual privacy rights

There are efforts in advancing the regulatory frameworks, such as the EU's AI Act and GDPR; still, the global ethical landscape of AI remains fragmented, creating gaps in consistency and oversight. Shared accountability and strict governance and compliance need to be ensured through cross-sector collaborations of all stakeholders in order to get societal benefits from AI. Only through coordinated ethical action can GenAI be steered toward inclusive, human-centered progress.

References

[1]   Jackson BR, Rashidi HH, Lennerz JK, and de Baca ME. Ethical and regulatory perspectives on generative artificial intelligence in pathology. *Archives of Pathology & Laboratory Medicine*. 2025;149(2):123–129.

[2]   Al-Kfairy M, Mustafa D, Kshetri N, Insiew M, and Alfandi O. Ethical challenges and solutions of generative AI: An interdisciplinary perspective. In *Informatics* 2024 (Vol. 11, No. 3, p. 58). Multidisciplinary Digital Publishing Institute.

[3]   Yu L, and Zhai X. Ethical and regulatory challenges of generative artificial intelligence in healthcare: A Chinese perspective. *Journal of Clinical Nursing*. 2024:1–17. Doi: 10.1111/jocn.17493.

[4]   Luk CY, Chung HL, Yim WK, and Leung CW. Regulating generative AI: Ethical considerations and explainability benchmarks [Internet]. 2024.

[5]   Wang X, and Wu YC. Balancing innovation and regulation in the age of generative artificial intelligence. *Journal of Information Policy*. 2024; 14:385–416.

[6]   Li J, Cai X, and Cheng L. Legal regulation of generative AI: A multi-dimensional construction. *International Journal of Legal Discourse*. 2023;8 (2):365–388.

[7]   Huang Y, Arora C, Houng WC, Kanij T, Madulgalla A, and Grundy J. Ethical concerns of generative AI and mitigation strategies: A systematic mapping study. *arXiv* preprint arXiv:2502.00015. 2025.

[8]   Al-kfairy M, Mustafa D, Kshetri N, Insiew M, and Alfandi O. A systematic review and analysis of ethical challenges of generative AI: An interdisciplinary perspective. Available at SSRN 4833030.

[9]   Laine J, Minkkinen M, and Mäntymäki M. Understanding the ethics of generative AI: Established and new ethical principles. *Communications of the Association for Information Systems*. 2025;56(1):7.

[10]   Atencio GS. The challenges and opportunities for ethics in generative artificial intelligence in the digital age. *DYNA: revista de la Facultad de Minas. Universidad Nacional de Colombia. Sede Medellín*. 2025;92(236):26–35.

[11]   Shumakova NI, Lloyd JJ, and Titova EV. Towards legal regulations of generative AI in the creative industry. *Journal of Digital Technologies and Law*. 2023;1(4):880–908.

[12]   Wach K, Duong CD, Ejdys J, *et al.* The dark side of generative artificial intelligence: A critical analysis of controversies and risks of ChatGPT. *Entrepreneurial Business and Economics Review*. 2023;11(2):7–30.

[13]   Saini H, Singh G, Dalal S, Lilhore UK, Simaiya S, and Dalal S. Enhancing cloud network security with a trust-based service mechanism using k-anonymity and statistical machine learning approach. *Peer-to-Peer Networking and Applications*. 2024;17(6):4084–4109.

[14]   Ordóñez JM. Creativity, ethics, and regulation in the age of generative AI. *AI Impacts on Branded Entertainment and Advertising*. 2025:45–64.

[15]   Ali H, and Aysan AF. Ethical dimensions of generative AI: A cross-domain analysis using machine learning structural topic modeling. *International Journal of Ethics and Systems*. 2025;41(1):3–4.

[16]   Raza S, Qureshi R, Zahid A, *et al.* Who is responsible? the data, models, users or regulations? a comprehensive survey on responsible generative AI for a sustainable future. *arXiv* preprint arXiv:2502.08650. 2025.

[17]   Bhutani M, Dalal S, Alhussein M, Lilhore UK, Aurangzeb K, and Hussain A. SAD-GAN: A novel secure anomaly detection framework for enhancing the resilience of cyber-physical systems. *Cognitive Computation*. 2025;17 (4):127.

[18]   Lilhore UK, Simaiya S, Dalal S, Alshuhail A, and Almusharraf A. A post-quantum hybrid encryption framework for securing biometric data in consumer electronics. *IEEE Transactions on Consumer Electronics*. 2025; 71(3):8289–8297.

[19]   Cath C Governing artificial intelligence: ethical, legal and technical opportunities and challenges. Philosophical Transactions of the Royal Society A: Mathematical. *Physical and Engineering Sciences*. 2018; 376(2133):20180080.

[20]   Dalal S, Rani U, Lilhore UK, *et al.* Optimized XGBoost model with whale optimization algorithm for detecting anomalies in manufacturing. *Journal of Computational and Cognitive Engineering*. 2024;4(4):1–17.

[21]   Dalal S, Poongodi M, Lilhore UK, *et al.* Optimized LightGBM model for security and privacy issues in cyber-physical systems. *Transactions on Emerging Telecommunications Technologies*. 2023;34(6):e4771.

Chapter 6

Risk assessment and management of generative AI systems

Generative artificial intelligence (GenAI) techniques permeate most industries and sectors, whether for content development or for critical decision support. Hence, demonstrating the transformational potential of GenAI along with different contexts of its application. On the other hand, GenAI presents its various limitations and risks that are intrinsically linked to other artificial intelligence contexts. These limitations and complex risks are commonly cited as bias, privacy invasion, dis/misinformation, intellectual property theft, data leak, and unknown outcome [1].

Therefore, a proactive risk assessment framework is necessary for the application of GenAI. This framework should possess the capability for effective risk management and reporting. This solution imposes an understanding of the opportunities of GenAI to build the foundation for proactive risk assessment, monitoring, reporting, and overall management. In this chapter, key mitigation strategies, ethical guidelines, and regulatory compliance are discussed to build the context for the responsible application of GenAI systems.

6.1 Introduction

Risk management in AI governance is very important as it is highlighted through strategies such as risk mitigation, monitoring, governance throughout the life-cycle, and compliance with regulations. In addition, ethical guidelines and reporting are also encouraged for the responsible application of generative AI [2]. The application of technological and legal measures therefore emphasizes robust monitoring mechanisms, ethical guidelines, and the use of synthetic data to prevent privacy infringements. This reflects techniques in medical and healthcare where GANs are usually used for generating synthetic datasets while preserving privacy during model training [3].

Likewise, some mitigation strategies for generative AI risks not just emphasize robust monitoring, ethical guidelines, and regulatory compliance, but also emphasize continuous improvement [4]. Many of the areas related to the governance of GenAI are not well explored; for instance, Ref. [5] does not present specific real-world case studies illustrating how organizations managed risks in their generative

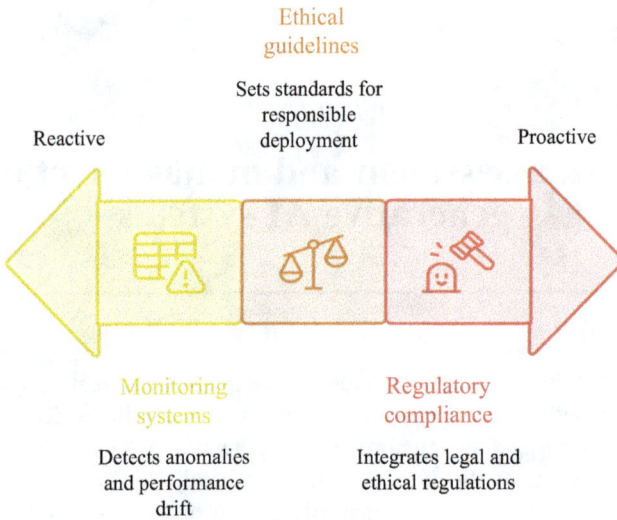

Figure 6.1   GenAI risk management strategies ranging from reactive to proactive

AI deployments. It discusses general challenges, benefits, and strategies for integration, but lacks detailed examples of successes and lessons learned (Figure 6.1). The real-world case studies showcasing AI's role in social cybersecurity, focusing on its application in detecting cyber threats and improving incident response, are presented in Ref. [6]. However, it does not specifically address generative AI deployments or the management of associated risks.

6.2   Robust monitoring systems

A cornerstone of GenAI risk management is the implementation of sophisticated, continuous monitoring systems. At present, advanced AI techniques, such as Generative Adversarial Networks (GANs), for real-time risk prediction (summarized in Table 6.1) can be embedded for robust monitoring systems to detect potential threats and anomalies [7]. The organization and industries using GenAI can take advantage of such a system and integrate for advanced risk management. To address other complicated and multilayered risks associated with the use of GenAI, ethical guidelines and regulatory compliance can be set [7–9].

Further, the effort to identify and mitigate risks in the granular details across the AI lifecycle to deploy it responsibly, and *The Generative AI Ethics Playbook* has practical resources to help practitioners [10,11]. Likewise, practical instances of risk management indicate lessons learned – as well as summating the successes achieved – to illustrate the need for approaches to continuous improvement in generative AI implementations [12]. Outputs from GenAI are more variable and context dependent (unlike conventional software) and must offer real-time

Table 6.1 Advanced AI techniques for real-time risk prediction in monitoring systems

Technique	How it works	Strengths for risk prediction	Limitations	Use cases	Maturity/readiness
Generative Adversarial Networks (GANs)	Two neural networks (generator + discriminator) learn normal vs. anomalous patterns.	Excellent at detecting anomalies and generating synthetic data for rare risks.	Training instability requires large datasets.	Fraud detection, cyber anomaly detection, insider threat modeling.	Emerging (active research, selective deployment)
Reinforcement Learning (RL)	Learns optimal policies through trial-and-error interactions.	Adapts dynamically to evolving risks, simulates "what-if" scenarios.	High computational cost, risk of unsafe exploration.	Adaptive cybersecurity, dynamic risk scoring.	Experimental (pilot-stage, limited production use)
Graph Neural Networks (GNNs)	Models entities and relationships as graphs to capture complex dependencies.	Detects risks in interconnected systems, excels at spotting hidden anomalies.	Computationally heavy, requires graph-structured data.	Supply chain risk, fraud rings, systemic financial risk.	Emerging (gaining traction)
Variational Autoencoders (VAEs)	Compresses and reconstructs data, detecting deviations as anomalies.	Effective at identifying subtle anomalies in high-dimensional data.	May miss complex anomalies.	Healthcare anomaly detection, IoT sensor monitoring.	Production-ready (commonly used)
Transformer-based Models	Uses self-attention to capture long-range dependencies in sequential data.	Effective at analyzing time-series risks in real-time.	Data-hungry, costly to deploy.	Market volatility prediction, real-time compliance monitoring.	Production-ready (widely adopted)

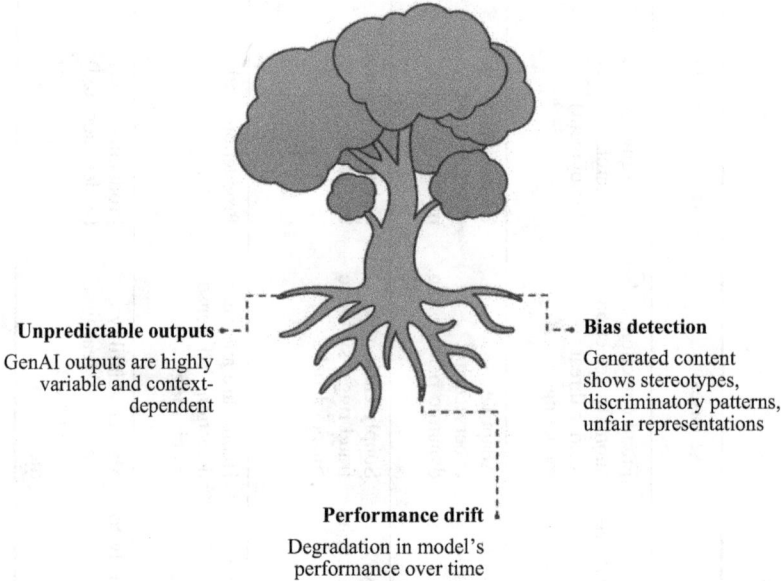

Unpredictable outputs
GenAI outputs are highly
variable and context-
dependent

Bias detection
Generated content
shows stereotypes,
discriminatory patterns,
unfair representations

Performance drift
Degradation in model's
performance over time

*Figure 6.2   Different indicators of risks that should be detected by the monitoring
systems*

oversight. An efficient and effective monitoring system (Figure 6.2) should include
monitoring of:

- **Output quality and consistency:** This comes in through checks, which occur
  as automated checks for coherence, and factual accuracy, as well as para, or
  content guidelines consistency, like writing quality from a human description
  of an article. The quality of the outputs, particularly images. Current Quality
  Assessments for Natural Language Processing (NLP) metrics and anomaly
  detection are typical in this process.
- **Bias scanning:** Bias is established through purposefully scanning for stereotypes,
  discriminatory patterns from the generated content, and or unfair representations.
  These three indicators are typically not the sole reason to show that bias is the
  outcome of bias acquired through the training data or, consequently, through model
  behavior. Automated bias detection can hence be accomplished to increase efficiency through decided intent using a variety of tools of fairness metrics and
  explainable AI (XAI) provided. Recent studies employing XAI illustrate how
  transparent models promote effective human-in-the-loop monitoring; this same
  strategy can be effectively applied to GenAI risk monitoring.
- **Monitoring drift and resource use:** Another verification type involves checks
  that detect potential model performance degradation over time, and thus signs of
  data drift, potential adversarial attacks, or model decay. Tracking the computational
  resources used to ensure an efficient, sustainable operation is also a risk indicator,
  especially when deploying on a larger scale. Also, user interactions and feedback

are collected (explicitly or implicitly) to capture problematic outputs and/or uncertain behavior that automated systems may overlook.

An ideal monitoring system would trigger alerts for human review when or if risks or anomalies occurred, thereby allowing for some sort of human-in-the-loop operational monitoring.

6.3   Ethical guidelines and principles

A second pillar for creating a responsible, trusted GenAI system is ethical guidelines (see Section 6.2). Ethical guidelines as established are a moral compass for the development, deployment, and use of AI technologies (see Section 5.2). Some of the key principles of the guidelines include:

- **Transparency and explainability:** This principle is intended to strive for understanding and the clarity of how generative AI (GenAI) systems generate their outputs, especially within serious applications. In other words, to foster trust while also facilitating effective auditing and debugging stages after GenAI has been used [13].
- **Fairness and non-discrimination:** The principle of fairness is about being proactive to identify and reduce bias both in data, algorithms, and outputs to provide fair treatment for every user or end-user from all user groups.
- **Accountability:** This principle is about being clear about who is responsible for the outputs and impacts of GenAI systems, including the designer, developer, deployer, this approach ensures data protection for the end user in accordance with the ethical guidelines.
- **Privacy and data security**: When writing ethical guidelines, the key here is to develop strong safeguards for the sensitive data collected for training and inference use, such as legally mandated measures such as those defined in GDPR, CCPA.
- **Human oversight and control:** This is another ethical guideline principle that is also embedded in the monitoring system. It deals with confirming that humans hold ultimate control over critical decisions and that GenAI systems are constructed just to augment, not replace, human judgment.

In addition, the ethical guidelines needed to be either co-developed with diverse stakeholders or regularly reviewed by them. This is necessary to adapt according to the evolving potentials of GenAI technologies and societal expectations [14–16].

6.4   Regulatory compliance

Another important part of the risk assessment strategies is that the evolving capabilities of GenAI need to meet the updated landscape of AI regulation (see Section 5.4). It must be determined that the GenAI deployments are complying with relevant laws and standards [17,18]. These compliances include:

- **Data privacy regulations:** Adherence to laws governing data collection, storage, and usage (e.g., GDPR, CCPA, HIPAA), as discussed in Section 5.4.1.
- **Content and copyright laws:** Ensuring that generated content respects intellectual property rights and avoids plagiarism or unauthorized use of copyrighted material.
- **Sector-specific regulations:** Compliance with industry-specific regulations is crucial for ensuring the reliability, safety, and fairness of AI systems, particularly in sectors like healthcare, finance, and education. These regulations usually emphasize ethical principles such as transparency, accountability, and privacy (as discussed in Section 6.3), which form the foundation of frameworks like IEEE's guidelines and UNESCO's AI ethics recommendations. For example, in healthcare, requirements for trustworthy AI include fairness, explainability, and robustness, all of which are essential for gaining the trust of healthcare stakeholders [19]. Likewise, AI-driven solutions enrich compliance by automating reporting and documentation in the finance industry, thus improving efficiency and accuracy while focusing on ethical concerns such as algorithmic bias. Furthermore, the AI compliance frameworks are also demanded to fulfill the unique challenges of each sector. Therefore, it required tailored standards and exchange of ideas among stakeholders for balancing innovation and risk management (Figure 6.3) [20].

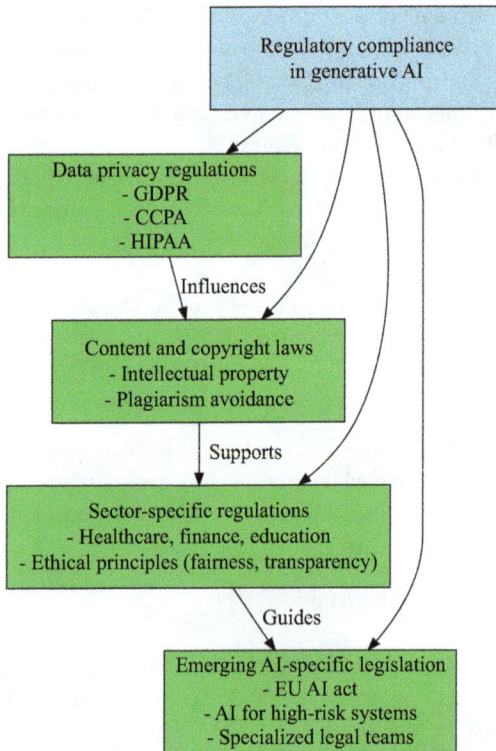

Figure 6.3   Ethical and regulatory cycle of GenAI

- **Emerging AI-specific legislation:** To establish specific obligations for developers and operators of high-risk artificial intelligence systems, it is imperative to proactively prepare for upcoming regulatory frameworks, for instance, the European Union's AI Act (discussed in Section 5.4.1). This can help in establishing specific obligations for developers and operators of high-risk GenAI systems. Additionally, maintaining a specialized legal and compliance team and engaging with subject matter experts is essential to effectively navigate these evolving requirements.

6.5   Continuous improvement practices

Risk assessment and management should be considered as an iterative and ongoing process rather than a singular event, especially in the context of generative AI (Figure 6.4). This continuous improvement approach entails the following activities:

- **Regular auditing and review:** Periodically auditing GenAI models, data pipelines, and deployment practices against established ethical guidelines and regulatory requirements.
- **Feedback loops:** This feedback mechanism(s) is derived from users, monitoring systems, and incident reports. It is essential for guiding the model retraining, fine-tuning the model, and system modifications.
- **Version control and documentation:** Maintaining clear documentation of model versions, training data, performance metrics, and any changes made over time.
- **Incident response planning:** Developing clear protocols for identifying, responding to, and mitigating the impact of unexpected or harmful GenAI outputs.

6.6   NIST AI Risk Management Framework (AI RMF)

For the effective implementation of AI risk management, the architecture is multilayered framework considered to be integrating governance, technical controls, and oversight throughout the AI lifecycle. A prominent architecture of AI risk management is the NIST AI Risk Management Framework (AI RMF). It is an iterated and multilayered architecture divided into four layers (depicted in Figure 6.5).

The Govern layer of this architecture remains the most important one, the first one. It is a process that is continuous and holistically centers on an organization's responsible AI ethical principles, policies, and culture (Table 6.2). This layer guarantees that key principles like fairness, accountability, and transparency are embedded and guide all successive activities by instituting a clear governance structure and an ethics committee with defined roles and responsibilities (briefly summarized in Table 6.3). This is a fundamental step. It is the organization's AI legal and ethical principles.

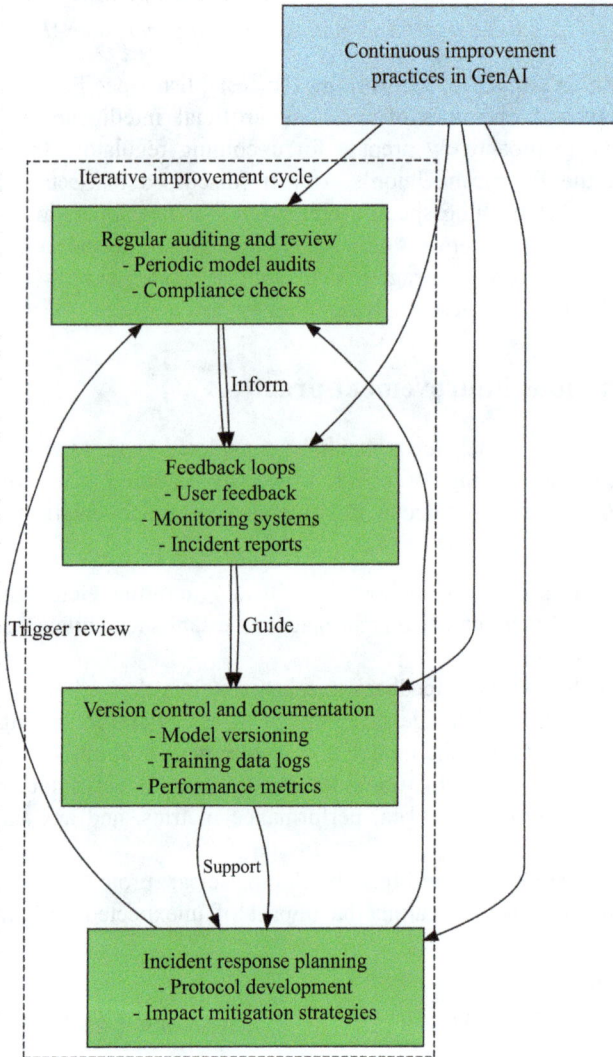

Figure 6.4   Continuous improvement practices

Table 6.2   Summary of key continuous improvement activities

Activity	Use	Benefits
Regular auditing and review	Periodically monitor and evaluate the AI system and its outputs.	Identifies emerging risks, prevents biases, and ensures compliance.
Feedback loops	Collect real-time feedback from users and stakeholders.	Improves model accuracy and reliability, builds trust.
Version control and documentation	Track all changes to model versions, training data, and code.	Ensures accountability, facilitates troubleshooting, and maintains system integrity.
Incident response planning	Develop procedures to address AI system failures or ethical breaches.	Minimizes harm, ensures quick resolution of issues.

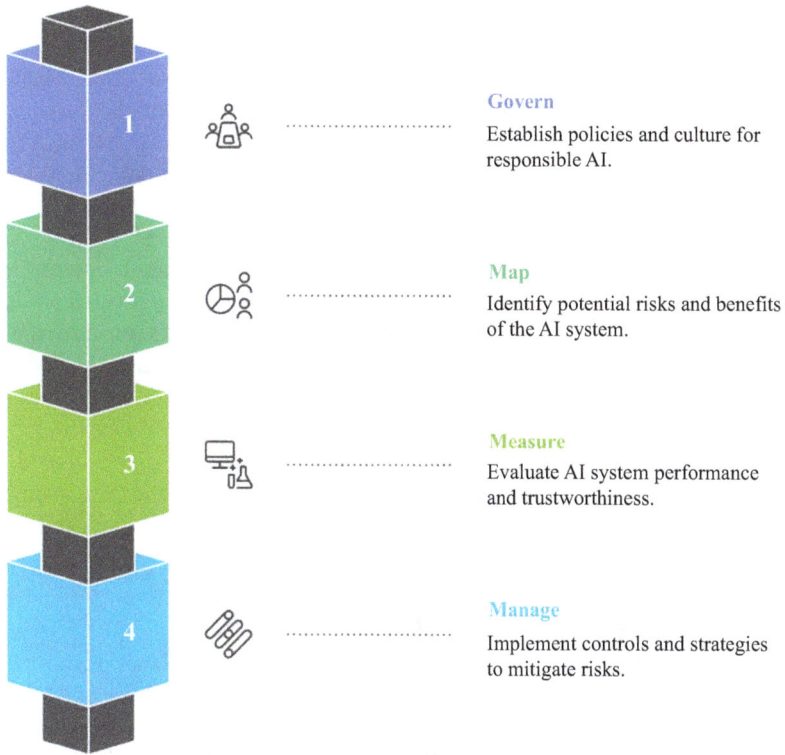

Figure 6.5   Implementing AI risk management using NIST AI Risk Management Framework

Table 6.3   Layers of NIST framework (AI RMF) with respective to their functions and benefits

Layer	Function	Priority	Benefits	Strategies
Govern	Policy foundation	Highest	Provides accountability, ensures compliance, and aligns AI with values.	Establish an ethics committee; define roles; create governance policies.
Map	Risk identification	High	Understands system risks early.	Conduct risk assessments; categorize AI systems; identify potential risks like bias and security.
Measure	Evaluation	Medium	Quantifies risk and monitors performance.	Use metrics to track fairness and accuracy; monitor performance over time.
Manage	Mitigation and action	High	Minimizes harm; enables effective crisis response.	Prioritize risks; implement controls; create incident response plans.

The ethics committee is responsible for the organization's AI risk assessment system. The architecture enters a continuous loop of Map and Measure. Here, the organization is able to categorize the AI system. This is called the "Map" stage, and it is described as the ability to contextualize and pinpoint potential benefits and risks for an AI system. Once potential risks are identified, such as problematic datasets that contain privacy, bias, and misleading and harmful data, the system is able to Measure. Assessment in the context of a people-to-people system where the AI system tiers risks is more human. This is called qualitative AI.

The last layer is Manage, which is the action-focused part. Using the information and insights derived during the "Measure" stage, this layer concentrates on the implementation of controls and management frameworks to curb the risk exposures. Some essential tasks revolve around the risk-by-risk ranking of potential consequences, grading the exposures using different techniques such as data set scrubbing or model tuning, and executing comprehensive and structured countermeasure response plans. This enables the organization to contain the adverse consequences, enables the organization to respond within reasonable time spans, and enables the organization to exploit the upside of a generative AI and use it safely and responsibly.

6.6.1　Critical aspects in implementing AI RMF

Although the framework outlined gives a significant resemblance to a practical approach to risk management in gender-active AI, its real-world use and adoption face severe adversities. While the model is sound in principle, its implementation has challenges, especially in the artificial intelligence domain and in the multifaceted complexities of organizations.

The first and perhaps the most significant in a list of challenges is that of risk measurement. Generative AI systems, in real-life applications, pose risks that challenge the established traditional systems model that is standard and predictive, and the systems model that employs AI that is sophisticated. Examples of the risks include hallucination, prompt injections, and model poisoning, and these types of risks are not only sophisticated but also novel and stimulative. Even in the most well- and deeply-established predictive and risk systems, the challenges of quantifying the probability and the repercussions of these risks are clear and glaring, especially in situations where the elements of consortia are not unified.

Furthermore, the opaque nature of many AI models, often referred to as the "black box" problem, complicates the "Measure" and "Manage" layers. It's difficult for organizations to understand how a model arrived at a specific decision, which hinders the ability to audit its processes, identify the source of a vulnerability, or implement targeted mitigation strategies. This lack of transparency also makes it challenging to establish a clear baseline for what constitutes a "human baseline" for comparison, as AI systems often perform tasks in fundamentally different ways than humans.

The Govern layer entails setting up an AI ethics committee and cultivating a culture of risk management. Smaller organizations may struggle with these

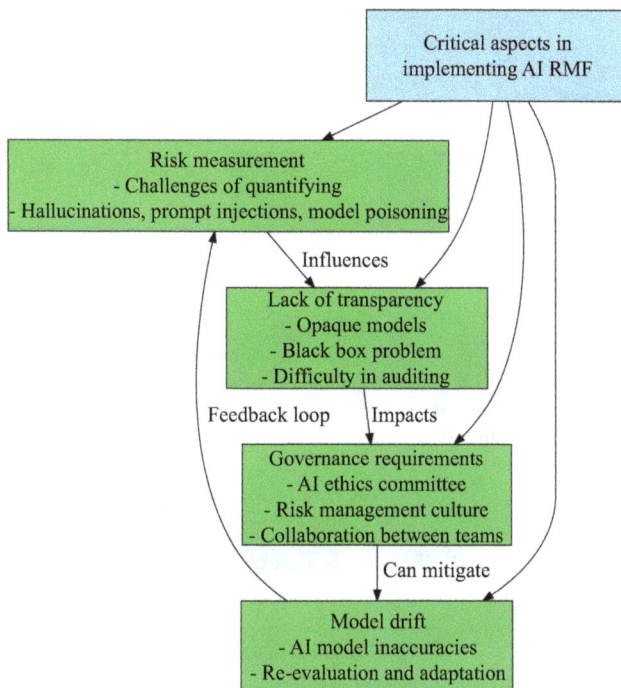

Figure 6.6 Critical aspects in implementing AI RMF

requirements. The framework's success in collaboration across diverse teams' collaboration which can be a challenge considering legal, technical, and executive teams need to work and agree on a risk tolerance (Figure 6.6). The nature of generative AI poses a challenge to AI frameworks. An AI model tends to suffer from model drift, which weakens its AI model, increases inaccuracy, and raises higher risks. This, therefore, means constant preparedness and reevaluation to avoid stasis. The framework needs to be a relentless, repetitive cycle. This vigilance requirement may serve as an operational and financial burden. This burden emphasizes the success blueprint the organization needs to go through systemic and practical challenges.

6.7 Risk assessment in generative AI

Risk assessment and management are undoubtedly crucial for GenAI systems due to their increased use in critical decision support and widespread use. Practical implementations of risk monitoring and management techniques underscore the critical importance of these strategies. For example, a leading media company implemented a robust monitoring program for its marketing materials generated by AI that was able to detect subtle biases before the materials were published, thus demonstrating the advantages of continuous monitoring. In contrast, first

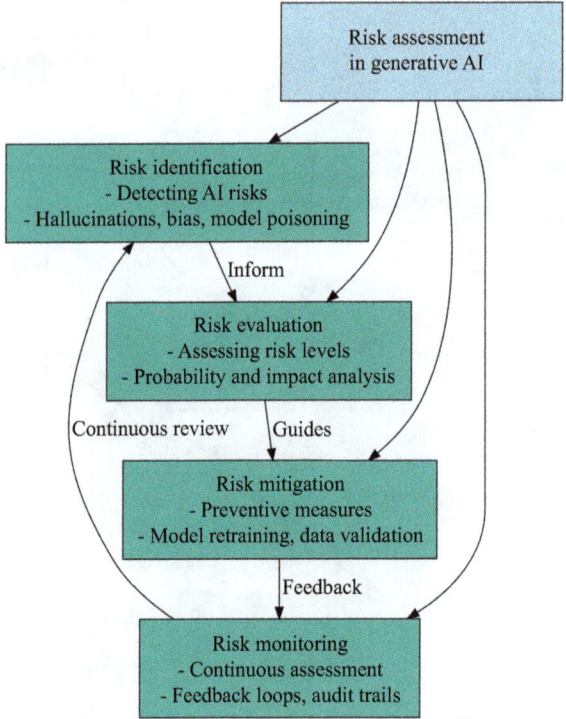

Figure 6.7   Risk assessment in generative AI

deployments of chatbots that were released without ethics guidelines received criticism from the public because they produced racist and otherwise inappropriate outputs that stressed the need for preemptive ethical protocols for AI (Figure 6.7).

The linguistic customization of AI systems—for example, designing a chatbot to use youth slang—has been shown to influence user affect and further provides evidence supporting the need for preemptive ethical design. In manufacturing, a smart factory had established continuous improvement cycles where operators provided their feedback into computerized predictive maintenance developed by generative AI. The computer recognized operator behavior and incorporated their feedback into the predictive maintenance system, which increased trust between humans and machines and lower unplanned downtime. Similar benefits have been evident in educational settings, where virtual reality-based chemistry learning contexts include interactive gamification strategies to support learner confidence and performance.

The application of generative AI on software development projects has demonstrated effective strategies for using chatbots for risk identification and assessment within various project contexts. Strategies of governance in these projects have been developed and can be seen in the public sector, where different countries and jurisdictions (i.e., Australia, Canada) have similar frameworks to govern public concerns and risks (e.g., data security, public trust), noting the importance also for a full regulatory framework. Table 6.3 outlines the key elements of risk assessment in generative AI (GenAI), including risk categories, evaluation methods, mitigation strategies, and monitoring practices.

Comparative studies have also shown how AI has demonstrated revolutionary potential for risk management through case studies in which AI has enhanced aspects of risk assessment, even with some challenges in its contextualization. In addition, governance frameworks for generative AI within corporate contexts are also important in order to balance various potential rewards against associated risks, etc., to provide "actionable" for organizations for the responsible integration of AI. Lastly, principles of an algorithmic governance framework can apply to public sector applications together with all stakeholders to support effective AI and collaborative implementation to further support existing structure, processes, and support roles within which they volunteer. These examples demonstrate that incorporating ethical considerations into AI system design is essential to ensure alignment with societal values, ethical principles, and human interests (Table 6.4).

Table 6.4   The key elements of risk assessment in generative AI

Risk category	Risk identification	Risk evaluation	Mitigation strategies	Monitoring practices
Hallucinations	AI generates incorrect or fabricated information	Assess the likelihood of hallucinations occurring based on model training and input data	Regular retraining, better data curation	Continuous model evaluation with user feedback
Bias	Identifying bias in model outputs based on datasets and historical data	Measure the extent of bias in various contexts (e.g., racial, gender)	Implement fairness algorithms, use diverse datasets	Monitor model performance across different demographic groups
Model poisoning	Detect malicious inputs affecting model behavior	Assess the potential impact on model reliability and security	Apply anomaly detection, secure training datasets	Continuously monitor input data and model outputs
Data privacy	Identifying risks of exposing sensitive data	Evaluate the risks of violating privacy regulations (e.g., GDPR)	Implement data anonymization, encryption	Audit and log model data usage to ensure compliance
Adversarial attacks	Detecting manipulation of model inputs to evade model defenses	Evaluate the model's robustness against adversarial attacks	Enhance model robustness through adversarial training	Continuously test for adversarial vulnerabilities

6.8   Case studies in risk assessment and management of generative AI

To better capture the practical use cases and lessons learned from managing the risk of generative AI (GenAI), we present case studies covering deployments in industry and coordinated regulatory compliance, ethical guidelines, as well as a preliminary taxonomy. This series of case studies illustrates successes and challenges, which have been instructive for developing effective risk management strategies for GenAI technologies.

6.8.1   Case 1: AI in healthcare – synthetic data for privacy protection

- **Background:** In the field of health, GANs have been used for the development of synthetic medical data for AI model training in order not to violate patient privacy. This is particularly important in industries, such as medical imaging, for which real patient data is extremely sensitive. With the help of several healthcare providers, UC Berkeley worked to use GANs to generate synthetic datasets that can mimic actual patient data for feeding into machine learning models without running afoul of privacy laws.
- **Risk management strategies:** The primary risk associated with this use case was that the simulated data should resemble original real-life data while at the same time not result in re-identification of individual patients. The group used strict validation methods to test the synthetic data for privacy and compare it with patient information, they said. They also complied with GDPR principles related to data protection and anonymization.
- **Outcome:** The deployment process effectively preserved the quality of training data and privacy. Through ongoing audits of model performance and guarantees for the fulfillment of data protection laws, this work showed how AI ethics can be embedded into healthcare systems to allow innovation without harming patient rights.
- **Challenges:** We just had to be careful that the synthetic data did not create any unwanted artificial biases or artifacts. Continuing partnership with ethics committees and regulatory agencies has been crucial to securing public trust in, and adherence to, health data protection practices.

6.8.2   Case 2: generative AI in marketing – mitigating bias in AI-generated content

- **Background:** One prominent global marketing agency turned to generative AI as a way to automate their content creation, from blog posts and social media ads, down to product descriptions. When the AI's productivity gains went through the roof, the company realized it had a consistent problem of biased representation in its content: of gender and race stereotypes that were propagated by the models' training data.

- **Risk management strategies:** The company created a holistic model for detecting and addressing bias. This structure consisted of leveraging explainable AI (XAI) tools as a means to detect and reduce any biases within the content that was produced. There were frequent bias audits, and the ML models used to generate text were retrained on more varied, balanced data. The association also created ethics recommendations to get ahead of questions of fairness and inclusion.
- **Outcome:** By constantly monitoring, the company was able to drastically cut down on biased content and enrich the diversity of its advertising materials. The proactive risk review and feedback loop allowed the company to establish trust with customers and show commitment to diversity in its AI-generated content.
- **Challenges:** One major problem here was to make sure that AI systems could detect subtle biases in their training data, for which meta-fairness metrics were integrated with AI. The team also needed to continue and maintain real-time surveillance of the data, detecting unintended trends in content as they arose.

6.8.3   *Case 3: AI in autonomous vehicles – handling adversarial attacks*

- **Background:** A top self-driving-vehicle company released a generative AI model to aid object recognition, road mapping, and decision-making in autonomous cars. Even though the system produced impressive results, it had one big weakness: adversarial attacks, under which subtle tweaks to visual inputs could cause the AI model to misrepresent objects and do unsafe things.
- **Risk management strategies:** The firm deployed adversarial training, which meant the AI was constantly bombarded with adversarial examples in a controlled setting to harden its defenses. They also deployed risk monitors and real-time prediction systems, which could point to systemic vulnerability. In addition, the company collaborated with regulators on safety standards and regulations for AVs.
- **Outcome:** With such procedures to continually update the system with adversarial trained samples and implement real-time monitoring, it was possible to improve the robustness of its so-called self-driving vehicles against adversarial attacks. The system also became more durable, offering safety and reliability on the real road for you.
- **Challenges:** The difficulty of adversarial attacks and the need for continual adaptation in alluvial environments, such as driving, were a huge hurdle. Creating an environment where the AI system could constantly learn to quickly detect and use new patterns of attacks in real time was an ongoing effort, and it needed cooperation between experts in AI, regulators, and technological companies.

6.8.4   *Case 4: customer support AI solution – addressing hallucination and inappropriate output*

- **Background:** A prominent customer service chatbot also used generative AI to automate replies for customer inquiries. However, people were beginning to note that the chatbot would occasionally offer a non-relevant or incorrect answer to more complex questions, potentially leading customers astray and damaging a brand's goodwill.

- **Risk management strategies:** To combat these risks, the company put in place a mix of hallucination detection and content filtering. To mitigate answer accuracy, we fine-tuned the model of the chatbot with additional high-quality domain-specific data. We also added a feedback loop where users could mark negative responses, which were subsequently examined and employed to retrain the model. A human-in-the-loop system was also established for oversight and escalation to address more difficult problems.
- **Outcome:** The accuracy of the system and customer satisfaction rates increased as the chatbot became more dependable in response to requests. The reliance on constant feedback loops ensured a high standard of service and that we could achieve rapid course corrections as issues invariably arose.
- **Challenges:** It was difficult to make hallucinations and then correct them on the fly, particularly when users input their questions in vague or unclear ways. Finding the right equilibrium between automation and human intervention was also a perpetual struggle, especially when dealing with complicated customer scenarios.

6.9 Conclusion

Generative AI technology has the power to redefine industries, but as with all powerful technologies, we must carefully consider how it should be used. The case examples in these studies show the potential as well as difficulties of risk estimation and management for practical GenAI applications. By taking a proactive risk management approach that includes ongoing surveillance, ethical guidance, and compliance with relevant regulations, companies can do more to minimize harm and maximize positive benefits from these technologies.

The risks of GenAI can be identified and mitigated early in the development cycle by real-time monitoring systems, ethical frameworks, and feedback loops. This forward-leaning approach builds trust and helps to ensure that GenAI systems are transparent and accountable, serving human values. As these case studies illustrate, the relationship between innovation and responsibility is not always smooth – but they also underscore the continued criticality of developers, regulators, and stakeholders working together to grapple with generative AI's complexities. Generative AI solutions, which have potential applications across healthcare, finance, entertainment, and security, among many others, hold the promise of altering our economic landscape. Yet the increasing use of these technologies requires that their risks be managed in a systematic manner.

Risk mitigation is not a one-off exercise but an ongoing loop that can only fall short due to incompleteness. This includes managing and tuning by AI models, while keeping it updated or performing periodic audits and operating feedback loops to perfect technologies over time. In doing so, they can also discover and address potential risks early to create trust with end-users and the public by demonstrating an ethical approach to AI.

Another challenge will be managing privacy risks, intellectual property concerns, and potential ethics breaches as the power dynamic within GenAI systems shifts. Given this changing landscape, companies should integrate their AI efforts with the increasingly complex and dynamic flow of national and international laws on issues such as data protection (GDPR), cybersecurity, and infrastructure (AI Act in the European Union) to protect both users and developers from harm.

How GenAI technologies can and should progress, in terms of governance, risk assessment, and ethical oversight, will need to evolve as well". Italians realize the potential for gain – or the potential for loss – in these systems is balance, it is transparency and accountability, and constant vigilant reforming. And only through this all-encompassing mindset can we guarantee generative AI technologies continue to be a benefit, lifting human experiences without jeopardizing their privacy, fairness, and security.

References

[1] Joshi S, and Joshi-Satyadhar S. Model risk management in the era of generative AI: Challenges, opportunities, and future directions. *International Journal of Scientific and Research Publications.* 2025;15(5):299–309.

[2] Bhattacharyya A, Yu Y, Yang H, *et al.* Model risk management for generative AI in financial institutions. *arXiv* preprint arXiv:2503.15668. 2025 Mar 19.

[3] Shabeena Shah W, Khadeeja Bilquees A, and Zubair MJ. Innovation unleashed charting a new course in risk evaluation with generative AI. *Generative Artificial Intelligence in Finance: Large Language Models, Interfaces, and Industry Use Cases to Transform Accounting and Finance Processes.* 2025:149–157. ISBN: 978-1-394-27105-4

[4] Hu Y, NA AN, Yellamati DD, and Goktas Y. Leveraging generative AI tools for proactive risk mitigation in design. In *2025 Annual Reliability and Maintainability Symposium (RAMS)* 2025 (pp. 1–6). IEEE.

[5] Mohawesh R, Ottom MA, and Salameh HB. A data-driven risk assessment of cybersecurity challenges posed by generative AI. *Decision Analytics Journal.* 2025;15:100580.

[6] Elgesem D. The AI Act and the risks posed by generative AI models. In *Proceedings of the 5th Symposium of the Norwegian AI Society (NAIS 2023)* 2023. CEUR.

[7] Buchicchio E, De Angelis A, Moschitta A, Santoni F, San Marco L, and Carbone P. Design, validation, and risk assessment of LLM-based generative AI systems operating in the legal sector. In *2024 IEEE International Symposium on Systems Engineering (ISSE)* 2024 (pp. 1–8). IEEE.

[8] Mohamed MA, Al-Mhdawi MK, Ojiako U, Dacre N, Qazi A, and Rahimian F. Generative AI in construction risk management: A bibliometric analysis of the associated benefits and risks. *Urbanization, Sustainability and Society.* 2025;2(1):196–228.

[9]   Wang Y. Generative AI in operational risk management: Harnessing the future of finance. *Operational Risk Management: Harnessing the Future of Finance.* 2023:1–17. http://dx.doi.org/10.2139/ssrn.4452504.

[10]   Tanaka H, Ide M, Yajima J, Onodera S, Munakata K, and Yoshioka N. Taxonomy of generative AI applications for risk assessment. In *Proceedings of the IEEE/ACM 3rd International Conference on AI Engineering-Software Engineering for AI* 2024 Apr 14 (pp. 288–289).

[11]   Beltran MA, Ruiz Mondragon MI, and Han SH. Comparative analysis of generative AI risks in the public sector. In *Proceedings of the 25th Annual International Conference on Digital Government Research* 2024 June 11 (pp. 610–617).

[12]   Mohamed MA, Al-Mhdawi MK, Rahimian FP, Ojiako U, O'Connor A, and Mahammedi C. Exploring the risks of integrating generative artificial intelligence into construction risk management: Insights from a systematic literature review. In *6th International Conference on Civil and Building Engineering Informatics: ICCBEI 2025.* 2025 Mar 24.

[13]   Humble N. Risk management strategy for generative AI in computing education: how to handle the strengths, weaknesses, opportunities, and threats? *International Journal of Educational Technology in Higher Education.* 2024; 21(1):61.

[14]   Saini H, Singh G, Dalal S, Lilhore UK, Simaiya S, and Dalal S. Enhancing cloud network security with a trust-based service mechanism using k-anonymity and statistical machine learning approach. *Peer-to-Peer Networking and Applications.* 2024;17(6):4084–4109.

[15]   Wach K, Duong CD, Ejdys J, *et al.* The dark side of generative artificial intelligence: A critical analysis of controversies and risks of ChatGPT. *Entrepreneurial Business and Economics Review.* 2023;11(2):7–30.

[16]   Hacker P, Engel A, and Mauer M. Regulating ChatGPT and other large generative AI models. In *Proceedings of the 2023 ACM Conference on Fairness, Accountability, and Transparency* 2023 June 12 (pp. 1112–1123).

[17]   Dalal S, Poongodi M, Lilhore UK, *et al.* Optimized LightGBM model for security and privacy issues in cyber-physical systems. *Transactions on Emerging Telecommunications Technologies.* 2023;34(6):e4771.

[18]   Lilhore UK, Simaiya S, Dalal S, Alshuhail A, and Almusharraf A. A post-quantum hybrid encryption framework for securing biometric data in consumer electronics. *IEEE Transactions on Consumer Electronics.* 2025; 71(3):8289–8297.

[19]   Bhutani M, Dalal S, Alhussein M, Lilhore UK, Aurangzeb K, and Hussain A. SAD-GAN: A novel secure anomaly detection framework for enhancing the resilience of cyber-physical systems. *Cognitive Computation.* 2025;17(4):127.

[20]   Dalal S, Rani U, Lilhore UK, *et al.* Optimized XGBoost model with whale optimization algorithm for detecting anomalies in manufacturing. *Journal of Computational and Cognitive Engineering.* 2024;4(4):1–17.

Chapter 7

Security challenges and innovative solutions for generative AI

In this chapter, we discuss the security issues and novel solutions for generative AI. However, with the advancement of these technologies comes both great promises and significant challenges. With the ever-growing privacy concern, adversarial attacks, and deepfakes, the necessity for secure techniques has never been felt more. The chapter also discusses these challenges in depth and discusses pragmatic, novel solutions such as federated learning, adversarial training, and deepfake detection. It also emphasizes practical use cases to illustrate how organizations are addressing these concerns and unlocking the potential of generative AI in a safe and ethical manner.

7.1 Introduction

Generative AI has kicked off a vast craze in various industries because it allows machines to come up with new data instead of merely predicting or classifying. These models, like GANs, VAEs, and transformer models such as GPT-4, have been applied across sectors, including healthcare and entertainment, to cybersecurity and finance. Being able to produce hyper-realistic content (images, audio, and text) has made generative AI a corollary tool for creativity. But with this power comes a new set of security challenges [1].

The generative nature of AI models means they are reproducing patterns from the real world and are thus exposed to internal and external security challenges. The data used to train these models can be stolen, abused, and exploited; the outputs they generate might be harnessed for nefarious purposes, from misinformation to privacy violations to assaults on other AI systems. These issues highlight the need for novel countermeasures that will protect both AI systems and their generated content from inappropriate use. This chapter presents a summary of these security challenges and details some innovative approaches that can be used to reduce the threat risk [2–4].

7.2 Security challenges in generative AI

Generative AI creates many security concerns with respect to the data and the generated content.

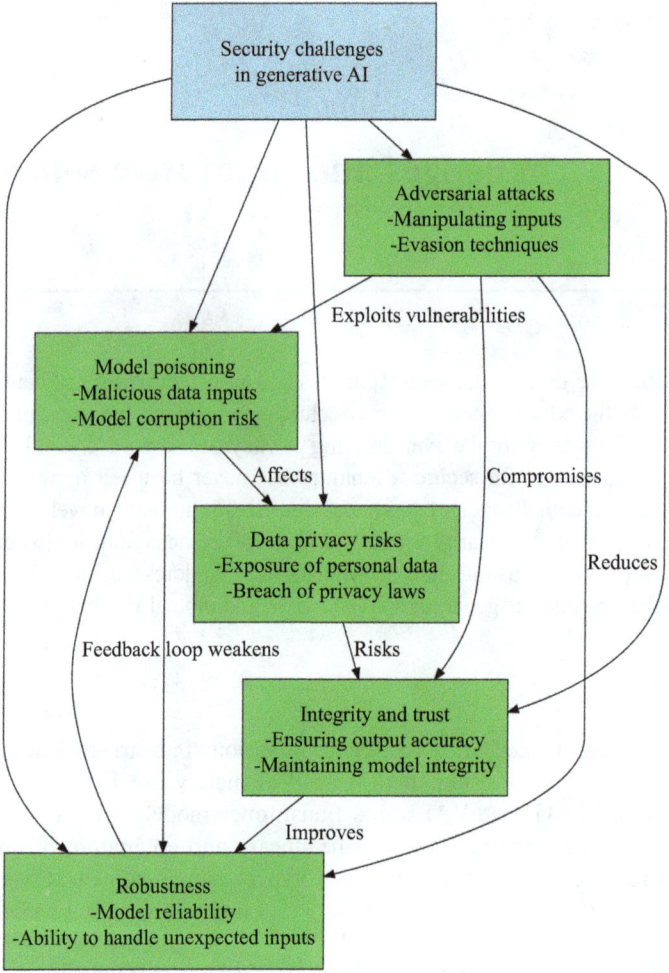

Figure 7.1   Security challenges in generative AI

These problems not only compromise AI system security but also concern the reliability and integrity of what AI produces. In the sections below, we explore the key pain points and their implications for the broader AI ecosystem (Figure 7.1).

7.2.1   Data privacy risks

This is a concern because generative AI models like this often need tons of data to train properly. Many of these models are trained on personal data relating to people's medical histories, financial transactions, or social media posts, and the misuse of this kind of information could result in data leakage. Due to the fact that generative AI is based on pattern and structure learning from training data, these models may "remember" specific identifiers in the process of generating new data, possibly leading to sensitive information exposure (Table 7.1 and Figure 7.2).

Table 7.1 Comparison of privacy-preserving techniques in generative AI

Privacy technique	Description	Benefits	Challenges
Differential privacy	Adding noise to datasets to prevent individual data identification.	Protects individual data privacy.	Can degrade model accuracy if not well-tuned.
Federated learning	Training models across decentralized devices.	Data remains local, improving privacy.	Needs substantial infrastructure and coordination.
Homomorphic encryption	Encrypted computation on data without decryption.	Secure model use without exposing data.	Computationally expensive.

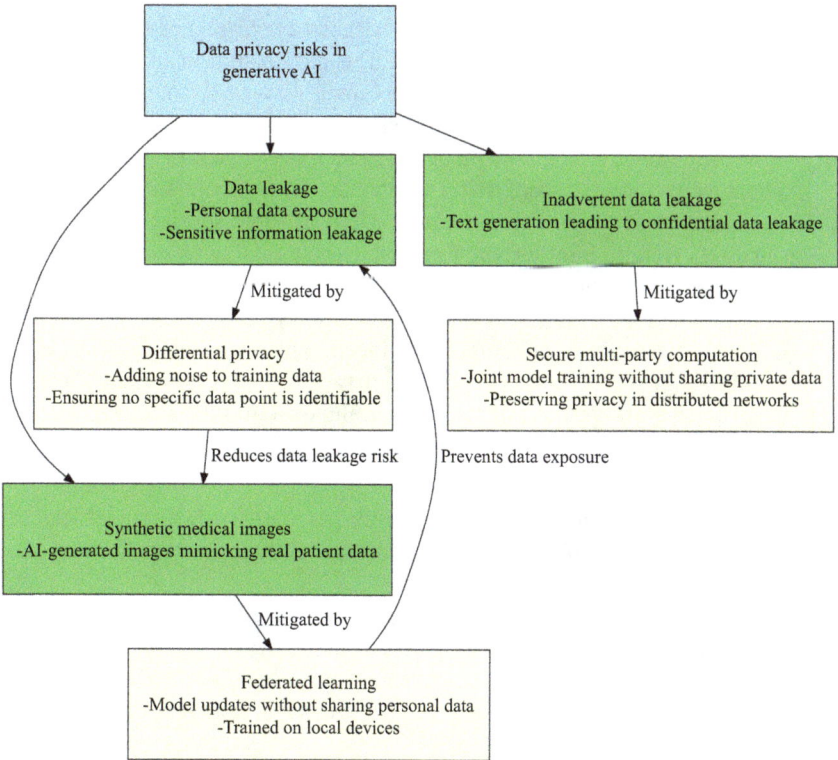

Figure 7.2 Data privacy risks overview for GAI

- **Example: Synthetic medical images:**
  Consider synthetic medical images, for example, an AI model trained to create synthetic medical images that can be used by a separate AI system for diagnosis support training. The model may produce fake images that may resemble the real ones of patients (generated by scanners themselves), which would violate privacy if not securely designed. This is especially perturbing in regulated industries, such as healthcare, because it requires adherence to HIPAA compliance for patient data handling [5].

  Furthermore, generative AI models sometimes produce outputs that are so close to the original training data that they can inadvertently leak people's private information. For instance, a generative model trained over text data may inadvertently generate personal or confidential information, and it can leak out to unauthorized users [6–8].

- **Mitigation strategies:**
  o *Differential privacy:* Through the addition of specially adjusted noise to the data at training time, differential privacy mathematically ensures that no specific data point can be inferred by the model during training. This guarantees that an adversary would have no way to obtain any personally identifiable information (PII), even if he or she gets hold of the trained model.
  o *Federated learning:* Rather than saving individuals' personal data onto central, vulnerable servers in the cloud, federated learning trains models based on user device or local server-held data. This approach maintains the privacy of personal data, forwarding back to a central server only model updates and ensuring that sensitive content never leaves the device. This approach has already proved a success in mobile apps such as Google's Gboard, which does not require users to share data when training the keyboard's language models.
  o *Secure Multi-Party Computation (SMC):* In some special cases, multiple parties wish to jointly train a model, and the goal is to enable those multiple parties to obtain a shared model without exchanging data representing their own private models. Secure multi-party computation (SMC) provides a method for computing with encrypted data while preserving the privacy of such data in a distributed network. This is important in medical research partnerships where private health data must be analyzed securely.

7.2.2   Adversarial attacks

Adversarial attacks pose a serious challenge for generative AI. These attacks take place by feeding input to AI models in order to trick them into generating false, biased, or even harmful content.

In generative AI, an adversarial attack may manipulate the input data such that a model produces fake or misleading results. Such attacks, when applied to applications where generative AI is employed and accuracy and trustworthiness are vital, e.g., in autonomous driving or medical diagnosis, can lead to serious consequences (Figure 7.3).

- **Example:** Imagine a generative model that is applied to self-driving cars. Adversarial example attacks could change road signs or pedestrian

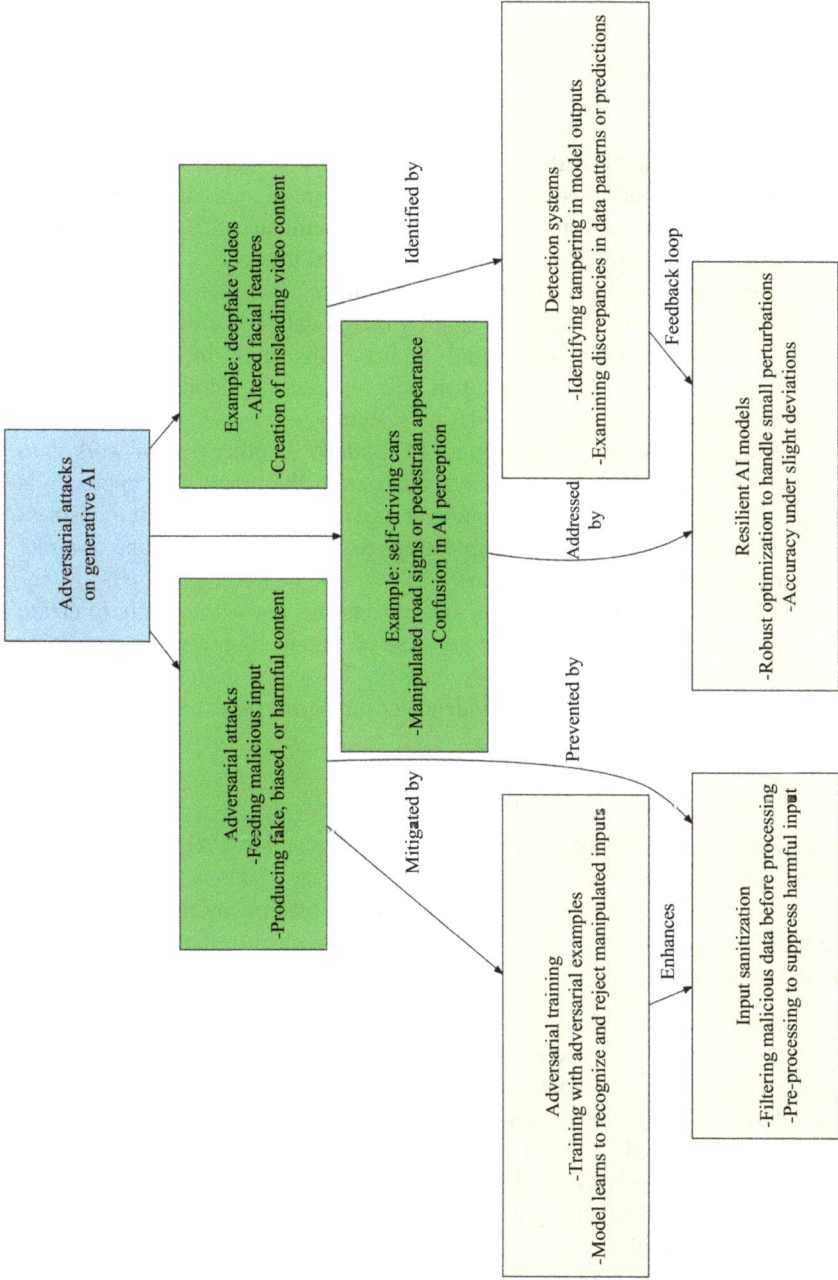

Adversarial attacks on generative AI

Example: deepfake videos
-Altered facial features
-Creation of misleading video content

Adversarial attacks
-Feeding malicious input
-Producing fake, biased, or harmful content

Example: self-driving cars
-Manipulated road signs or pedestrian appearance
-Confusion in AI perception

Detection systems
-Identifying tampering in model outputs
-Examining discrepancies in data patterns or predictions

Resilient AI models
-Robust optimization to handle small perturbations
-Accuracy under slight deviations

Adversarial training
-Training with adversarial examples
-Model learns to recognize and reject manipulated inputs

Input sanitization
-Filtering malicious data before processing
-Pre-processing to suppress harmful input

Identified by

Addressed by

Feedback loop

Mitigated by

Prevented by

Enhances

Figure 7.3   Adversarial attacks overview of GAI

appearances, and the car's AI model would be confused about what is in front of them [9–11]. Likewise, attackers may perform small changes in a video of facial features at a deepfake technology level that can lead to an enactment of a realistic but fake video by a generative model.

- **Mitigation strategies:**
  - ○ **Adversarial training:** One of the most effective methods to defend generative AI is labeled as adversarial training. In this approach, the model is trained with adversarial examples of input that have been intentionally modified to cause it to be incorrectly classified and/or generated. The model learns to recognize and eliminate such perturbed inputs during training by exposure to these distorted inputs.
  - ○ **Input sanitization:** Applying some form of filtering/sanitizing of incoming data prior to processing by the model can be used as a defense mechanism against adversarial inputs. This may include data preprocessing techniques to discover and suppress malicious input patterns before they are submitted to the AI system.
  - ○ **Resilient to small perturbation AI models:** Another line of work is to make AI models robust to minor changes in the input. This approach is called robust optimization, aiming at providing the model with robustness against such adversarial manipulations that allow for generating accurate outputs under slight deviations.
  - ○ **Detection systems:** Detection systems can be applied not only to create more robust models against adversarial inputs but also to recognize adversarial attempts once they happen. These are designed to examine outputs from the model for evidence of tampering, say differences in data patterns or bizarre predictions.

7.2.3 Deepfakes and misinformation

Deepfakes are one of the most worrying iterations of generative AI, as they make it possible to generate entirely fictional content that looks real – whether that is an image, video, or audio. Generative models' ability to manipulate real-world media has sounded alarms over their potential for misuse in misinformation campaigns, fraud, and defamation.

- **Example:** Imagine a deepfake video that can be used to depict a politician saying something outrageous. It only takes one click of a "share" button on your webcam to turn this into an outbreak on social media, leading the whole public to be thrown into confusion, political instability, or loss of reputation for whoever was filmed [12] (Table 7.2). A deepfake video of a company's chief executive falsely promising higher earnings or compensation could hammer the stock price in financial markets (Figure 7.4).
- **Mitigation strategies:**
  - ○ **Deepfake detection models:** As deepfakes continue to grow increasingly uncanny, AI-based deepfake detection models are being trained to detect small discrepancies in video and audio. These models examine facial

Table 7.2   Comparison of deepfake detection approaches

Detection approach	Description	Strengths	Limitations
Deep Learning models	Using AI models trained to recognize manipulated media.	High accuracy and scalability.	May fail on highly realistic deepfakes.
Blockchain provenance	Embedding digital fingerprints in media files to track their authenticity.	Immutable, verifiable record.	Requires industry-wide adoption.
Signature-based detection	Identifying signature artifacts from previous manipulation techniques.	Fast and lightweight.	Can be bypassed by newer techniques.

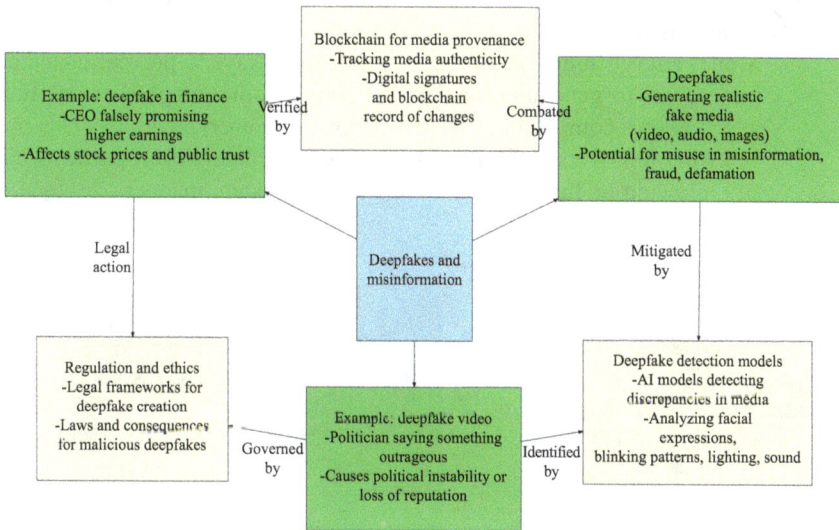

Figure 7.4   Deepfakes and misinformation

expressions, patterns of blinking, inconsistencies in lighting, and the soundtrack to detect if a media file is doctored.

○ **Blockchain for media provenance:** In the blockchain-based solution, we explore a new way of tracking media provenance and history. With the addition of a digital signature on media files, blockchain could thus enable verification of the authenticity of content. If an operation is applied repeatedly, the process of verification becomes increasingly complex and computationally expensive.

○   **Regulation and ethics:** Legal frameworks to govern the creation and dissemination of deepfakes are being established by governments as well as organizations. Such laws would enact consequences for the production of harmful deepfakes and make creators responsible to minimize malicious media propagation. Some social media platforms are also now deploying detection tools to automatically flag or take down deepfake videos [13–15].

7.2.4   Model exploitation

Generative AIs are very useful and valuable things, but they also have an issue of being somewhat prone to model theft or abuse. Once an adversary has access to a trained generative model, they can generate politically sensitive or other damaging content that is easily shareable or lift intellectual property (Figure 7.5).

- **Example:** A hacker might pilfer a generative model that generates realistic avatars for VR apps. That would allow them to copy the model and apply it to new avatars with less Savory intentions, like stealing someone's identity or committing fraud.
- **Mitigation strategies:**
  ○   **Model encryption:** One of the most effective ways to prevent unauthorized access to generative models is through **homomorphic encryption**, which allows computations to be performed on encrypted data. This prevents the model itself from being exposed to unauthorized parties while still allowing its functionality to be used in a secure manner.

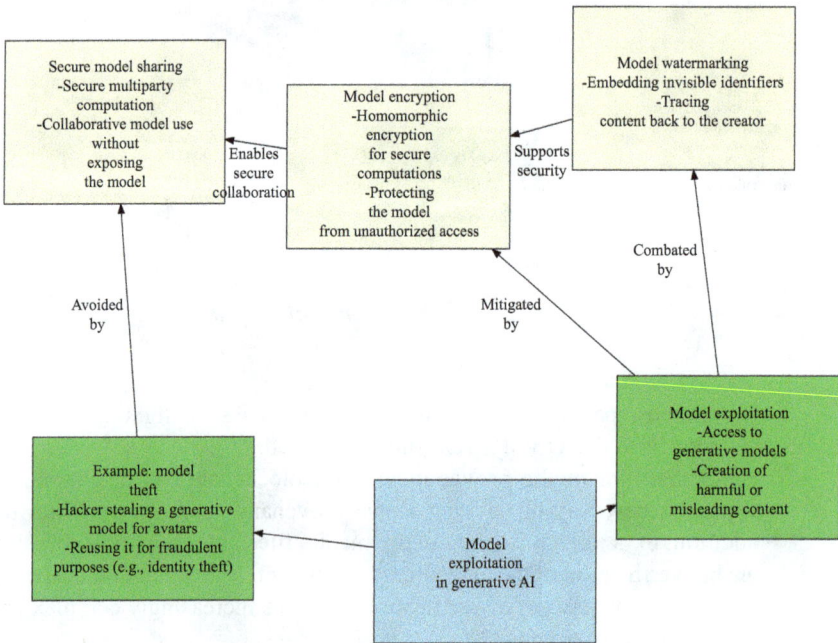

Figure 7.5   Model exploitation in generative AI

- **Model watermarking:** Watermarking involves embedding unique, invisible identifiers in the model or its generated content. This ensures that the output can be traced back to its creator, helping to detect unauthorized use or theft of the model.
- **Secure model sharing:** Techniques such as **SMC** enable multiple parties to securely collaborate using an AI model without exposing the model or data to any party outside the collaboration. This prevents unauthorized sharing or theft of models while allowing for safe collaboration.

7.2.5   Bias and fairness in generated content

Generative AI models are very reactive to their training data. For training data with biases, the biases may also propagate to model predictions. This results in fairness concerns, which occur when some groups are impaired or discriminated against in the generation based on how a model creates content (Figure 7.6).

- **Bias auditing:** Performing constant bias audits of generative models helps identify policy-based biases and redress them. These audits shall check if there are hidden patterns in the data that unfairly favor some demographic groups and we can modify our training process to make it fairer.
- **Fairness-constrained training:** Fairness-constrained training alters the objective of model training so as to guarantee fair outputs in some sense. This may involve the requirement of equal representation among all demographic groups in creating content, or that the model does not unduly prefer one group over another.
- **Synthetic data generation:** Generative AI can also generate synthetic data that can help mitigate the under-representation of demographic groups in training datasets. By tagging the synthetic data along with the training data, the model can learn to produce content that is fairer and more representative [16].

- **Example:** A Generative AI model fed a bias training data set about hiring could produce résumés that are biased in favor of male rather than female applicants, thereby compounding gender biases in hiring.
- **Mitigation strategies:** See Table 7.3.

Table 7.3   Methods for bias mitigation in generative AI

Method	Description	Benefits	Challenges
Bias auditing	Systematic review of model outputs for fairness	Identifies and mitigates biases	Time-consuming and costly
Fairness-constrained training	Introducing fairness constraints during training	Promotes fairness in model output	Requires detailed fairness metrics
Synthetic data generation	Using generative AI to produce unbiased data	Balances underrepresented groups	May introduce new forms of bias

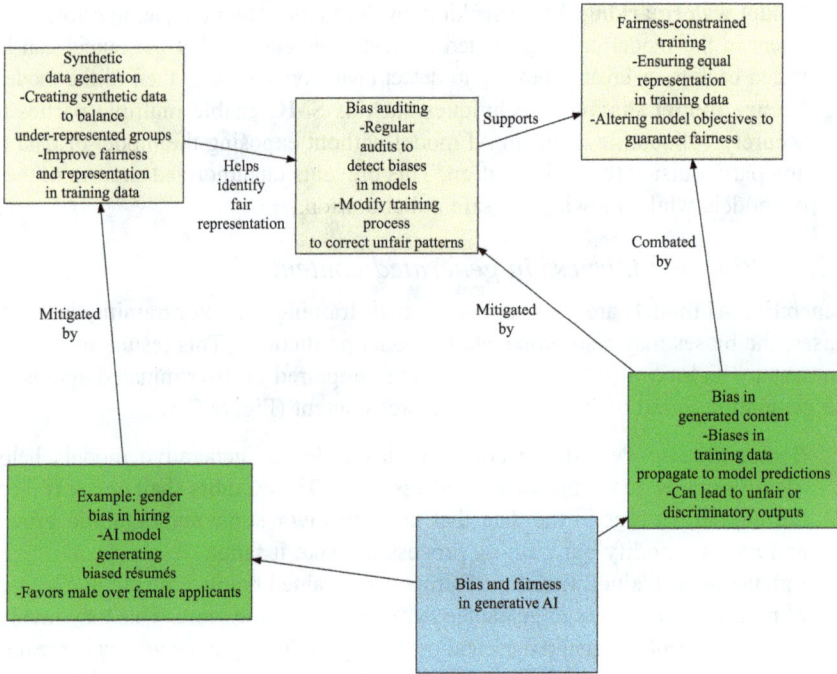

Figure 7.6   Bias and fairness in generated content

7.3   Novel strategies for generated secure GAI models

Generative AI models present significant security challenges that necessitate new, pragmatic solutions to enable privacy, fairness, robustness, and intellectual property protection. Below, we explain the innovative ways that are being developed to secure generative AI (Figure 7.7).

7.3.1   Privacy-preserving GAI

Generative AI models must work in a setting where data privacy is of utmost concern. Two state-of-the-art techniques that help to defend your privacy during training are Federated learning and Differential Privacy.

Federated Learning: In the scenario of federated learning, training is conducted locally on users' devices, instead of centralized servers. This approach also ensures that sensitive personal data, such as health records or financial information, is never stored or leaves the mobile phone. The only model updates are sent back to a central server, thus enabling data privacy and learning from the entire dataset [17–19].

Differential Privacy: Differential privacy adds random noise to training data such that no one can be categorized from the model's output. The method, also used in AI models from big tech firms such as Apple and Google, allows for personalization while protecting user data.

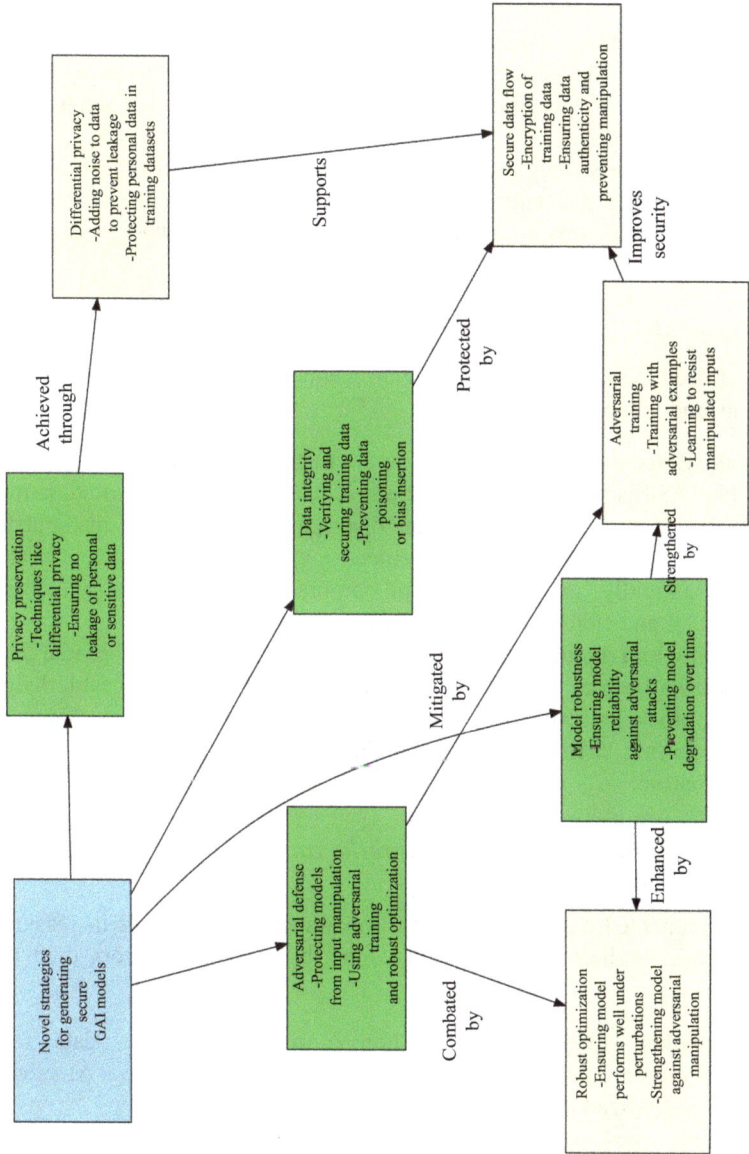

Figure 7.7 Novel strategies for generated secure GAI models

7.3.2   Robustness against adversarial attacks

AI models can also be tricked by adversarial attacks through manipulating the inputs at places where they are not performing as expected. Robustness of GI is a vital concern when deploying generative AI models at scale.

- **Adversarial training:** Training the model on adversarial examples enables each model to learn how to handle them. This can be expected to strengthen the robustness of the model against attacks and maintain more stable outputs, even in adverse scenarios.
- **Ensemble methods:** Aggregating the predictions of several models through ensemble methods can enhance robustness. This mitigates the risk that all models become victims of one and the same adversarial attack, making the system more robust as a whole.

7.3.3   Deepfake detection and media authentication

In the era of deepfakes, authenticating digital media has become a top priority for governments and companies (Figure 7.8).

- **Deepfake detection models:** Deepfakes are getting harder and harder for us to spot, but AI-based deepfake detection is based on sophisticated pattern recognition that can notice common discrepancies typical of manipulated videos, such as unnatural face movements or audio artifacts. Such models allow us to rapidly comb through large corpora of media to identify manipulated content and stop it from being disseminated.
- **Blockchain and media:** Blockchain can be used to verify the source of digital media (reduce tampering). Through minting an unchangeable ledger of media, blockchain allows individuals to validate the legitimacy of content prior to putting their trust in a crucial element at play when fighting misinformation.

7.3.4   Secure sharing model and intellectual property protection

Policing uncommented on code is gaining importance as AI models increasingly become valuable intellectual property that must be safeguarded from theft and unauthorized use.

- **Homomorphic encryption:** With homomorphic encryption, data stays encrypted during calculation, helping protect access to sensitive AI models against unauthorized users.
- **Model watermarking:** Insertion of invisible watermarks in models, and the model output becomes a mechanism for tracking content's origins. This ensures that the AI model and/or outputs cannot be copied or used without proper authorization.

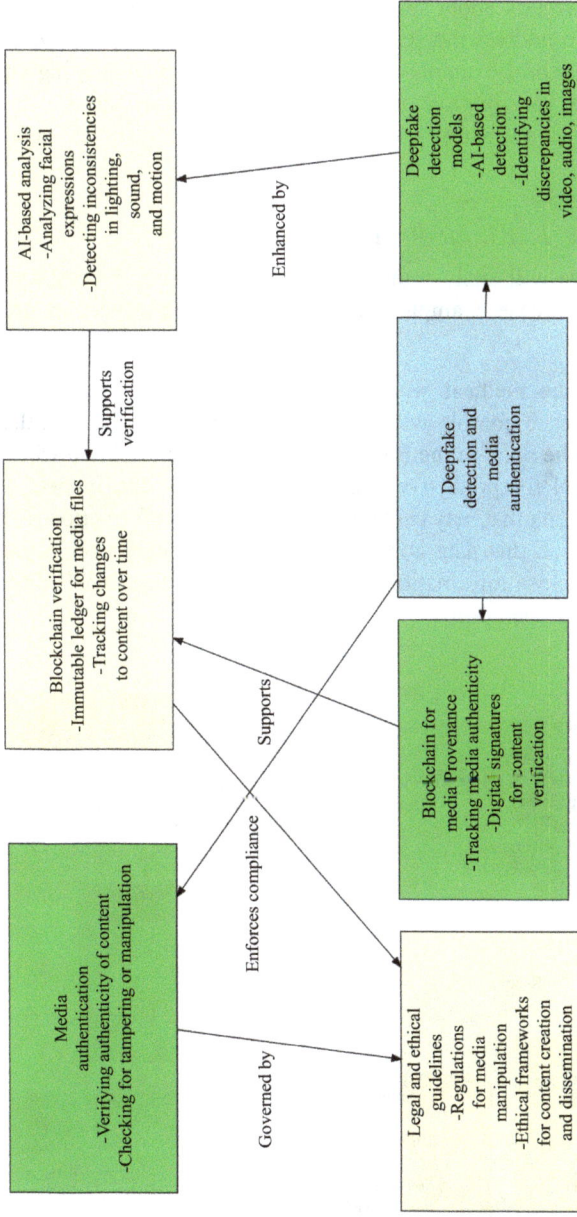

Figure 7.8 Deepfake detection and media authentication using GAI

7.4   Examples of new approaches for security to generative AI

In the following, we talk about specific examples where new approaches are successfully applied to address the security implications of generative AI. These use cases provide real-world examples of how enterprises are managing presumptive risk around things like privacy risks in data, adversarial attacks, or deepfake manipulation while allowing for ethical and secure use of generative AI technologies.

7.4.1   Use case 1: FL for healthcare security

In this example, we will analyze the healthcare situation with security of Google Health as in the use case example (subdivision of Google Inc.), as presented by Figure 7.9.

- **Problem:** In the medical world, one needs to respect patient information privacy in order to comply with regulations like HIPAA here in the U.S. and GDPR across the pond in the E.U. This comes to be a problem when you want to train a GAN for predictive tasks in healthcare – the models need to be trained on big data that may contain Personal Health Information (PHI). Due to the way in which this data is recorded centrally, central access may make it possible to disclose information not meant for that diagnosis/ consult request (enabling rogue operation).

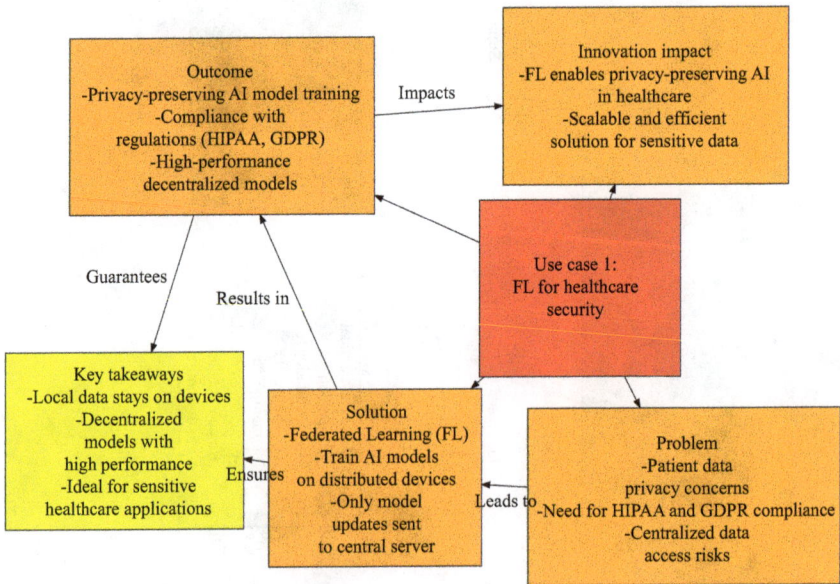

Figure 7.9   Use case 1: FL for healthcare security

- **Solution:** Google Health used federated learning to develop AI models on distributed devices without sharing raw patient data with a central server. Rather than shipping sensitive data back and forth, we ship AI updates (updates to the AI's weights and parameters) instead of a central server that collects them to make the model better. This process keeps patient data on local devices, such as hospital servers or even the user's own device, which protects privacy while still providing powerful AI training.
    - **Outcome:** With the use of federated learning, Google Health was able to train machine learning models that can diagnose diseases (e.g., diabetic retinopathy in eye images) while preserving patient privacy. It provides not only regulatory compliance guarantees but also a scalable and efficient approach for privacy-preserving AI in healthcare.
    - **Innovation impact:** This case study shows that federated learning is a promising privacy-preserving approach for AI model training in healthcare, especially within highly sensitive settings.
- **Key takeaways:**
    - Federated learning guarantees that all the local data cannot leave without a proper transmission, which avoids the risk of a data leak.
    - Decentralized models can potentially achieve high performance on tasks, such as medical imaging or diagnostics, which is a practical and private solution for healthcare settings.

7.4.2 *Adversarial training case: autonomous vehicles (Tesla) for adversarial training in autonomous vehicles like Tesla*

- **Problem:** Self-driving vehicles use machine learning systems to interpret images of the world captured by cameras, radar, and LiDAR sensors. But these models are vulnerable to adversarial examples due to the fact that slight modifications in multimedia signs or objects in the scene can lead the car to make wrong decisions and even go into collisions (Figure 7.10).
- **Solution:** Tesla has adopted adversarial training for harder, secure autonomous driving. By producing and including adversarial samples in the model training data, Tesla's AI can be trained to identify manipulated inputs and output responses as well. For example, adversarial examples can be modified traffic signs or pedestrians that are wearing designed clothing to deceive the vehicle's vision system.
    - **Outcome:** Tesla's self-driving models are more robust to adversarial inputs, which are less likely to cause misclassification and prevent unsafe driving behaviors. The addition of adversarial training made Tesla's self-driving systems more robust/durable in real-world usage.
    - **Innovation impact:** In this article, we show that GAT is a general defense technique against other adversaries attacking the input space, which can help mitigate intentional input data manipulations and enhance the safety

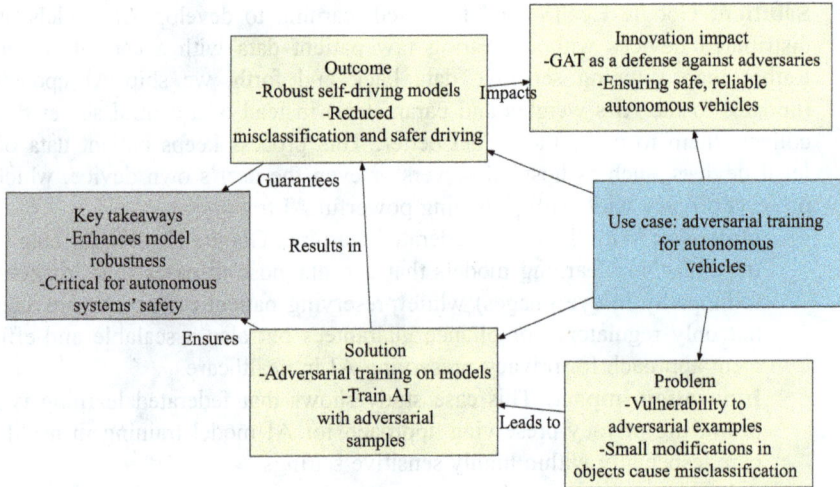

Figure 7.10   Use case: adversarial training for autonomous vehicles (Tesla)

and reliability of critical-generation AI systems in deployment (e.g., autonomous vehicles).

- **Key takeaways:**
  o Adversarial training enhances the robustness of AI models so that they can better understand adversarial altered inputs.
  o Techniques of this type are necessary to guarantee the safety and dependability of autonomous systems operating in unpredictable real-world scenarios.

7.4.3   Case study 3: deepfake detection and misinformation prevention (Microsoft's Video Authenticator)

- **Problem:** The third case study we consider is of a use case that leverages ANNs to detect deepfakes through a web-scale application, which requires high accuracy with low latency. The emergence of deepfake technology has made it easier for bad actors to produce realistic but false videos and audio recordings. Such deepfakes can be employed for disinformation, slander, or political manipulation as well as put news sources and public discourse in jeopardy (Figure 7.11).
- **Solution:** Video Authenticator, a tool which has been built by Microsoft Researchers and is being made available today in the Azure cloud as well as through its recently formed Defending Democracy Program, is designed to analyze videos and images for signs of manipulation or splicing. The system relies on a blend of deep learning models to analyze videos that help determine their authenticity. It does so by identifying artifacts or small inconsistencies that are typically found in deepfake content, even high-quality ones.

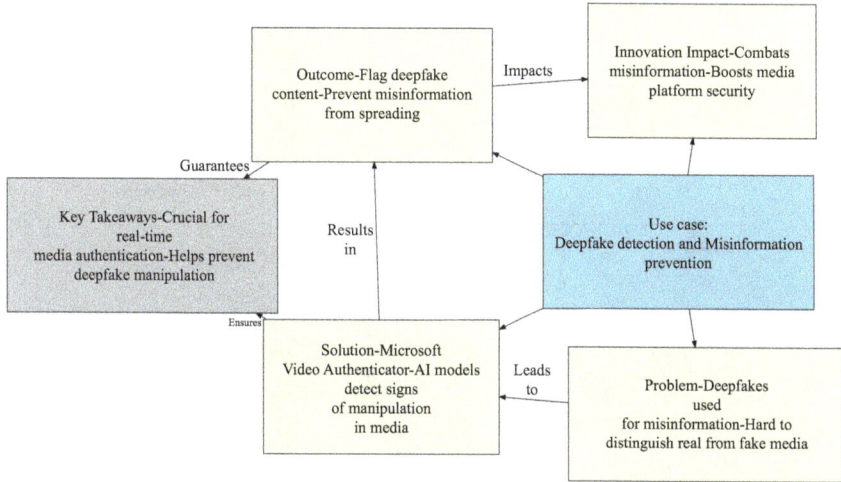

*Figure 7.11   Case study 3: deepfake detection and misinformation prevention
(Microsoft's Video Authenticator)*

- o **Outcome:** Microsoft's tool has been used by platforms such as Twitter to identify and flag deepfake videos before they go viral. This has empowered platforms to intervene against misinformation and suppress the dangerous effect on public opinion of deepfake videos.
- o **Innovation impact:** This example demonstrates the significance of deepfake detection systems in combating misinformation. Fusing AI for detection and provenance tracking with the legal and normative framework will allow us to guarantee the traceability of media and trustworthiness in digital content.
- **Key takeaways:**
  - o Deepfake detection methods such as Microsoft's Video Authenticator are crucial for identifying and blunting the impact of manipulated media.
  - o AI-driven detection capabilities can be added to media platforms, helping to prevent the spread of fake or harmful digital content in real time.

7.4.4   Use case 4: blockchain to protect IP for AI models (OpenAI)

- **Problem:** AI models, and especially generative AI models, are important intellectual properties (IP). But these devices are frequently stolen or used by unauthorized persons. Attackers might be able to steal trained models, or deconstruct them to create fake content or replicate proprietary technology (Figure 7.12).
- **Solution:** OpenAI has also turned to blockchain in an attempt to curtail model theft and protect its intellectual property. With the use of blockchain-based provenance systems, OpenAI can offer each model a unique identity on a

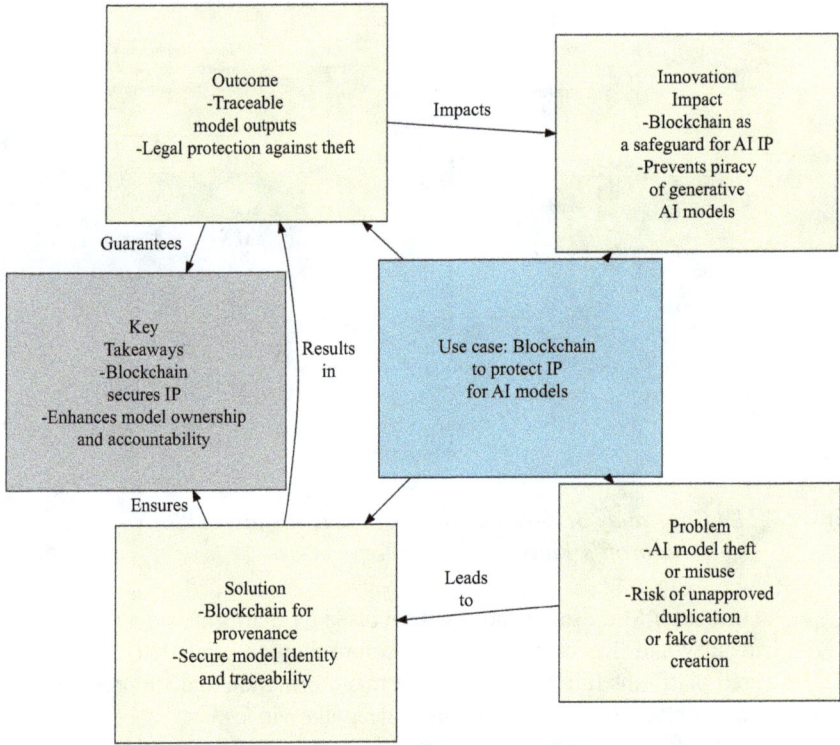

Figure 7.12   Use case 4: blockchain to protect IP for AI models (OpenAI)

digital ledger that keeps track of where it came from and who altered it. This digital fingerprint is held securely on the blockchain, so every output can be traced back to the source model and creator.

○ **Outcome:** The mechanism allows the developer to trace their models and outputs and make sure nobody abuses them or uses them without permission. It also offers legal support by making unlawful reproduction trackable and actionable through the courts.

○ **The innovation:** By using blockchain to verify that content is created by AI, and protect it as intellectual property, this represents a new protocol helping fight model theft and piracy of generative AI.

• **Key takeaways:**
○ Generative AI: Protecting intellectual property with blockchain is a powerful mechanism to protect IP in generative AI.
○ By allowing for traceability of models and their outputs, blockchain serves to discourage unauthorized use of proprietary AI technologies.

7.4.5   *Case study 5: fairness-constrained training for bias reduction in hiring algorithms (IBM Watson)*

- **Problem:** Generative AI models can replicate and increase bias if they are trained on biased data. In the context of machine learning models for hiring, if your training data encoded historical biases (such as gender or racial bias in hiring), you could produce outputs that arbitrarily disadvantage certain demographic groups relative to other groups (Figure 7.13).
- **Solution:** IBM Watson applied fair-constrained training to eliminate biases in recommendations for hiring made by AI. IBM Watson makes sure that this AI model treats all applicants equally across gender, race, and other demographic information by deploying fair singling algorithms during the training. The company employed an algorithmic auditing system that constantly monitored the process for hiring, tweaking the models to stamp out any skewed patterns.
  - ○ **Outcome:** This solution helped IBM Watson AI models generate recommendations for selection that were fairer and more equitable, resulting in a fairer job opportunity set for the group of underrepresented populations. The recommended list could be balanced by the models according to qualifications, but not demographics.
  - ○ **Innovation impact:** This case illustrates how fairness constraints can always be placed into the process of generative AI to prevent the entrenchment of societal bias and provide ethical use in AI technologies.

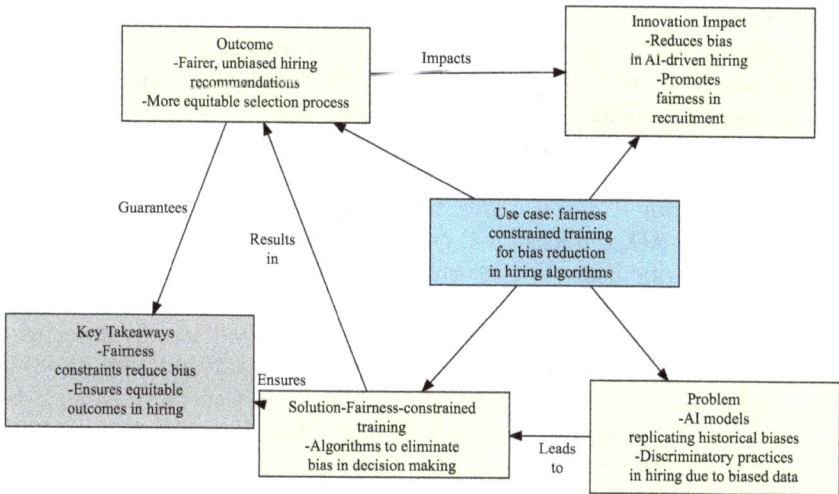

Figure 7.13   *Case study 5: fairness-constrained training for bias reduction in hiring algorithms (IBM Watson)*

- **Key takeaways:**
  - ○ Fairness-constrained training is a key tool to help deal with biases in the generative AI models, especially when it comes to hiring, finance, and education applications.
  - ○ By continuing to audit algorithms and refine models, we can lend a helping hand in developing AI systems that are fair and avoid adding fuel to existing biases.

7.5 Conclusion

These use cases illustrate the real-world application of novel ways to solve the security problems that come along with generative AI. Federated learning in healthcare, adversarial training in autonomous vehicles, and blockchain for the protection of intellectual property – these concrete use cases demonstrate how admissible generations or expectations may be evaluated safely and ethically. Organizations are doing a ton to responsibly mitigate generative AI risks with advanced detection systems, privacy-contained methods, and fairness criteria. In the ongoing development of generative AI, research and deployment in practice will be important for drawing out the positives and negating the negatives. Recent studies highlight that adversarial misuse of generative AI systems poses long-term security and societal challenges that require coordinated technical and policy-level interventions [20].

References

[1] López Delgado JL, and López Ramos JA. A Comprehensive survey on generative AI solutions in IoT security. *Electronics*. 2024;13(24):4965.

[2] Huang K, Wang Y, Goertzel B, Li Y, Wright S, and Ponnapalli J. *Generative AI Security*. Future of Business and Finance. 2024.

[3] Khan A, Jhanjhi N, Hamid DH, Omar HA, Amsaad F, and Wassan S. Future trends and challenges in cybersecurity and generative AI. *Reshaping CyberSecurity With Generative AI Techniques*. 2025:491–522.

[4] Almagrabi AO, and Khan RA. Optimizing secure AI lifecycle model management with innovative generative AI strategies. *IEEE Access*. 2024; 13:12889–12920.

[5] Golda A, Mekonen K, Pandey A, *et al.* Privacy and security concerns in generative AI: A comprehensive survey. *IEEE Access*. 2024;12:48126–48144.

[6] Sai S, Yashvardhan U, Chamola V, and Sikdar B. Generative AI for cyber security: Analyzing the potential of ChatGPT, DALL-E, and other models for enhancing the security space. *IEEE Access*. 2024;12:53497–53516.

[7] Chen Y, and Esmaeilzadeh P. Generative AI in medical practice: in-depth exploration of privacy and security challenges. *Journal of Medical Internet Research*. 2024;26:e53008.

[8] Dalal S, Poongodi M, Lilhore UK, *et al.* Optimized LightGBM model for security and privacy issues in cyber-physical systems. *Transactions on Emerging Telecommunications Technologies.* 2023;34(6):e4771.

[9] Saini H, Singh G, Dalal S, Lilhore UK, Simaiya S, and Dalal S. Enhancing cloud network security with a trust-based service mechanism using k-anonymity and statistical machine learning approach. *Peer-to-Peer Networking and Applications.* 2024;17(6):4084–4109.

[10] Bhardwaj YK. Securing generative AI: Navigating data security challenges in the AI era. *Journal of Computer Science and Technology Studies.* 2025; 7(4):147–155.

[11] Rana R, and Bhambri P. Generative AI-Driven Security frameworks for web engineering: Innovations and challenges. In *Generative AI for Web Engineering Models* 2025 (pp. 285–296). IGI Global.

[12] Pasupuleti R, Vadapalli R, and Mader C. Cyber security issues and challenges related to generative AI and ChatGPT. In *2023 tenth International Conference on Social Networks Analysis, Management and Security (SNAMS)* 2023 (pp. 1–5). IEEE.

[13] Andreoni M, Lunardi WT, Lawton G, and Thakkar S. Enhancing autonomous system security and resilience with generative AI: A comprehensive survey. *IEEE Access.* 2024;12:109470–109493.

[14] Sindiramutty SR, Prabagaran KR, Jhanjhi NZ, Murugesan RK, Brohi SN, and Masud M. Generative AI in network security and intrusion detection. In *Reshaping CyberSecurity With Generative AI Techniques* 2025 (pp. 77–124). IGI Global.

[15] Zeng M, Xie M, Meng L, Zhang H, Wu T, and Wang J. Generative AI Enabled Secure Communication in Smart Grid: Challenges and Solutions. *IEEE Network.* 2025;39(5):81–87.

[16] Khan MA, Alasiry A, Marzougui M, *et al.* Securing intelligent transportation systems: A dual-framework approach for privacy protection and cybersecurity using generative AI. *IEEE Transactions on Intelligent Transportation Systems.* 2025:1–12. (Early Access). doi:10.1109/TITS.2025.3591007.

[17] Bhutani M, Dalal S, Alhussein M, Lilhore UK, Aurangzeb K, and Hussain A. SAD-GAN: A novel secure anomaly detection framework for enhancing the resilience of cyber-physical systems. *Cognitive Computation.* 2025;17(4):127.

[18] Lilhore UK, Simaiya S, Dalal S, Alshuhail A, and Almusharraf A. A post-quantum hybrid encryption framework for securing biometric data in consumer electronics. *IEEE Transactions on Consumer Electronics.* 2025; 71(3):8289–8297.

[19] Dalal S, Rani U, Lilhore UK, *et al.* Optimized XGBoost model with whale optimization algorithm for detecting anomalies in manufacturing. *Journal of Computational and Cognitive Engineering.* 2024;4(4):1–17.

[20] Liu B. Network security issues caused by generative artificial intelligence. In *Proceedings of the 2024 International Conference on Artificial Intelligence, Digital Media Technology and Interaction Design* 2024 Nov 29 (pp. 132–136).

Chapter 8

Privacy-preserving techniques and mitigation strategies for generative AI

With generative AI rapidly becoming a part of everyday applications, the demand for robust privacy-preserving solutions has reached an all-time high. In summary, this chapter discusses emerging generative AI privacy risks, including unintentional data disclosures, inference attacks, and risks associated with information that could be sensitive. We address privacy at three main phases: during training, when the model is deployed, and when users interact with the model. In addressing these risks, we assess the implications of several known strategies for matching privacy with continued AI progress, including federated learning, differential privacy, data minimization, and model auditing.

We also emphasize Secure Multi-Party Computation (SMPC), a cryptographic method to share computation while preserving data privacy. We show the integration of SMPC in privacy by design systems through an example use case: in a setting where privacy constraints are crucial, due to inter-organizational collaboration, and where the privacy of data is key to its reuse. In this chapter, we deliver – from the perspectives of practitioners, researchers, and policymakers – that full picture of the privacy problems that generative AI presents and of the novel solutions to better preserve sensitive data while promoting the responsible use of AI technologies going forward.

8.1 Introduction

As artificial intelligence continues to grow, it is starting to become more integrated and personal by being incorporated into applications that are more commonplace. From photorealistic content creation to personalized recommendations, AI systems are increasingly processing, generating, and interacting with data that may include or reveal sensitive information. In generative AI, where models learn from datasets and produce outputs that mirror the original, real-world data, this capability creates an imminent risk that places privacy at the center of the conversation.

8.1.1 Overview of privacy concerns in AI

Artificial intelligence depends on significant years of data to establish trends and predict. Such data includes personally identifiable or sensitive information in the fields of medical records, financial transactions, bodily identifiers, or private communications. In the absence of sufficient protection, AI systems can leak this information either through direct exposure or via subtle leaks encoded in their outputs (Figure 8.1).

AI has long been beset by privacy fears, but they have become more complicated because of advances in ML models. Even when anonymized, the capacity of models to retain content from training data poses significant issues. It is about leaking information that a model could take away illegitimately through the behavior it is made to execute.

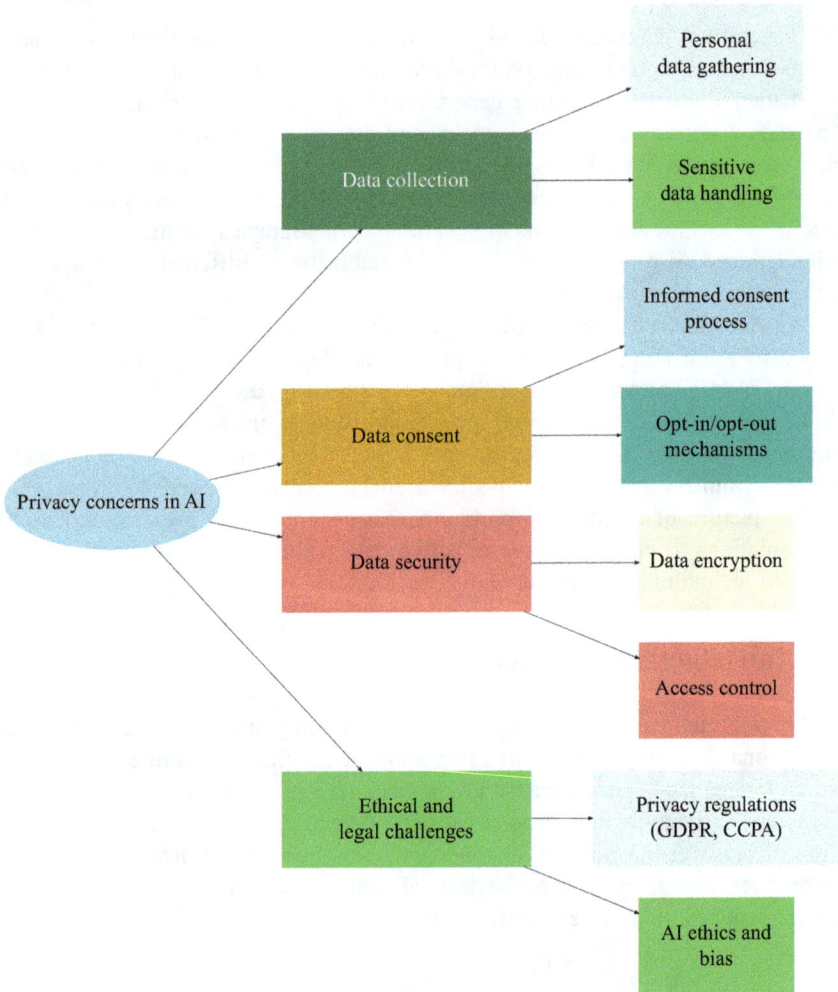

Figure 8.1   Overview of privacy concerns in AI

8.1.2 Specific challenges in the context of generative AI

On the other hand, we have generative AI, models like GPT, DALL·E, etc., which pose their own unique set of privacy issues [1]. These models are trained on large volumes of data that have at times been scraped from the internet or compiled without the express permission of data owners. However, because they are designed to create new content based on patterns they have learned, they can sometimes accidentally recombine the data they were trained on, such as confidential documents, passages of text, or images of people, especially when asked to do so in particular ways (Figure 8.2).

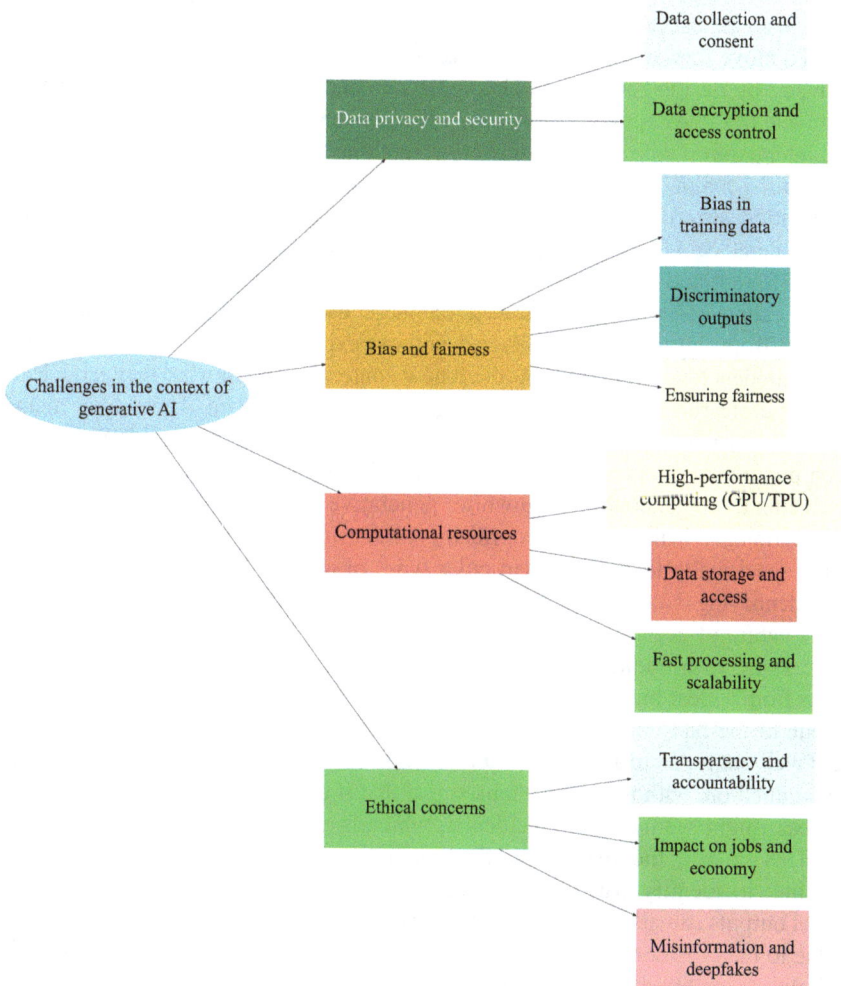

Figure 8.2 Challenges in the context of generative AI

What is more, identifying where there is a leak can be rather difficult. Was that just a lucky coincidence, or was it straight-up memorization by the model? This is an area of periodic uncertainty, making audit and responsibility challenging. It also raises vital questions about data provenance, whether consent is required, and what recourse, if any, individuals whose information may have been used without their knowledge to develop these systems have [2,3].

8.1.3   Importance of privacy-preserving strategies

In light of these concerns, strategies for preserving privacy [4] are thus not optional; they are mandatory. With generative AI being implemented in a wide range of sectors from healthcare to finance to education and even public services, the implications of a data breach become more severe. User data protection is not only a technical aspect but also an ethical responsibility, regulatory obligation, and a matter of trust.

To move forward ethically, AI developers and organizations should embrace a "privacy by design" approach. This means embedding safeguards over the entire life cycle of the AI system – from data collection and model training to deployment and interaction – with the user in every step along the way. In this chapter, we will discuss the major privacy threats associated with generative models and a set of pragmatics, tested solutions to balance privacy rights with innovation [5–7].

Generative AI models, especially well-known models like GPT and DALL·E, raise different and unique privacy challenges compared to traditional AI systems. These callbacks are usually trained on large datasets, which can include data scraped from the internet or collected without explicit consent from data holders. These models tend to recreate/produce new content based on what they have learnt and therefore run the risk of generating a portion of the data. These may include something private or sensitive, such as full-text fragments, private documents, or even pictures of yourself that may be included in your training data, but the model inadvertently regenerates. Meanwhile, generative models can produce texts that unintentionally leak private, proprietary, or sensitive information if the model is asked specifically to generate particular types of text.

Identifying data leakage in your generative AI is not even possible because it is in the nature of generative AI, after all, to not even keep track of where something came from. In a traditional setting, it is relatively easy to identify the leak as it stems from a clear breach of data; however, in generative models, the leakage could be due to the fact that a model memorized the training data. Thus, the model can very well output an exact copy, or a high similarity match of a section of the data it was trained on, without any obvious signal that it exposed privacy. At other times, the leak might seem entirely incidental, which is even worse [8].

This is also the reason for the massive difficulties of accountability and auditing; to identify where the source of a leak is inherently ambiguous. If the model outputs something sensitive, it can be non-trivial to demonstrate whether this is due to data memorization, a weakness of the training process, or something else entirely. In addition, this issue leads us to at least two basic ethical questions, namely regarding the nature and permission of the data with which these models have been trained. For example, if personal data were scraped without consent, it raises questions about the rights of people whose data has been included in the model's training set. Without realizing, hundreds of millions of people used their data for training AI or providing permission, and it was also used against them.

In addition, generative AI algorithms can reinforce biases, stereotypes, and other negative externalities found in the training data. For instance, if the training data has bias or discriminatory content and the model prompts to generate contents, these biases may reflect in the model outputs. It also adds another dimension to privacy violations if the system recreates things that violate privacy, but also to reinforce social biases. As a result, the privacy and data protection risks of generative AI models are multidimensional and linked with a larger conversation on the ethical use of AI, transparency in data collection, and the changes in the digital age surrounding consent. Combating these challenges involves a mix of tech solutions, ethical principles, and regulatory oversight.

8.1.4 Importance of privacy-preserving strategies

The risk concerning privacy from the generative AI models is huge, and thus privacy-preserving techniques are no longer recommended but rather mandatory. In sensitive domains, such as public services, education, finance, and healthcare, where generative AI is increasingly being deployed, the ramifications of privacy violations are particularly serious. In these areas, a privacy attack would give rise to exposing personal and sensitive data and thus also violates the trust that users have in these services. This means that data protection is not only a technical problem, but also an ethical and legal one, and a question of trust in AI. For an individual, a privacy breach can alter their life, while for the organization behind data management, it can lead to loss of millions of dollars [9–11].

There is a need to adopt a "privacy by design" approach in developing systems to encourage the responsible and ethical development of AI systems; this is necessary for developers and companies working on these systems. This approach advocates for the integration of privacy protections into the full life cycle of an AI system – from data gathering to model training and final use and deployment by persons. It needs to be ensured that at every stage of development, privacy is given the first priority and the rights of the users are protected. A change is needed to ensure that AI technologies serve the public good without violating individual privacy.

Here, we explore the greatest privacy issues around generative AI models. We discuss specific deployable, end-to-end solutions that have been tested over time for these problems, including differential privacy and federated learning, Secure Multi-Party Computation (SMPC), and others. These strategies provide unique routes to push the boundaries of AI without infringing on the rights of people. These privacy-preserving approaches allow developers to innovate responsibly and help create AI systems that can ensure compliance with legal standards while building user trust and safeguarding privacy in an ever-increasing data-driven world. Figure 8.3 presents the flowchart of privacy-preserving mechanisms in generative AI systems [12,13].

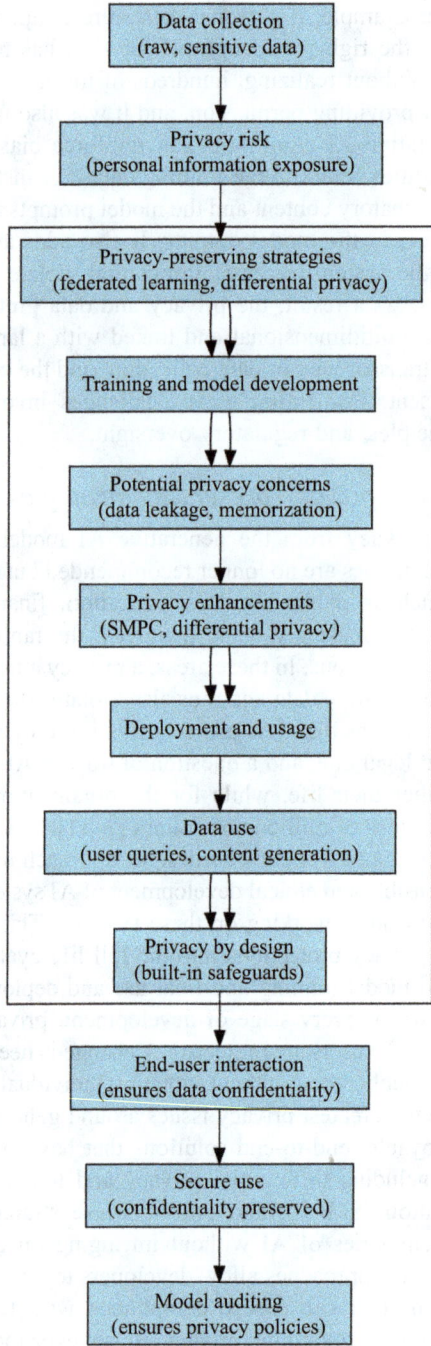

Figure 8.3   Flow of privacy-preserving mechanisms in generative AI systems

8.2 Understanding privacy risks in generative AI

Artificial Intelligence is considered by the majority of people to be a genius, which is going to assist us in doing our tasks, writing new content for us, and providing us with solutions to complex problems in a much easier way than a human can ever do (Figure 8.4).

However, the data behind the base of these AI systems is often glossed over. We only miss data when something goes wrong, as data is not always the sexiest of topics but probably one part of the process that requires more attention, as generative AI is highly dependent on huge datasets of data, developed from real-world human-sourced data. Large data sets of content and language, base models, such as generative AI for text or images, are trained on vast supplies of data. The training

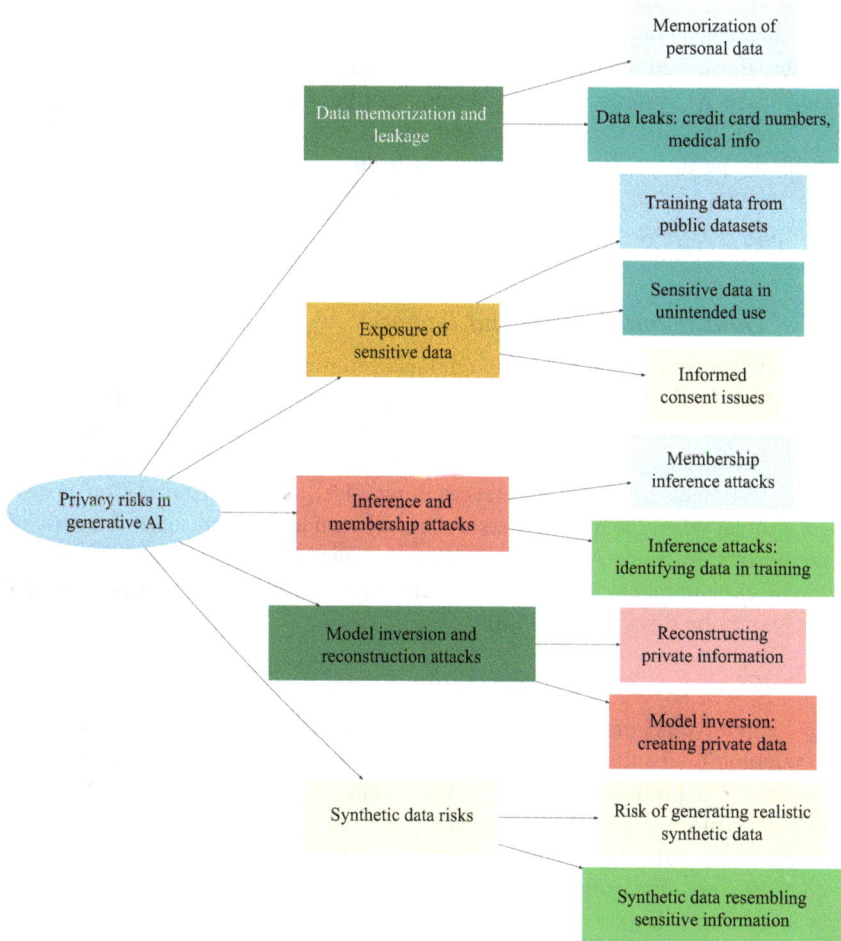

Figure 8.4 Understanding privacy risks in generative AI

sets are where it synthesizes text and other media (images, videos, etc.) collected from diverse datasets. Often this data comes from human beings, and often this is personal, sensitive, or proprietary data. While generative AI models generate answers comparable to the best of human creativity in art and other creative expressions, they also amplify privacy issues. What exactly is in those models, and, even more significantly, how much of that information is basically confidential, or secret?

The dilemma is deciding whether these AI techniques could expose sensitive data. The problem is, e.g., whether a generative AI model can suffer "data leaks", i.e., whether the model can output non-public or confidential information, even when a dataset it was pretrained on is otherwise not subclassified as confidential. When it comes to privacy, this is another thing to think about, because if it is trained with private and proprietary data, it may still generate content that discloses some private information about people or organizations, which can impose potential privacy risks [14–16].

Two, this question underscores the need for research on how privacy risk arises in generative AI systems and how privacy can be mitigated through data governance, model training transparency, and model output recommendations. This is particularly pertinent now that there has been mass adoption of generative AI across various sectors, which has called for systems to be in place to safeguard against privacy risks and, more importantly, to prevent the unintended exposure of data.

8.2.1   Data memorization and leakage

One major concern is that generative models can memorize their training datasets. Unlike traditional algorithms, which are designed to find patterns while ignoring exact values, large language and image models have been shown, at times, to retain exact information, including full email addresses, full names, or excerpts from private documents of a few sentences long [4,7]. Such memorization poses a privacy threat when the user triggers the model with a text that causes it to disclose its memorization. Some AI models have been shown to produce sensitive data, such as credit card numbers or private medical notes, in certain conditions (none of which should be disclosable!) [5,6].

8.2.2   Exposure of sensitive training data

Many generative AI models are trained on huge datasets collected from the internet, including blogs, forums, social media posts, and other types of publicly shared documents. The problem occurs when these data sets contain clinical or Personally Identifiable Information (PII) that was never meant to be used to train an AI model. Although these datasets might have been available to collect on public resources when they were first gathered, the availability of data does not imply access to include it in an ML model. This poses both a legal and moral nonvolume, did the people who formed part of these datasets do it by giving informed consent? Do users have a way to opt out or control how their data is being used?

When data is present in the training set, especially sensitive data, it is impossible to clear it completely. While the model learns patterns from this data, it has the unfortunate potential of memorizing or retaining this private information in model parameters. Privacy risk follows as a logical consequence since the model may produce outputs that leak the sensitive information contained within this data. Further, there exists an ethical quandary about using such information without the express consent of the individuals. This leads to further issues about whether developers and organizations are accountable for ensuring the data privacy of the end-users if the models may potentially leak private information without their awareness. Moreover, it is often unclear how privacy laws like GDPR or HIPAA are transgressed when these models are deployed in the real world, opening a legal grey area for AI data use cases.

For starters, this speaks to the bigger problem of data ownership and the rights of people. Often, users may never have even known that the content they posted in public could be used for training to begin with, raising concerns of potential privacy violations and a lack of transparency. As well as this, the inability to track where particular information that a model has been trained on originated from makes accountability and model auditing even harder. These issues will only become more pressing as AI systems become more powerful, and will demand clear ethical standards, strong regulatory systems, and transparency from those involved in developing and deploying these technologies.

8.2.3   Inference and membership attacks

The risks to privacy are not always evident. In some situations, attackers might deploy a model through inference or membership inference attacks. These techniques endeavor to determine if a piece of data was used to train the model, sifting through the material for signs of its past. What does this all mean? A new context for privacy arises: if you query a model and find out you were included in the training set, then you have a right to know and the right to exclude. Privacy may be violated if glancing at a model can tell you what your old medical condition is when a model is applied to a dataset that includes your old medical condition [8,13].

Membership inference calculates whether a data sample x belongs to the training set D [9]. The adversary observes by using (8.1).

$$f(x) = Model(x) \tag{8.1}$$

If the model behaves differently (e.g., lower loss or higher confidence) for previously seen samples, this can be used to guess using (8.2).

$$P(x \in D) > threshold \tag{8.2}$$

8.2.3.1   Simulating a membership inference test

A very intuitive but illustrative simulation is provided in this section to demonstrate the theory behind membership inference attacks. The intent is to show how an

Membership inference: confidence distribution

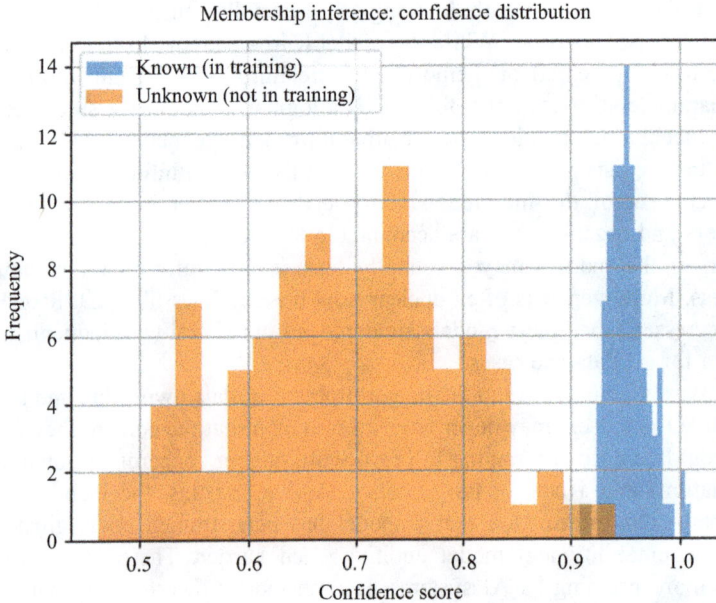

Figure 8.5   Membership interference confidence distribution

attacker could exploit a model to get the model to output a certain way, specifically in terms of confidence, to learn whether a specific piece of data appeared in the training set [10,12]. Such an approach would unearth one sizable privacy threat in generative AI systems and other ML models. Membership inference attacks leverage the different behaviors of a model on training data vs new/unseen data. In broader terms, when given the familiar (training) data, the model will be more confident in its predictions [11–13]. Its confidence is usually lower on out-of-distribution inputs and often with higher uncertainty. This gap can expose new information about the base training set, in particular, whether the source has sensitive data (like real health records, financials, or user identities). In order to stimulate such behavior, we generate two batches of confident scores as shown in Figure 8.5.

• A set for data presumed to be in the training set (known),
• One for data that are not in the training set ("unknown").

These simulated model responses are visualized and statistically analyzed to test the ease with which an attacker could discriminate between the two [14–16].

8.2.4   Model inversion and reconstruction attacks

There is another threat hidden in the owner system, model inversion, where an attacker will want to break the output indication and reconstruct the training input data nearby. In the context of generative AI, this can mean inpainting a warped face, infilling a portion of a sensitive text, or reconstructing a conversation that should have been private [15–18]. These attacks are not a spit from the pages of science fiction. Research labs today are developing them with advanced sophistication. The tools to employ generative models also grow sophisticated with the capabilities of the models themselves [1–4].

8.2.5   Synthetic data risks

But not everything is so simple; surprisingly, even synthetic data (a lot of hype about it to preserve privacy) is not so safe. Text generated using a generative model trained on sensitive data may, in some cases, still resemble real people or events, particularly when the model has not been appropriately constrained. In other words, new data may have been the data processed with staleness [19,20], preserving old private information.

Generated data can be too perfectly realistic. The risk to privacy remains even though we train a model on the patient records and get the "fake" records that look exactly like us. Generic (8.3) is used to evaluate the privacy risk of synthetic data.

$$\text{Revelation Risk} = \max_{x \in x} \text{synthetic}\left(\min_{y \in x} \text{real\_sim}(x,y)\right) \qquad (8.3)$$

where sim (x, y) quantifies similarity (e.g., cosine, Euclidean), a disclosure risk approaching 1 suggests that the synthetic data may closely resemble actual individuals [2–5].

8.3   Privacy by design: principles and frameworks

As generative AI systems become more powerful and as they are deployed in sensitive domains, thinking about privacy by design is critical. Placing privacy as a secondary goal is not the right approach because privacy by design is an approach to the personal data environment where privacy-preserving mechanisms are going to be part of the system architecture, and the processes of developing models are part of the system processes [6]. These three touchpoints of data minimization, transparency, and accountability are explored here.

8.3.1   Data minimization and purpose limitation

The principle of data minimization dictates that only the data essential for a particular task should be collected, processed, or retained. This principle is vital to mitigating exposure risks in generative AI, which frequently utilizes extensive uncrated datasets [3,19]. Conceptual equation: Let:

$D = Complete\ dataset$

$T \subset D = Subset\ pertinent\ to\ the\ task$

$I \subset T = Privacy\text{-}preserving\ input$

Data minimization simulation

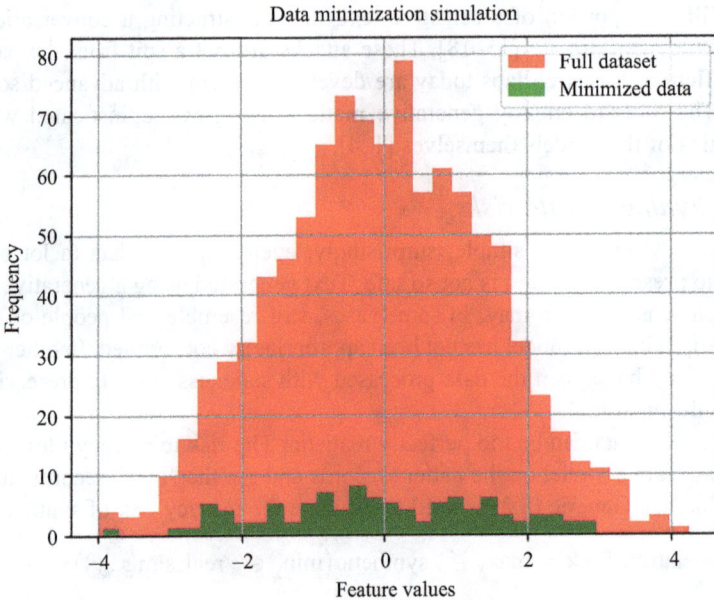

Figure 8.6   Comparison of full vs. minimized dataset usage

Subsequently, the system must guarantee (8.4).

$$\text{Utilize exclusively } I \subseteq T \subseteq D, \tag{8.4}$$

where: T ensures objective limitation, while I ensures minimal, privacy-preserving input.

This is the histogram from Figure 8.6, which illustrates the effects of data minimization, showing the distribution from the full dataset vs that from a reduced subset. The smaller dataset retains statistical properties but at a lower risk to privacy and exposure [6–11], when compared to the original dataset, despite its being a fraction of the original dataset. This illustration shows how the characteristics in an entire data set differ from the characteristics in a sample of that data (in this case, a narrow bandwidth). Although statistically similar, the minimized version can receive significantly less exposure, giving an adversary a much smaller attack surface, all the while preserving comparably high data quality.

8.3.2   Transparency and explainability

Transparency is an important characteristic of AI systems where users and stake-holders must be aware of how data is collected, managed, and utilized. With gen-erative AI, transparency means telling people where training data came from, how it was collected, and what algorithms were used to create the model. That is the disclosure of the inner workings of AI systems by making them available to the public, which includes ensuring users are aware of how their data is being used, stored, and potentially shared. This is crucial for the development of trust, as AI systems are used in high-stakes industries such as healthcare, finance, and education. It also helps users make informed decisions about their data and how they should understand these AI-powered tools' risks and rewards.

Explainability, as the name suggests, is about explaining and justifying what AI models are doing and why. This means creating processes and techniques for understanding and explaining AI results to other people in a consumable manner, even to non-technical audiences. With generative AI, the emphasis on explainability is on how the model produces content and why it is making some predictions or production. For instance, when a generative model generates text, images, or music, what features in the input data led the model to create a particular output, and what role does each feature play in the outcome? This is critical for decision makers, stakeholders, and users to trust the model as they will have to be assured that the behavior of the model is not random and arbitrary but logical, principled, and consistent. If explainability is absent, the AI systems turn into opaque boxes of sorts, where a user questions how the system has made certain decisions and hence hesitates to trust them, particularly when the consequences of failure or wrong decisions can be so severe as in autonomous driving or medical diagnosis.

Transparency and explainability go hand-in-hand and help in creating trust in AI systems. Transparency and explainability are measures of trust: Trust in the sense that when users know how their data is being used and handled, they are more likely to trust it; and that when users understand how the AI model works and how it justifies its predictions and outputs, they can trust the process. Nonetheless, achieving a transparent and explainable AI system can be challenging, as it is with complex models such as deep learning networks. Due to the complexity and obscure nature of these "black-box" models, new techniques for model explanation and interpretability are needed. To overcome the discrepancy between interpretability and real-world requirements, researchers and practitioners are developing novel techniques like model-agnostic interpretability methods [1], attention [2], and visualization tools [3].

$$Trust = Transparency \times Interpretability \qquad (8.5)$$

Let: *Level of transparency*, *I* : *Interpretability*, *Trust*: *Assessed model reliability* A trust can be measured by using (8.6).

$$Trust \propto T \times I \qquad (8.6)$$

Here:

- Transparency means the degree to which users are aware of how their data is obtained, utilized, and processed.
- Explainability means that decisions and outputs of the model need to be comprehensible and justifiable.

- Risk takes into consideration the potential negative impacts and uncertainty created from AI model predictions/outputs (e.g., bias, error, or misuse).

This equation shows that trust in AI linearly scales with transparency and explainability, but behaves inversely to risk. This means that greater transparency and explainability of an AI system lead to an increased trust level, and the perceived risk decreases. Thus, efforts to improve transparency and explainability in technical terms can significantly raise user trust, thus resulting in a high potential for the technology to be widely accepted and contribute to the success of applications. With AI even more complex than before and widespread impact across sectors, solving transparency and explainability from an ethical and responsible deployment perspective will be critical.

8.3.3   Accountability and auditability

Privacy-preserving AI systems, particularly in the domain of generative AI, are built on two fundamental principles of accountability and auditability. These principles go beyond technical functionality. They lay the foundation for ethical, transparent, and legally compliant AI systems. While privacy-preserving algorithms reduce the risk of exposure, the traceability of the events (related to timing and why) strengthens the trust of developers, auditors, and regulators in the AI system. Even the most secure systems may become black boxes – not able to be verified, ultimately, we argue, dangerous without accountability and auditability [8–14]. Table 8.1 summarizes the key components of the proposed framework for privacy-aware generative AI systems.

- *Accountability: Assigning responsibility:* Assigning blame for the actions and results of a system is known as accountability. It guarantees a transparent chain of accountability in case of an issue, such as a data leak, privacy violation, or model hallucination [15–17]. This comprises:
  o   Logging model training setups and iterations
  o   Tracking who has accessed or changed data
  o   Determining who is responsible for making decisions

    In high-stakes industries where generative models have the potential to directly or indirectly affect people's lives, such as healthcare, finance, and national security, accountability is crucial.
- *Auditability: Making AI decisions traceable:* The ability to examine, track, and replicate an AI system's actions is known as auditability [18]. Usually, this entails the methodical recording of:
  o   Pipelines for data
  o   Configurations and checkpoints for the model
  o   Events of inference
  o   Interactions between users and AI outputs

These logs comprise the audit trail, a record of occurrences that enables compliance validation and post hoc analysis [19], as presented by Table 8.1.

Table 8.1 Audit log elements in generative AI systems

Component	Audit information logged	Purpose
Data ingestion	Timestamp, source, hash of data batch	Verifies data provenance
Model training	Version ID, hyperparameters, training logs	Enables reproducibility
Inference requests	Input prompt, model version, user ID (if applicable)	Tracks misuse or unauthorized queries
Output generation	Generated content, timestamp, content hash	Supports accountability in content use
Access logs	User access records, IP, session duration	Detects abnormal or unauthorized behavior

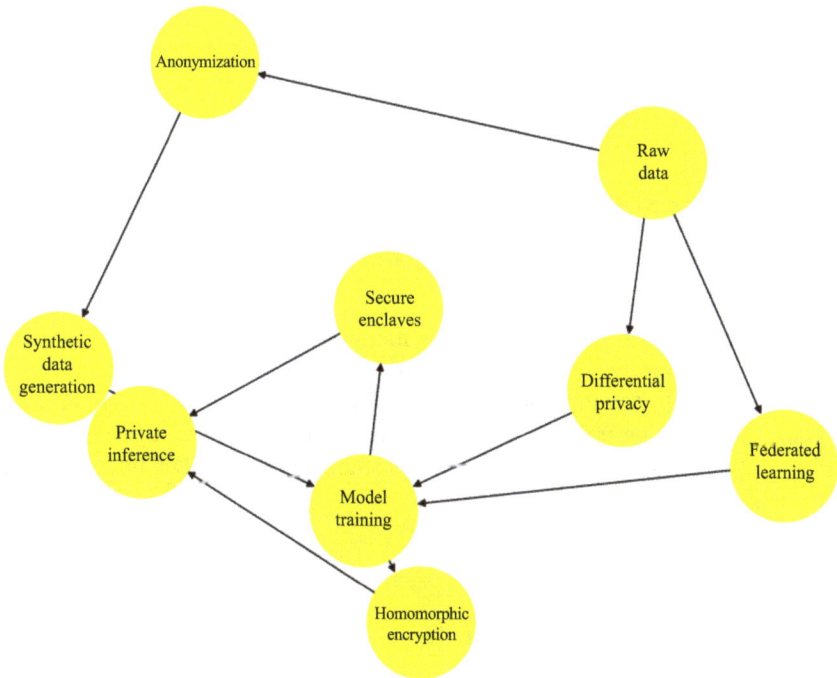

Figure 8.7 Privacy-preserving techniques in generative AI

8.4 Techniques for privacy preservation in generative AI

Generative AI systems need to be built with safeguards that actively prevent the exposure of sensitive data as they grow in strength and prevalence. This section balances usability, security, and performance by outlining the fundamental methods currently used to protect privacy in generative AI systems [18–20]. Figure 8.7 presents the privacy-preserving techniques in generative AI.

Table 8.2   Effects of epsilon on model privacy

Epsilon (ε)	Privacy level	Model utility
0.1	Very strong privacy	Lower accuracy
1	Moderate privacy	Moderate utility
10	Weak privacy	Higher accuracy

8.4.1 Differential privacy

- **Concepts and guarantees:** Differential Privacy (DP) offers a formal privacy assurance by ensuring that adding or removing any individual data point minimally influences the outcome of a computation [1–3]. The objective is mathematically concealing individual-level data while permitting significant aggregate statistics by (8.7). Table 8.2 presents the impact of Epsilon on model privacy.

Let M be a randomized algorithm. For datasets D_1 and D_2 that differ by one element

$$P_r[M(D_1) \in S] \leq e^{\varepsilon} \cdot P_r[M(D_2) \in S] + \delta \tag{8.7}$$

where: ε controls privacy loss (smaller is better), δ allows for a negligible probability of failure.

- **Applications in training generative models**
  The key applications [6] are as follows.
  - *DP-SGD:* A widely utilized algorithm that incorporates noise into gradients during training to mitigate overfitting specific data points.
  - *OpenDP and Opacus:* Libraries offering seamless DP integration for PyTorch models.

8.4.2 Federated learning

- **Decentralized training and data locality**

Federated Learning (FL) is a decentralized training approach allowing multiple clients, such as smartphones, hospitals, or organizations, to train a machine learning model collaboratively without disclosing raw data. Clients download a global model, train it locally with their private data, and upload only the model updates, such as gradients or weights, to a central server. The server consolidates these updates to enhance the global model [10]. This paradigm facilitates privacy preservation by maintaining data localization, thereby reducing the risk of data breaches or exposure. In a healthcare context, hospitals can cooperate to develop a model for disease detection without exchanging patient records [13]. Figure 8.8 presents the FL workflow.

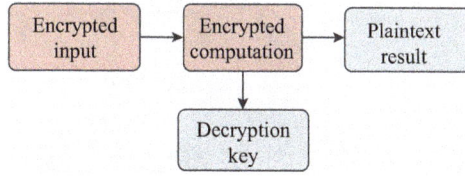

Figure 8.8 Federated learning workflow

Table 8.3 Challenges in generative model use

Challenge	Description
Non-IID data	Clients may have highly diverse data distributions, hurting model convergence.
Large model sizes	Generative models often have millions of parameters, increasing bandwidth cost.
Privacy leakage from updates	Gradients can still leak sensitive info through inference or inversion attacks.
Training instability	Generative models are notoriously unstable, requiring precise tuning that FL complicates.

Federated averaging can be expressed by using (8.8), the updated global model w_t at round t is computed as presented by (8.8). This approach preserves data locality, aligning with privacy by design principles.

$$wt = \frac{1}{N} \sum_{i=1}^{N} w_t^i \qquad (8.8)$$

where: N is the number of clients, and $wt(i)$ is the local model trained by client i at time t.

- **Challenges in generative model use**

Even though FL has many benefits, it is very hard to use with generative models like GANs or diffusion models, as presented in Table 8.3.

8.4.3 Homomorphic encryption

- **Computation on encrypted data**

A revolutionary development in computation that protects privacy is Homomorphic Encryption (HE). HE allows mathematical operations to be performed directly on encrypted data, unlike traditional encryption methods that require data to be decrypted before computation. These calculations produce encrypted results that, when decrypted, produce the same results as if they had been carried out on raw data. This characteristic makes HE very desirable for use in delicate industries like finance, healthcare, and artificial intelligence, particularly in cases where strict data security and confidentiality are required by laws like GDPR or HIPAA [14–19]. Figure 8.9 presents the HE.

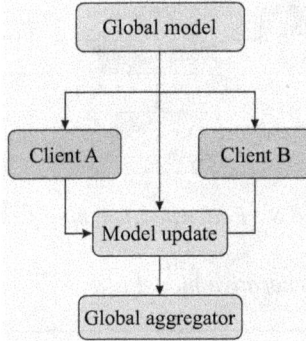

Figure 8.9   Homomorphic encryption

Table 8.4   Main categories of homomorphic encryption

Type	Operations supported	Use case
Partially Homomorphic Encryption (PHE)	One operation (e.g., only addition or multiplication)	Simple statistics, voting systems
Somewhat Homomorphic Encryption (SHE)	Limited number of operations	Basic encrypted ML, small AI tasks
Fully Homomorphic Encryption (FHE)	Arbitrary computation on encrypted data	General-purpose encrypted computation

- **Mathematical foundation for HE**

Let E be an encryption function and f a function to compute [10]. A homomorphic encryption scheme satisfies the following equation:

$$E(f(x,y)) = f'(E(x), E(y)) \qquad (8.9)$$

where: f is a plaintext operation (e.g., addition, multiplication), f' is the corresponding operation under encryption, $E(x)$ and $E(y)$ are encrypted values, and decrypting $f'(E(x), E(y))$ gives the same result as $f(x,y)$.

For example, in an additively homomorphic scheme like Parlier encryption as presented in (8.10).

$$E(x) \cdot E(y) = E(x+y) \qquad (8.10)$$

This allows summing encrypted values without ever decrypting them, an essential feature for privacy-preserving data analytics and inference.

- **Types of homomorphic encryption**

There are three primary categories of HE, each exhibiting differing levels of computational complexity and capability as presented in Table 8.4.

Table 8.5   Limitations for large-scale AI

Limitation	Impact on AI Workflows
Computation overhead	Operations on ciphertexts are 100–1000× slower than plaintext.
Memory expansion	Encrypted data can be 10–100× larger than raw data.
No GPU acceleration (yet)	Most HE libraries do not leverage GPUs effectively, limiting scalability.
Complexity of integration	HE frameworks are hard to integrate into mainstream ML platforms like PyTorch.
Limited supported functions	Non-linear functions (like ReLU or SoftMax) are hard to approximate accurately.

- **Limitations for large-scale AI**

HE is currently confronted with a number of significant limitations, particularly when it comes to the training or deployment of large-scale generative models such as GPT, GANs, or diffusion networks, even though it holds a great deal of promise as presented in Table 8.5.

8.4.4   Secure enclaves and trusted execution environments (TEE)

TEEs are secure, isolated hardware regions within a processor that offer a safe-guarded environment for executing code and data. These environments guarantee that, even if the operating system or hypervisor is breached, the data within the enclave remains secure and impervious to tampering. The foremost implementation of a TEE is Intel Software Guard Extensions (SGX). TEEs facilitate privacy-preserving computation by maintaining both the data and the computation encrypted externally to the enclave, decrypting them solely within this secure environment [10,20].

- **TEE workflow**
  - ○ Code and data Provisioning: The model code and encrypted user data are safely supplied to the enclave [11].
  - ○ Computation in the enclave: The TEE is where data is processed and decrypted.
  - ○ Result encryption: Prior to leaving the enclave, the output is once more encrypted.

- **Challenges in generative AI use**
  The use of TEEs in large-scale generative artificial intelligence models is restricted, despite the fact that they provide robust security as presented in Table 8.6.

Table 8.6   Challenges in generative AI use

Challenge	Impact
Limited memory	Most TEEs (like Intel SGX) support only a few hundred MBs.
Restricted GPU access	TEEs cannot leverage external accelerators, limiting training.
Complex programming	Writing enclave-compatible code requires low-level expertise.
Performance overhead	Encryption/decryption and memory copying incur delays.

Table 8.7   Anonymization techniques

Method	Description
Generalization	Replacing values with broader categories (e.g., age 27 → 20–30).
Suppression	Removing sensitive fields (e.g., names, SSNs).
K-Anonymity	Ensuring each record is indistinguishable from at least *k–1* other.
L-Diversity/ T-Closeness	Enhancements to prevent attribute inference.

8.4.5   Data anonymization and synthetic data generation

- **Need for anonymization in generative AI**

Data anonymization denotes the conversion of personal data into a format that precludes the identification of individuals, whether directly or indirectly. In the realm of generative AI, training models on user-generated or sensitive data such as medical images, chat logs, or financial records requires stringent anonymization methods to safeguard user identities and adhere to legal regulations (e.g., GDPR, HIPAA) [13]. Table 8.7 presents the anonymization techniques.

A k-anonymity constraint can be defined by (8.11). Let a dataset D satisfy *k*-anonymity if, for every combination of quasi-identifiers, each equivalence class in D contains at least k records sharing the same set of quasi-identifier values

$$\forall r \in D, \exists \{r1, r2, \ldots, rk - 1\} \subset D : QI(r) = QI(ri) \qquad (8.11)$$

where QI(r) represents the quasi-identifier set of record r.

8.5   Secure multi-party computation (SMPC): a case study

8.5.1   What is SMPC and how it works

A SMPC is a cryptographic protocol that allows several parties to collaboratively compute a function based on their individual inputs while maintaining the confidentiality of those inputs from one another. The concept relies on distributed trust, ensuring that no individual can reconstruct another's private information, while all participants can contribute to and benefit from the final outcome [15]. Figure 8.10 presents the working of SMPC, and Table 8.8 presents the SMPC overview.

- **Mathematical foundation**

Let $x_1, x_2, ..., x_n$ be private inputs from parties. SMPC enables the computation of a public function $f(x_1, x_2, ..., x_n)$ such that:

$$Each \ x_i \ remains \ private, \ yet \ f(x_1, ..., x_n) \ is \ revealed \ to \ all. \tag{8.12}$$

This is often achieved using techniques like secret sharing, oblivious transfer, or garbled circuits (Equation (8.12)) [19].

- **Secret sharing example (Shamir's scheme)**

Each private value x is split into n shares using a polynomial (Equation (8.13))

$$f(i) = a0 + a1i + a2i2 + \cdots + at - 1it - 1 \tag{8.13}$$

Each participant gets a point $(i, f(i))$. Only t participants can reconstruct the original value using Lagrange interpolation. Less than t reveals nothing.

8.5.2   Benefits for collaborative AI use

In artificial intelligence, SMPC enables organizations to collaboratively train models without centralizing their data, providing robust privacy assurances for sensitive applications, as illustrated in Table 8.9.

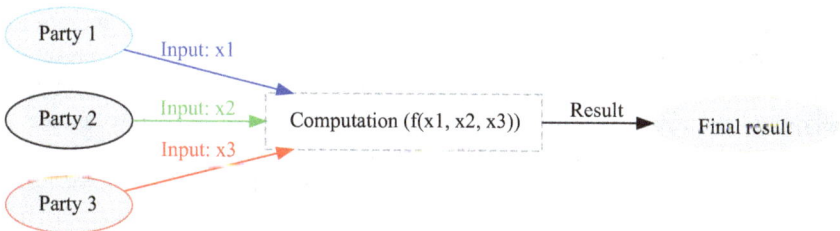

Figure 8.10   SMPC workflow

Table 8.8   SMPC overview

Aspect	Description
Core principle	Joint computation on private inputs without revealing them
Use in generative AI	Enables collaborative training on sensitive data (e.g., medical or financial)
Implementation methods	Secret sharing, garbled circuits, oblivious transfer
Strengths	Data confidentiality, compliance with privacy laws, decentralization
Weaknesses	High overhead, complex integration, scaling difficulty

Table 8.9   Benefits for collaborative AI use case

Use case	How SMPC helps
Healthcare AI	Hospitals can collaboratively train on patient data without sharing it
Finance	Banks can build shared fraud detection systems while preserving client privacy
Federated learning extension	SMPC can enhance federated learning with cryptographic security

8.6   Conclusion

In this chapter, we explored the fuzzy relationship of generative AI and privacy, another growing topic of relevance in AI today. In addition to assisting with data-basing and searching at best, the generative model itself becomes a major privacy risk as it strengthens and pervades more segments of society with offerings such as in healthcare, finance, content creation, and security; purposefully kept secrets are at risk of feed into the model that will mistakenly memorize copies of original samples, being exploited to generate artificial copies, and accidentally leaking further user info that the system must otherwise keep secret. Addressing these risks will require not just technical mitigation but also a fundamental shift to privacy-preserving design and governance.

Our starting point was projecting the major privacy issues of generative AI since training on large datasets is often scraped from public or semi-private sources that could lead to leakage of information. We then deployed various privacy-preserving methods of differential privacy, federated learning, secure enclaves, homomorphic encryption, and data anonymization methods. We also reviewed each technique for its rationale, use cases, shortcomings, and utility when sociotechnical systems are trained and used with generative models. This chapter analyzed the principle of privacy by design and how it supports transparency and accountability, and least data collection, as important foundational elements in the development of generative AI. These principles are at once ethical imperatives and practical guides for building data protection-compliant and socially palatable systems.

Much of the chapter then examined a case study of SMPC, or "Secure Multi-Party Computation", a cryptographic approach that allows several parties to collaboratively train generative models while never needing to disclose their own data. The SMPC was regularly demonstrated in a case study on cross-institutional model training, showing that even highly competitive sectors like healthcare, defense, or finance can benefit from collaborative innovations while protecting sensitive data.

Ultimately, privacy-preserving techniques are essential building blocks for the ethical evolution of generative AI. The rapid evolution of the field calls for robust, scalable, and legally compliant privacy measures to nurture public confidence, secure user data, and sustain innovation. Future research should continue to explore hybrid approaches that combine technical and non-technical solutions to provide cryptographic security, regulatory compliance, and algorithmic fairness in order to ensure safe and responsible use of generative technologies.

References

[1]   Feretzakis G, Papaspyridis K, Gkoulalas-Divanis A, and Verykios VS. Privacy-preserving techniques in generative AI and large language models: a narrative review. *Information*. 2024;15(11):697.

[2]   Liu Y, Huang J, Li Y, Wang D, and Xiao B. Generative AI model privacy: a survey. *Artificial Intelligence Review*. 2024;58(1):33.

[3]   Uddagiri C, and Isunuri BV. Ethical and privacy challenges of generative AI. In *Generative AI: Current Trends and Applications* 2024 (pp. 219–244). Singapore: Springer Nature Singapore.

[4]   Golda A, Mekonen K, Pandey A, *et al*. Privacy and security concerns in generative AI: A comprehensive survey. *IEEE Access*. 2024;12:48126–48144.

[5]   Mumtaz M, Tayyab M, Jhanjhi NZ, Muzammal SM, and Hameed K. Privacy preserving data analysis with generative AI. In *AI Techniques for Securing Medical and Business Practices*. 2025 (pp. 391–410). IGI Global.

[6]   Yang Y, Zhang B, Guo D, *et al*. Generative AI for secure and privacy-preserving mobile crowdsensing. *IEEE Wireless Communications*. 2024; 31(6):29–38.

[7]   Veluru CS. Impact of artificial intelligence and generative AI on healthcare: Security, privacy concerns and mitigations. *Journal of Artificial Intelligence & Cloud Computing*. SRC/JAICC-364. DOI: doi. org/10.47363/JAICC/2024 (3). 2024;347:2–6.

[8]   Dalal S, Poongodi M, Lilhore UK, *et al*. Optimized LightGBM model for security and privacy issues in cyber-physical systems. *Transactions on Emerging Telecommunications Technologies*. 2023;34(6):e4771.

[9]   Zheng Y, Chang CH, Huang SH, Chen PY, and Picek S. An overview of trustworthy AI: Advances in IP protection, privacy-preserving federated learning, security verification, and GAI safety alignment. *IEEE Journal on Emerging and Selected Topics in Circuits and Systems*. 2024;14(4):582–607.

[10] Arora A. Developing generative AI models that comply with privacy regulations and ethical principles. Available at SSRN 5268204. 2025.

[11] Shafik W. Generative adversarial networks: Security, privacy, and ethical considerations. In *Generative Artificial Intelligence (AI) Approaches for Industrial Applications*. 2025 (pp. 93–117). Cham: Springer Nature Switzerland.

[12] Huang Y, Arora C, Houng WC, Kanij T, Madulgalla A, and Grundy J. Ethical concerns of generative AI and mitigation strategies: a systematic mapping study. *arXiv* preprint arXiv:2502.00015. 2025.

[13] Khan MA, Alasiry A, Marzougui M, *et al*. Securing intelligent transportation systems: A dual-framework approach for privacy protection and

cybersecurity using generative AI. *IEEE Transactions on Intelligent Transportation Systems*. 2025:1–12. (Early Access).

[14]   Lilhore UK, Simaiya S, Dalal S, Sharma YK, Tomar S, and Hashmi A. Secure WSN architecture utilizing hybrid encryption with DKM to ensure consistent IoV communication. *Wireless Personal Communications*. 2024: 1–29. https://doi.org/10.1007/s11277-024-10859-0

[15]   Ullah I, Hassan N, Gill SS, *et al.* Privacy preserving large language models: ChatGPT case study based vision and framework. *IET Blockchain*. 2024; 4:706–724.

[16]   Shahriar S, Allana S, Hazratifard SM, and Dara R. A survey of privacy risks and mitigation strategies in the artificial intelligence life cycle. *IEEE Access*. 2023 11:61829–61854.

[17]   Mohialden YM, Salman SA, Mijwil MM, *et al.* Enhancing security and privacy in healthcare with generative artificial intelligence-based detection and mitigation of data poisoning attacks software. *Jordan Medical Journal*. 2024;58(4):279–291.

[18]   Bhutani M, Dalal S, Alhussein M, Lilhore UK, Aurangzeb K, and Hussain A. SAD-GAN: A novel secure anomaly detection framework for enhancing the resilience of cyber-physical systems. *Cognitive Computation*. 2025; 17(4):127.

[19]   Lilhore UK, Simaiya S, Dalal S, Alshuhail A, Almusharraf A. A post-quantum hybrid encryption framework for securing biometric data in consumer electronics. *IEEE Transactions on Consumer Electronics*. 2025; 71(3):8289–8297.

[20]   Dalal S, Lilhore UK, Faujdar N, Simaiya S, Ayadi M, Almujally NA, and Ksibi A. Next-generation cyber attack prediction for IoT systems: Leveraging multi-class SVM and optimized CHAID decision tree. *Journal of Cloud Computing*. 2023;12(1):137.

Chapter 9

Case studies and real-world applications in generative AI

This chapter explores the real-world application of generative AI technologies in multiple sectors. Case studies of successes and failures give the reader an understanding of the potential and pitfalls of generative models in real-world systems. Our focus lies in industry-specific case studies from entertainment, the cybersecurity space, finance, banking, and the healthcare subsector.

9.1 Introduction

Generative artificial intelligence has changed the landscape in many areas of intelligent systems, such as data synthesis, automatic creative artifacts generation, and content generation in various multimedia forms. Unlike conventional models that mainly focus on classification or prediction [1,8], generative models are designed to generate new instances of data that adhere to a specific dataset. The power of this capability of cloning, refining, and augmenting the real data has enabled various applications from marketing to entertainment, to cyber security, to healthcare, to financial modeling [2].

Significant progress has been made in the past years with novel deep learning architectures, including transformer-based architectures such as DALLE and GPT, as well as Variational Autoencoders (VAEs) and Generative Adversarial Networks (GANs). These models have been impressive in their generation of realistic images, coherent text, synthetic tabular datasets, and artificial voices [3, 11]. Now, while there is no shortage of these technologies, they are hard to deploy into the hands of practical settings. The vicissitudes and diversity of the real estate often mean that matters fail not on an ideal or technical level [1], but on subtler challenges of ethics, regulations, and robustness of generative results [4].

In an attempt to bridge the theory-practice gap, this chapter explores the deployment of generative AI across different sectors. We explore several in-depth case studies that illustrate the use of generative models to solve real-world challenges, enrich current systems, or create new ideas across various companies. In each of the case studies [5], the use case, model design, implementation details, performance metrics, privacy and security concerns, and the outcome, whether it is success, limitation, or failure, are critically analyzed.

This process highlights a few unexpected outcomes and errors made when generative models are deployed without consideration. A considerable number of issues have arisen, such as the misuse of deepfake technologies through social media, bias in AI-generated clinical images, and unchecked dissemination of synthetic financial data. These drawings emphasize the importance of responsible AI development and are suggestive of future research and business practices [6,10]. The chapter starts with a formal framework for accessing real-world use cases of generative AI. The ensuing domain-specific case studies, spanning entertainment, cybersecurity, finance and banking, and healthcare, evaluate each in terms of technical feasibility, societal impact, and the security-privacy trade-off. The chapter closes by sharing some of the most interesting failures and the lessons learned with that will guide the future application of generative technologies in the real world.

9.2 Framework for case study evaluation

Evaluating the real value that generative AI can deliver is more than a reflection of the capability of the underlying algorithms. Unlike traditional machine learning, which produces preservative metrics, generative models output original text, images, audio, or structured data that need to be assessed for correctness, naturalness, usefulness, fairness, and safety in given application contexts [7]. It is this mixture of a sufficiently rigid, yet still flexible framework, which is absolutely essential to be prepared to correctly compare and analyze case studies from many other fields. The framework presents five key dimensions: purpose, technology, integration, outcomes, and implications. Each dimension offers one way to examine the deployment of generative models and their impact (in the short-term and long-term potential effects) [8].

The major theme is the most important question of all – why? Problem statement: Why is this a problem, and how is generative methodology better than traditional methods? Generative models are often used by organizations to generate data for training, improve creativity workflow, or personalize content in granular detail. Understanding the use case provides the necessary background for every subsequent decision, including model selection, data strategy, and deployment architecture [9].

The second dimension is the underlying technology: model architecture (e.g., GANs, VAEs, transformers), training and inference methods, and the data pipeline. It also includes a consideration of the availability of data, the pre-processing, and the approaches for bias mitigation. We also see some distinct use cases between StyleGAN2, which seems to be dominating the entertainment world, and CTGAN, which is more capable of generating synthetic tabular data for finance applications. A model can only be effective depending on the data and the structure of the computational system it resides on [3,11]. Table 9.1 presents the evaluation framework for GAI case studies.

The third dimension focuses on the need to unify systems and successfully execute campaigns. This assessment examines the effectiveness of the generative model in real-world settings. This includes concerns over growth opportunities,

Table 9.1   *Evaluation framework for generative AI case studies*

Dimension	Description
Purpose	The business or research motivation behind the use of generative AI
Technology	Model architecture, training data, tools used, and data quality considerations
Integration	Deployment environment, scalability, human interaction, and feedback loops
Outcomes	Quantitative results (e.g., accuracy, FID) and qualitative impacts
Implications	Ethical, security, privacy, and societal impact

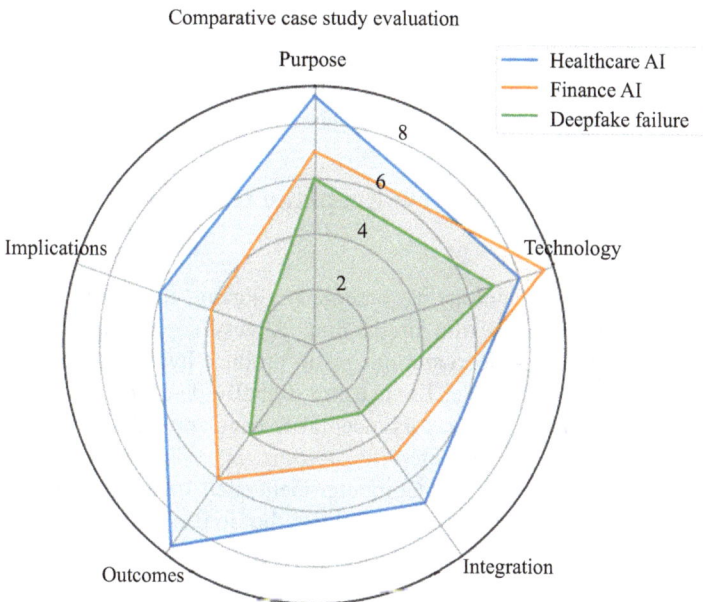

Figure 9.1   Comparative case study evaluation

timeframes, buy-in, and outputs [12]. In some cases, outputs generated from generative processes are validated by human domain experts before they reach final production (synthetic medical imagery), while in other cases, they directly aid in making autonomous decisions (simulated malware during a cybersecurity training). System integration maturity is often the defining factor in the effectiveness of generative AI applications [7,13].

This next dimension is result (both quantitative and qualitative) based. Although accuracy, similarity indices (SSIM, FID), or perplexity provide a quantitative measure of quality, we must be mindful of the end-to-end experience for the user and the business that we are delivering. For specific case studies, value with generative AI is not necessarily driven by the accuracy of the model but often by cost or time savings it affords, or its unique ability to scale content generation [8,19]. This discussion leads to a comparative case study evaluation, as illustrated in Figure 9.1.

Ultimately, any practical assessment must acknowledge the ethical, safety, and social costs of generative systems. Data privacy, intellectual property, model exploitation, and unintentional bias and constraints in the implementation of these principles and ethical usage of AI [14]. Synthetic financial records must comply with GDPR or CCPA-like privacy rules, while synthetic media used in entertainment must be regulated to prevent its abuse as deepfakes. It assesses mechanisms to mitigate risk, such as differential privacy, federated learning, and human-in-the-loop validation [15,20].

The five dimensions (purpose, technology, integration, outcomes, and implications) to review generative AI case studies can together act as a gentry framework. This framework enables comparisons across domains while reflecting the unique constraints and opportunities of each sector. And as generative models improve and enter into mission-critical systems, that sort of framework seems indispensable for researchers and practitioners who want to understand not just what these systems can do, but what they should do, and how they should be governed [12].

9.3   Entertainment industry: deepfake technology for film production

Work due to deepfake technology has emerged as a game-changer in the domain of entertainment, especially in film production. A very sophisticated AI tool that enables you to edit audio–video and images to produce hyper-realistic representations of real or fictional people. From using digitally de-aged actors, to creating full-length films with deceased actors, deepfakes have entered the film-production realm, often for recreating characters for a scene, or adding special-effects shots without as hefty of a price tag as Computer-Generated Imagery (CGI) may. This technology offers thrilling creative possibilities, but it also raises important ethical and legal issues about consent, authenticity, and abuse (Figure 9.2).

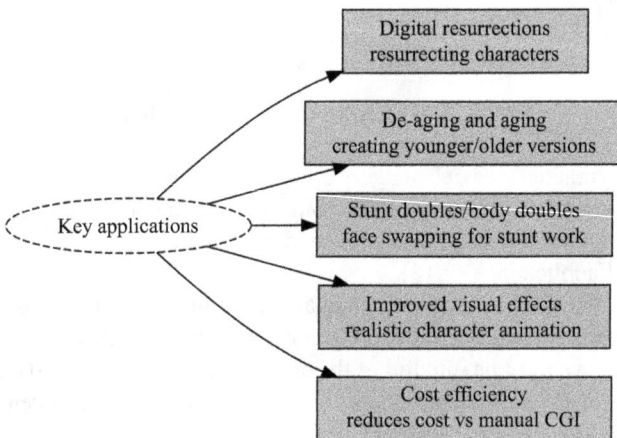

Figure 9.2   Key application of generative AI in deepfake technology for film production

9.3.1   Introduction and context

One of the earliest notable applications of generative AI is the utilization of deepfake technology in the entertainment industry. To artificially generate or modify features in audiovisual content, deepfakes utilize advanced neural networks, particularly GANs. The film industry has adopted these tools to produce scenes that would be unfeasible, risky, or expensive to film otherwise [2,13].

Deepfake technology allows for the reversal of aging, the mimicking of voices, the swapping of faces, and the reanimation of deceased actors in order to preserve the consistency of the narrative. For instance, the film Rogue One (2016) utilized generative models to enhance the CGI that restored the late Peter Cushing's appearance as Grand Moff Tarkin. In recent years, there has been a transition from manual animation to AI-driven automation, which is facilitated by tools like DeepFaceLab, FaceSwap, and NVIDIA's StyleGAN [3,10].

9.3.2   Technological implementation

These systems operate by training a neural network on extensive datasets of an actor's face in a variety of lighting conditions, expressions, and angles. The trained model employs deep learning-based video processing to map and blend the target face onto the actor's body during post-production. To enhance temporal consistency and fidelity across frames, numerous contemporary solutions implement attention modules and encoder-decoder architectures [4,16]. Despite technological advancements, the use of deepfakes in media raises ethical and legal concerns. These encompass audience manipulation, intellectual property rights, misinformation risks, and actor consent [5,18]. Table 9.2 presents the benefits and challenges of deepfakes in film production.

9.3.3   Key applications in film production

The key applications are as follows (Figure 9.3).

Table 9.2   Benefits and challenges of deepfakes in film production

Aspect	Details
Creative control	Enables artistic freedom – resurrecting characters, de-aging actors, or shooting impossible scenes with ease.
Cost efficiency	Reduces reliance on manual CGI and reshoots. Deepfakes can be generated in hours compared to days of manual VFX work.
Technical risk	Requires high-quality training datasets. Inconsistent lighting or emotion representation can lead to uncanny or unrealistic outcomes.
Ethical risk	High potential for misuse outside of entertainment (e.g., misinformation, pornography). Legal guidelines are still evolving.
Industry practice	Studios often combine AI output with manual touch-ups and watermarking strategies to indicate generated content.

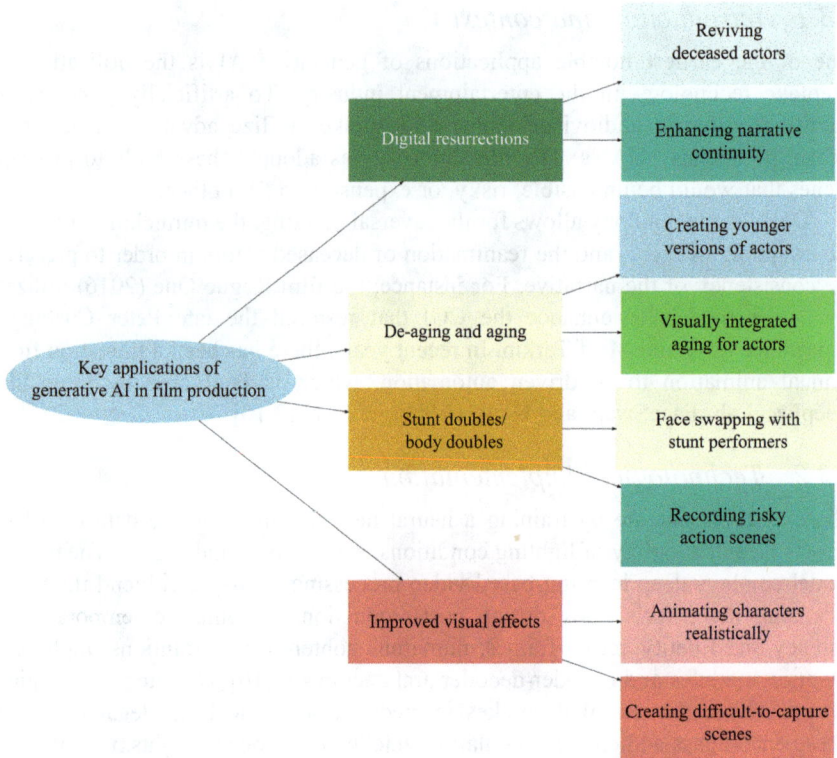

Figure 9.3   Generative AI key applications of generative AI in film production

- *Digital resurrections:* Let us face it, deepfake technology has allowed film-makers to raise actors from the tomb and bring them back into the world, and some will almost always remain so. In 2019, the film The Irishman used deepfake-like technology to digitally de-age young versions of actors like Robert De Niro and Al Pacino. This may enable filmmakers to tell stories between periods or have actors appear after their deaths.
- *De-aging and aging:* By applying deepfake tech, a literal younger or older version of the actor can be created without complex makeup or CGI. Most of the time, it is more economical and visually integrated, enhancing the production value.
- *Stunt doubles/Body doubles:* Producers can use deepfake to digitally swap an actor's face with that of a stunt double, safely recording the risky action scenes involving the stunt performer in place of the actor. This is also something you could use to not be present on set, and you still need the presence of an actor.
- *Improved visual effects:* Most of the blockbuster films use CGI, but deepfake technology is a better and more realistic option for animating a character or scene. This is especially visible in movies where characters need to act in settings that live-action shots would have difficulty capturing.

9.4   Cybersecurity: GANs for malware simulation

9.4.1   Introduction and motivation

Cybersecurity has always been a cat-and-mouse game where the creators of high-end malware constantly look for ways to beat defenders, who continue to enhance their detection mechanisms. Polymorphic malware can evade traditional malware detection systems that rely on static signatures or heuristic detection [6,19].

While not directly related to designing any known form of defense, GANs have emerged as a new tool in this space with the objective of providing a solution to simulate realistic, evolving malware variants (Figure 9.4). By leveraging these samples, a stronger detection model can be trained and validated (serving as a red teaming mechanism in AI cybersecurity research [2,14]).

9.4.2   Generative approach in threat simulation

A brief description of some of the threats included in the standard malware GAN architecture, below [18–20].

- Artificial malware binaries (or feature vectors based on them) are prepared by a device.
- A device that separates real malware from fake malware.
- A mechanism that encourages the generator to generate examples that cannot be distinguished from real threats.

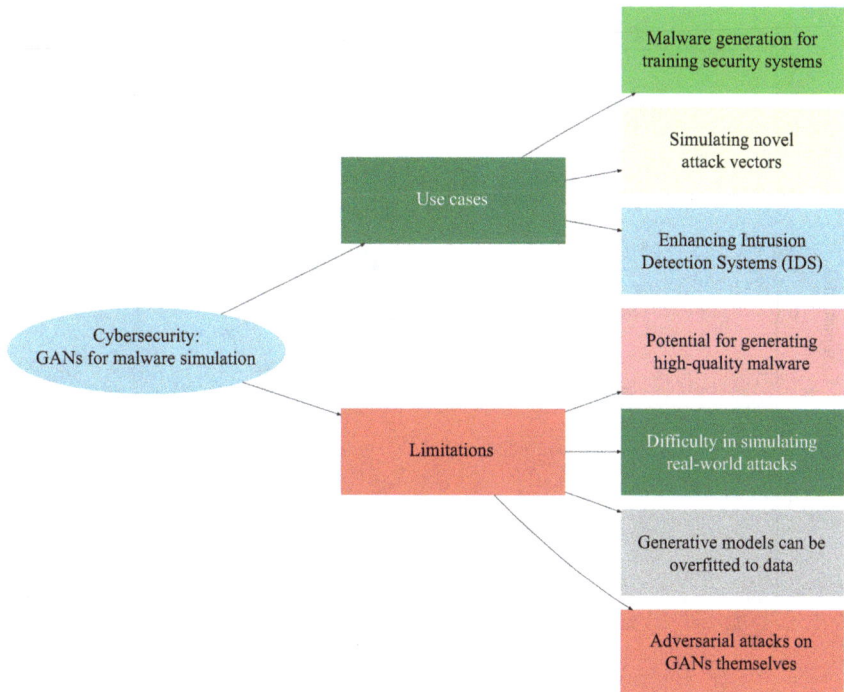

Figure 9.4   GANs for malware simulation use cases and limitations

The best approach leverages representation learning on sequences of opcodes, API calls, and/or behavioral traces. Feature vectors are normally constructed from binary embeddings or dynamic trace logs, which are collected using sandbox environments [13].

Key Findings: As reported in 2021, a GAN, once trained on 20,000 ransomware binaries, was tested to create new variants that were able to bypass 35% of commercial antivirus engines when independently evaluated in a lab setting [5–9].

Figure 9.5 depicts the feature-space similarity of synthetic and real malware as projected using t-SNE. The overlapping distributions confirm the efficacy of GAN-generated malware for defensive training without requiring real-world malicious code in deployment [6,19].

9.4.3   Use cases and limitations

GANs constitute an emerging field in cybersecurity; it simulates new forms of malware to find stronger defense systems. The fake samples thus generated can emulate existing attack patterns, but their differences differ from traditional malware signatures, leading modern antivirus and intrusion detection systems to stretch their muscle. GAN approach for malware generation is mainly to train the defender, red team the threat, and measure the attack [7,19]. Such cases have their security models evaluated with malware types that were unseen during training. This brings the tests to the real-world scenario of zero-time attacks. Figure 9.5 presents the GANs for malware simulation use cases and limitations.

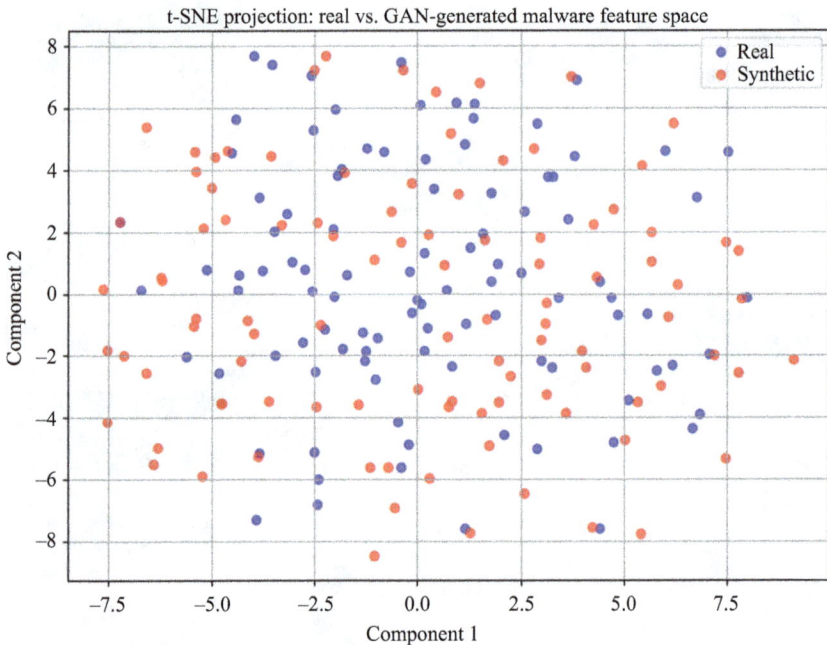

Figure 9.5   t-SNE projection real vs. GAN-generated malware feature space

Table 9.3   Practical use cases and limitations of GAN-generated malware in cybersecurity

Category	Aspect	Description
Use cases	Adversarial training	Creation of diverse synthetic malware to train more robust threat detection models.
	Red team simulation	Emulation of polymorphic or zero-day malware for penetration testing and system hardening.
	Research and benchmarking	Generation of controlled datasets to evaluate machine learning-based antivirus performance.
Risks and limitations	Dual-use Risk	Potential misuse of generated samples for real-world attacks by malicious actors.
	Legal uncertainty	Ambiguities in laws governing the creation and use of synthetic malware in academic or private settings.
	Operational risk	If mishandled, synthetic malware could escape secure environments and cause harm.
Recommended safeguards	Isolated execution	Training and testing are restricted to sandboxed or air-gapped systems to prevent uncontrolled propagation.
	Access controls	Limited datasets, source code, and results access to approved researchers or red teams.
	Purpose-bound use	Ensuring generated malware is only used for simulation and never embedded in real-world systems.

Security companies and schools use these methods to make highly variable datasets and have an improved machine-learning-based classification model. But it works both ways; that same technology can also be misused. If misused, cybercriminals may use a GAN to develop different classes of time-variant and undetectable malware, as well as automated polymorphic and metamorphic attack patterns. And this dual-use potential is bound to raise some serious ethical and legal debates. The researchers investigating GAN malware usually do so in isolated areas like air-gapped labs, as they are not permitted to submit datasets or models to other researchers. Table 9.3 lists cases and challenges using GAN-generated malware in cybersecurity.

9.5   Finance: synthetic data for credit risk modeling

9.5.1   Introduction and context

In the financial sector, data plays a crucial role in determining risk, compliance, detection of fraud, and decision-making. Introduction credit risk modeling is one of the most important applications since it informs a lender about the probability of default of a borrower that immediately influences its risk exposure and profitability [2,15].

Such models typically employ private real-life information, including credit histories, income levels, payment behaviors, and demographic profiles. But privacy law (as with GDPR and CCPA), insufficient data, and concerns of bias can prevent companies from opening access to big, diverse, and representative datasets. Using them internally restricts innovation and collaboration with the outside [6]. Generative AI, more specifically VAEs, GANs, and tabular data generators, is being used to synthesize financial datasets. These datasets preserve the statistical properties and correlation structures of real credit data after the removal of direct identifiers. This makes them perfect for research, model training, and regulatory sandbox environments [7,10].

9.5.2   Generative techniques for tabular data

Unlike images or text, financial data is mostly structured and tabular, often containing a mix of categorical, numerical, and ordinal variables (Figure 9.6). Generative models must maintain [11]:

- Statistical dependencies (e.g., loan amount ↔ income level),
- Distributional characteristics (e.g., non-Gaussian skew),
- Regulatory variables (e.g., credit score thresholds, default labels).
- **Popular models used include:**
  - Conditional Tabular GAN (CTGAN) – handles imbalanced classes and mixed data types [13].
  - Tabular VAE (TVAE) – captures non-linear correlations in multi-modal tabular datasets [16].
  - Gaussian Copula + DP-Synthesizers – for privacy-preserving statistical generation.
- **Applications of synthetic data in credit risk**

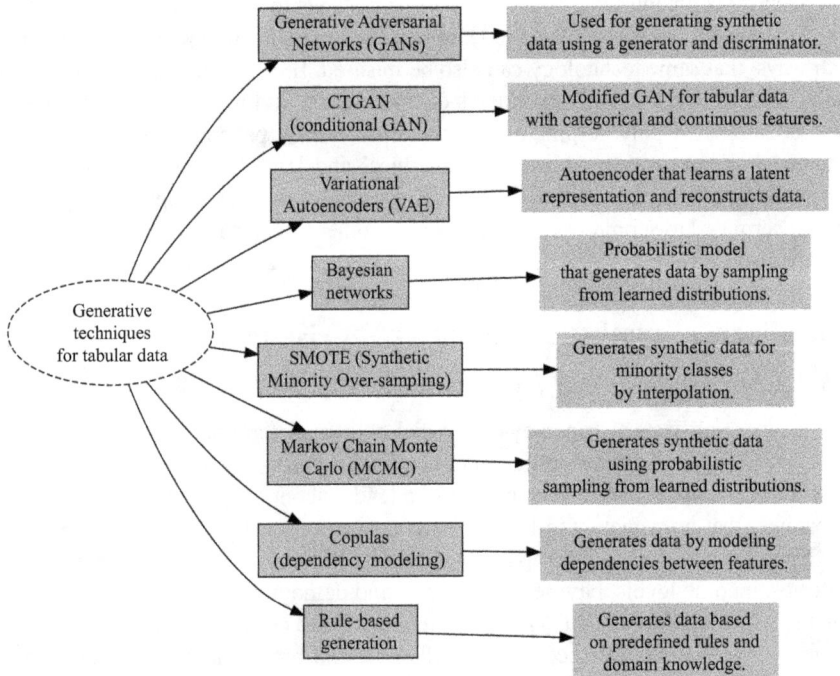

Figure 9.6   Generative techniques for tabular data

Table 9.4 Key applications of synthetic data in credit risk score analysis

Application area	Use case
Model development	Train and validate credit scoring models without accessing production data.
Regulatory testing	Generate plausible but non-sensitive customer data to test compliance models (e.g., Basel III).
Stress testing	Simulate economic downturn scenarios (e.g., increased defaults) for resilience testing.
Data sharing and outsourcing	Enable data collaboration with fintechs, partners, or researchers without privacy violations.

Table 9.5 Evaluation of synthetic data for credit risk modeling

Evaluation dimension	Real dataset	Synthetic dataset	Comments
Sample size	50,000 credit applications	50,000 synthetic records (CTGAN)	Match the size for balanced modeling
Default rate (%)	12.5%	12.3%	Statistically consistent
Correlation (Loan ↔ Income)	0.78	0.76	Preserved economic relationships
Model AUC (XGBoost)	0.89	0.87	Minor performance loss, acceptable trade-off for privacy
KL divergence	–	0.043	Indicates high similarity in distributions
Privacy score (Yale DP Tool)	0.94	0.99	Indicates stronger anonymity in the synthetic version

The key applications of synthetic data in credit risk score analysis are as follows (Table 9.4).

9.5.3 A case study

A big European bank trained a machine learning credit risk model with fake data made by CTGAN from loan records from 2015–2020 that had been made anonymous. The fake dataset was statistically similar to the real one (KL divergence < 0.05), so internal teams and external auditors could test the models without accessing the real data (Table 9.5). What it led to was [19]:

- Thirty percent faster cycles for development (no need for lengthy approval processes for data).
- Ninety-five percent of the model's performance is kept when trained on real data.
- Internal compliance audits have found no regulatory red flags.

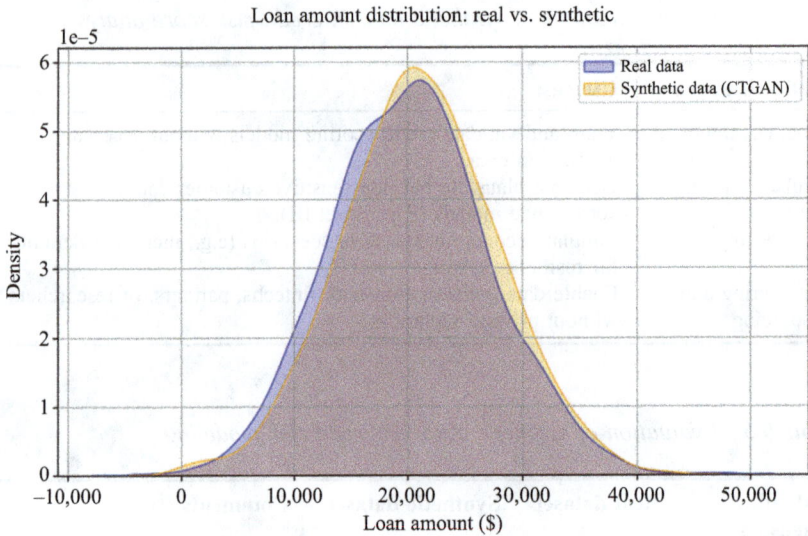

Figure 9.7   Comparative analysis of loan amount distribution: real vs. synthetic

In Table 9.7, you can see a comparison between real and fake credit application data that was made using a CTGAN model. The fake dataset has many statistical features that are similar to those of the real one. For example, the default rate is 12.3% compared to 12.5%, and the correlation between loan amount and income is 0.76 compared to 0.78. This shows that the generative process kept meaningful financial relationships needed for credit risk modeling. The model's performance stayed strong, too. When trained on fake data, the AUC was 0.87, but it was 0.89 when trained on real data, showing only minor degradation. It's important to note that the synthetic version had a higher privacy score (0.99), which shows that it can be used in ways that are safe for regulators [20].

Figure 9.7, which shows the kernel density estimates for loan amounts in both datasets, shows that these estimates are the same. The distribution curves for real and fake data are similar, with only minor differences in the peak density and spread. This visual alignment proves that synthetic data accurately captures real patterns while protecting privacy. This makes it a valuable tool for building, testing, and sharing models across institutions [12].

9.6   Healthcare: generative models for medical imaging training

9.6.1   Introduction and context

The healthcare sector increasingly depends on data-driven approaches to facilitate diagnostics, treatment planning, and medical education. Medical imaging, encompassing modalities such as X-rays, CT scans, MRIs, and histopathological slides, is pivotal [5–9]. However, the advancement of AI models for medical image analysis is frequently obstructed by several significant challenges:

- Insufficient data, particularly for uncommon conditions or marginalized populations.
- Privacy regulations, such as HIPAA and GDPR, restrict data sharing.
- The annotation burden arises from expert clinicians' need to label medical images.

Generative AI methodologies, including generative adversarial networks and diffusion models, are employed to generate high-fidelity synthetic medical images to mitigate these limitations. Synthetic datasets can be utilized for AI training, medical education, and algorithm benchmarking, frequently without jeopardizing patient privacy [11–17]. Table 9.6 presents the types of generative models used in medical imaging, and Table 9.7 presents the key applications in medical imaging.

9.6.2 Case example: synthetic retinal fundus images

We have created high-resolution synthetic retinal fundus images using StyleGAN2 in a multicenter study. A Convolutional Neural Network (CNN) was

Table 9.6 Types of generative models used in medical imaging

Model type	Use case	Strengths
DCGAN/ Progressive GAN	Generation of realistic X-rays or histology images	Simple structure, fast convergence
Conditional GAN (cGAN)	Conditioned on disease type or region	Targeted generation based on clinical labels
StyleGAN2/ StyleGAN3	High-resolution brain or retina scans	Photorealistic output, fine control over features
Diffusion models	Simulating complex anatomical variations	High-quality generation with improved diversity
CycleGAN/pix2pix	Domain translation (e.g., MRI ↔ CT)	Useful for cross-modality synthesis

Table 9.7 Applications in medical imaging

Application area	Use case
Data augmentation	Improve model generalization by training on rare or minority pathology cases.
Education and simulation	Provide diverse case studies for student radiologists and clinicians.
Cross-domain translation	Convert between imaging modalities (e.g., CT to MRI).
Privacy-preserving AI	Train or share models without exposing real patient data.
Annotation efficiency	Reduce the need for expert annotations via self-supervised learning.

trained using these pictures to identify symptoms of diabetic retinopathy. The accuracy of the model trained on synthetic data was 91.2% when tested on a real validation set, which is only slightly less than that of a model trained on real data, which was 93.8%. The synthetic images were visually identical to the real samples in terms of pathological markers and anatomical structure, according to a review by a clinician [4,18]. Table 9.8 and Figure 9.8 present the evaluation of synthetic medical imaging for training AI models.

Table 9.8 presents an empirical evaluation of the effective utilization of synthetic medical images in deep learning models. The findings indicate a negligible reduction in diagnostic precision and robust visual fidelity, corroborated by clinician assessments. Furthermore, synthetic data produced greater diversity and markedly diminished privacy risks. This corresponds with Figure 9.9, in which a

Table 9.8   Evaluation of synthetic medical imaging for training AI models

Evaluation metric	Real dataset	Synthetic dataset	Comment
Sample size (Images)	25,000	25,000 (StyleGAN2)	Size-matched for performance comparison.
Model accuracy (ResNet50)	93.8%	91.2%	Slight drop, acceptable for training purposes.
Expert visual quality score	4.7/5	4.5/5	Clinicians rated realism on a blind test.
Diversity score (LPIPS)	0.82	0.85	The synthetic set showed slightly higher diversity.
Privacy risk (Membership inference attack)	High	Low	Synthetic data showed strong resistance to inversion attacks.

Real retinal image (simulated)   Synthetic retinal image (simulated)

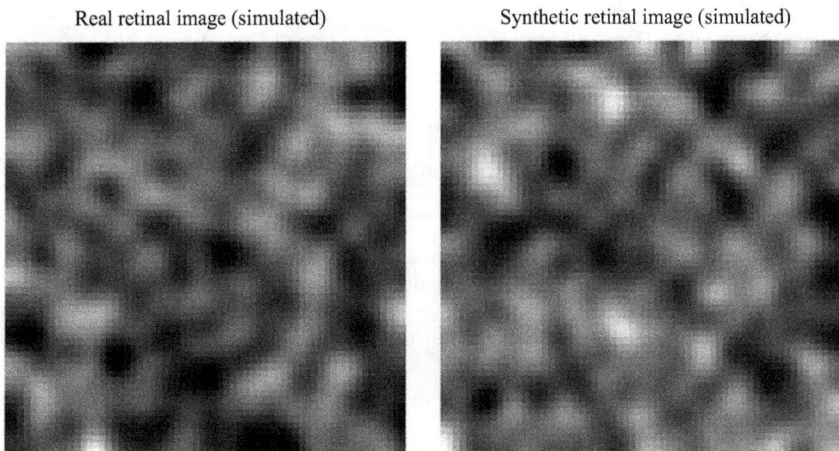

Figure 9.8   Real retinal vs synthetic retinal image (simulated)

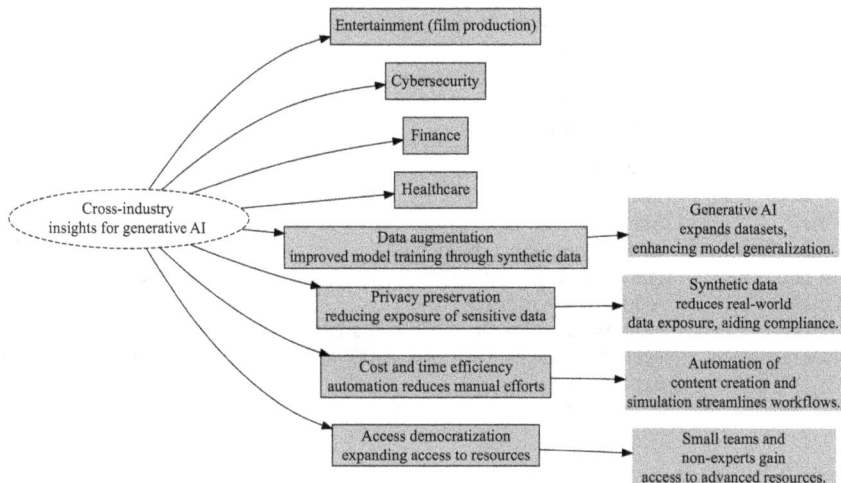

Figure 9.9   Cross-industry insights of generative AI

visual comparison of simulated real and synthetic retinal-like images illustrates perceptual similarity, thereby validating the generative model's ability to reproduce significant structures without directly replicating actual patient data.

9.7   Cross-industry insights

9.7.1   Introduction

The utilization of generative AI in various sectors – entertainment, cybersecurity, finance, and healthcare – has uncovered both industry-specific opportunities and several common themes, challenges, and best practices. This section synthesizes cross-disciplinary insights from the previously presented case studies, identifying patterns in deployment strategies, ethical dilemmas, model evaluation, and risk mitigation. Comprehending these standard dimensions offers strategic direction for stakeholders aiming to implement generative technologies across diverse sectors.

9.7.2   Common benefits observed

Despite the vast number of applications, which include everything from deepfake-assisted film production to synthetic medical imaging, Table 9.9 presents a few fundamental benefits that have consistently been revealed.

9.7.3   Shared technical and ethical challenges

Numerous cross-industry challenges require constant attention, despite the fact that the benefits are widespread, as presented by Table 9.10.

Table 9.9   Diversity of use cases from deepfake-assisted film production to synthetic medical imaging

Shared benefit	Description
Data augmentation	Generative AI expands limited datasets, allowing better generalization in model training.
Privacy preservation	Synthetic data reduces the exposure of sensitive real-world records, easing compliance burdens.
Cost and time efficiency	Automated content creation and simulation accelerate workflows and reduce manual effort.
Access democratization	Non-expert users or small teams gain access to resources (e.g., synthetic images, malware, data) that would otherwise be restricted or expensive.

Table 9.10   Shared technical and ethical challenges

Challenge	Industries affected	Description
Dual-use risk	Cybersecurity, entertainment, and healthcare	Tools used for good (e.g., training, simulation) can be exploited maliciously.
Synthetic bias	Finance, healthcare	Biases in training data may be amplified or concealed in generated outputs.
Model evaluation difficulty	All	Lack of standard benchmarks for assessing realism, diversity, and fidelity.
Regulatory uncertainty	Finance, healthcare	Legal frameworks are still evolving around the use of synthetic or altered data.
Trust and transparency	All	Concerns about how generative outputs are produced, validated, and used.

9.7.4   Privacy, security, and explainability trade-offs

A lot of the time, generative systems are where privacy protection and data utility meet. For instance:

- In finance, synthetic credit data makes modeling easier for compliance, but it might not have the edge-case realism needed for making high-risk decisions.
- In cybersecurity, GAN-generated malware makes adversarial training better, but it needs to be kept in a tight container to keep it from getting out of hand.
- In healthcare, synthetic scans lower privacy risk, but they must be checked for clinical relevance and diagnostic accuracy.

The prioritization of five target dimensions, Privacy, Security, Explainability, Utility, and Compliance, as defined in the report between the input dataset entertainment, cybersecurity, finance, and healthcare outcome dimensions in the deployment of generative AI systems, was shown in Figure 9.10.

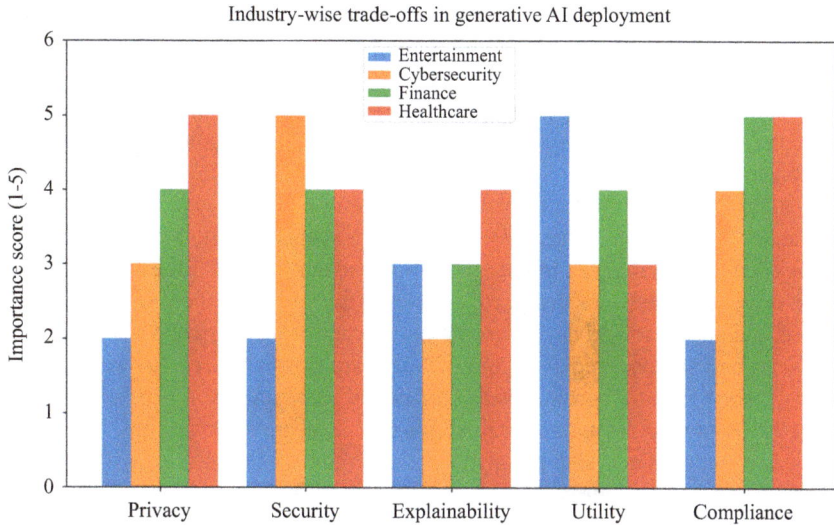

Figure 9.10   Comparative analysis of industry-wise trade-offs in generative AI deployment

Despite GANs being highly effective, Security is prioritized in cybersecurity as it demands strong defense mechanisms when GANs are used for malware simulation/benign malware simulation/penetration testing. Despite the fact that compliance and privacy are top priorities, explainability is still down on the list, reflecting the complexity and ambiguity in adversarial models. Across the four dimensions, finance displays an average profile, with even good scores on privacy, compliance, and utility. This is an important alignment where generative models like the ones used, for example, in synthetic credit risk modeling need a strong regulatory infrastructure in order to be operationally and legally sound, as they depend heavily on explainability and accountability.

The privacy, compliance, and explainability columns all gained the top score in healthcare, due to the sensitive nature of the data (patient information) and the necessary transparency on clinical decision-making. Generative models in this space must balance compliance with ethical and medical guidelines against providing real-world utility. The radar chart shows that no sector has its sweet spot aligned on all dimensions equally, which implies that the design and implementation of generative AI systems would need to be very sector-specific. Figure 6 illustrates an example of alignment with the proposed ethical and governance framework.

9.8   Conclusion

The case studies in this chapter exemplify how generative AI solutions are becoming more impactful and converging across industries. In entertainment, creative production is now being transformed using deepfake technologies, and adversarial threat simulation can improve defenses in cybersecurity. Synthetic financial data also allows for more equitable risk modeling, and generative technologies are doing amazing things in medical imaging, with each type of application coming with its own unique set of opportunities, challenges, and ethical considerations.

An important takeaway from these cases is the deeply contextual nature of generative AI adoption. Generative systems are shaped by the push of regulation and risk sensitivity, the pull of data privacy mandates, and the Fiber of the domain of use into which they are designed, implemented, and governed. Certain sectors, like entertainment, are driven by creativity and performance, while others, such as healthcare and finance, require more of a focus on compliance, transparency, and safety. Something of a constant is the duality of risk and return. These same generative tools that can be used to make training better, create edge-case simulations, or augment datasets can also simply be turned against you, hijacked, weaponized, and used to subvert security and trust. Keywords: dual-use dilemma, responsible development, experts from social sciences and humanities, policy, responsible innovation, harm mitigation.

We briefly outline visual analyses and a performance framework that, at least in principle, systematically assesses generative applications in a more holistic way that integrates social, ethical, and operational dimensions alongside technical dimensions both at and after the moment that generative applications are developed or deployed. In the wake of generative AI progress, practitioners and researchers should adopt a measured, reflective approach focused on real-world outcomes and social aspects. Chapters to follow will focus respectively on design philosophy, policy implications, and safe architectures that these lessons, trade-offs, and interdisciplinary perspectives can inform the foundations of trustworthy generative systems.

References

[1]   Khan A, Jhanjhi NZ, Alı GA, Ray SK, and Wassan S. Case studies and applications of generative AI in real-world cybersecurity scenarios. In *AI Techniques for Securing Medical and Business Practices* 2025 (pp. 61–100). IGI Global Scientific Publishing.

[2]   Balasubramanian P, Liyana S, Sankaran H, *et al.* Generative AI for cyber threat intelligence: Applications, challenges, and analysis of real-world case studies. *Artificial Intelligence Review*. 2025;58(11):1–34.

[3]   Sai S, Gaur A, Sai R, Chamola V, Guizani M, and Rodrigues JJ. Generative AI for transformative healthcare: A comprehensive study of emerging models, applications, case studies, and limitations. *IEEE Access*. 2024; 12:31078–31106.

[4]   Dewan B, Bhattacharyya S, Sharma I, and Sheybani E. Generative AI in practice: From core principles to real-world use. In *Exploring Generative AI*

for Collaborative Robots in Agriculture 6.0 2026 (pp. 203–224). IGI Global Scientific Publishing.

[5] Lee B. Emerging applications of generative: Techniques, use cases, and challenges. *International Journal of Artificial Intelligence and Machine Learning.* 2013;13(10):346–352.

[6] Sai S, Arunakar K, Chamola V, Hussain A, Bisht P, and Kumar S. Generative AI for finance: Applications, case studies and challenges. *Expert Systems.* 2025;42(3):e70018.

[7] Pandey MK, Pal TL, and Gupta P. Case studies and real-world application of deep generative models in Alzheimer's research. In *Deep Generative Models for Integrative Analysis of Alzheimer's Biomarkers* 2025 (pp. 341–360). IGI Global.

[8] Ghosh S, and Jana O. Generative AI in practice: Case studies and implementation frameworks for industry professionals. In *Generative AI in Software Engineering* 2025 (pp. 195–228). IGI Global Scientific Publishing.

[9] Lilhore UK, Dalal S, Varshney N, *et al.* Prevalence and risk factors analysis of postpartum depression at early stage using hybrid deep learning model. *Scientific Reports.* 2024;14(1):4533.

[10] Cronin I. Applications and real-world case studies. In *Understanding Generative AI Business Applications: A Guide to Technical Principles and Real-World Applications* 2024 (pp. 195–209). Berkeley, CA: Apress.

[11] Dalal S, Rani U, Lilhore UK, *et al.* Optimized XGBoost model with whale optimization algorithm for detecting anomalies in manufacturing. *Journal of Computational and Cognitive Engineering.* 2024;4(3):1–11.

[12] Ghalibafan S, Gonzalez DJ, Cai LZ, *et al.* Applications of multimodal generative artificial intelligence in a real-world retina clinic setting. *Retina.* 2024;44(10):1732–1740.

[13] Qin X, and Weaver G. Utilizing generative AI for VR exploration testing: A case study. In *Proceedings of the 39th IEEE/ACM International Conference on Automated Software Engineering Workshops* 2024 (pp. 228–232).

[14] Dalal S, Manoharan P, Lilhore UK, *et al.* Extremely boosted neural network for more accurate multi-stage Cyber attack prediction in cloud computing environment. *Journal of Cloud Computing.* 2023;12(1):1–22.

[15] Kenthapadi K, Lakkaraju H, and Rajani N. Generative AI meets responsible AI: Practical challenges and opportunities. In *Proceedings of the 29th ACM SIGKDD Conference on Knowledge Discovery and Data Mining* 2023 (pp. 5805–5806).

[16] Sandelin F. A multi-case study on generative AI use in work and decision-making: Exploring applications and potential departmental effects. Masterthesis, Svenska handelshögskolan. 2024.

[17] Nguyen CT, Liu Y, Du H, *et al.* Generative AI-enabled blockchain networks: Fundamentals, applications, and case study. *IEEE Network.* 2024;39(2):232–241.

[18] Ashwini A, Saranya R, and Balasubramaniam S. 11 Real-World software solutions through generative AI in transforming code and beyond. *Generative*

AI for Software Development: Code Generation, Error Detection, Software Testing. 2025:263. https://doi.org/10.1515/9783111677798-011

[19]　Lilhore UK, Simaiya S, Dalal S, Alshuhail A, and Almusharraf A. A post-quantum hybrid encryption framework for securing biometric data in consumer electronics. *IEEE Transactions on Consumer Electronics.* 2025;71 (3):8289–8297.

[20]　Bhutani M, Dalal S, Alhussein M, Lilhore UK, Aurangzeb K, and Hussain A. SAD-GAN: A novel secure anomaly detection framework for enhancing the resilience of cyber-physical systems. *Cognitive Computation.* 2025;17(4):127.

Chapter 10

Generative AI collaborative approaches and open-source initiatives

Open-source AI means that anybody can use, study, change, and share these AI systems for whatever they choose, without asking anyone for permission. These liberties are in line with what the Open-Source Initiative (OSI), widely recognized as the guardian of open-source policies and principles, has defined as open-source Artificial Intelligence (AI). The emergence of generative AI has accelerated the transition to this new era of open-source AI. Economist Impact revealed that in 2023, the majority of Large Language Models (LLMs) were released as open source. LLMs are foundation models, and they are often utilized to create genAI applications such as chatbots and coding assistants.

10.1 Open-source AI software

AI is driving digital transformation in practically every industry, from healthcare and education to manufacturing and transportation. While proprietary AI platforms from huge enterprises make headlines, open-source AI software has grown equally significant. This ecosystem includes code repositories and a mindset of collaboration, transparency, and shared progress. Open-source AI allows researchers, developers, entrepreneurs, and communities worldwide to innovate without expense by sharing algorithms, datasets, and development tools. Openness affects ethical dilemmas, governance models, educational opportunities, and even the democratization of information in nations with restricted access to cutting-edge technology [1].

Open-source AI is not new. Linux and Apache showed the power of distributed collaboration in earlier open-source computer revolutions. Theano, Torch, TensorFlow, PyTorch, and JAX established an open-source culture in AI. Open-source groups create and maintain many of the most advanced models, from massive language models to computer vision systems. To comprehend this ecosystem, one must examine three dimensions: the evolution of open-source AI software, its difficulties and debates, and its future potential [2–4].

10.1.1 Evolution and ecosystem of open-source AI

Open-source AI software has made quick and transformational progress. Machine learning packages like scikit-learn made regression and clustering algorithms easy

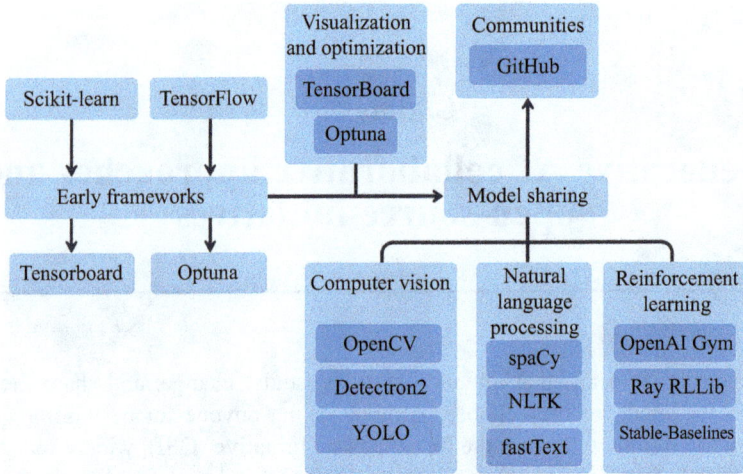

Figure 10.1   Evolution of open-source AI

to implement in the early 2000s. These libraries were built in Python, which became popular due to its open and community-driven approach. Scalable deep learning frameworks became necessary as AI advanced from theory to practice. This led to Theano, a popular GPU-accelerated neural network training framework. TensorFlow, published by Google, and PyTorch, supported by Facebook's AI Research lab, followed Theano. Both frameworks had liberal open-source licenses for worldwide cooperation and quick iteration (Figure 10.1).

The technological sophistication and communities that surrounded these frameworks made them successful. Thousands of graduate students and engineers changed documentation, added features, and produced tutorials [5]. GitHub became a common location for bugs, pull requests, and conversations. These platforms created ecosystems of products like TensorBoard, Optuna, and Hugging Face, which provide visualization, optimization, and model-sharing. Hugging Face improved open-source AI by centralizing pretrained models like BERT and GPT derivatives and multimodal transformers. It allowed small teams to implement cutting-edge solutions by lowering the entrance barrier to high-performance models.

Open-source contributions helped specialized domains as well as generic frameworks. Developers without computer vision knowledge could use OpenCV, Detectron2, and YOLO to detect objects and recognize images. FastText from Meta improved word embeddings for speed and scalability, while spaCy and NLTK provided text preprocessing and linguistic features for natural language processing. OpenAI Gym, Ray RLlib, and Stable-Baselines provide standardized environments and baselines for reinforcement learning. These tools help academics and practitioners duplicate results, benchmark new methods, and innovate on shared foundations [6–8].

The rise of open-source AI emphasizes cross-institutional collaboration. Repositories often house large enterprises, academic organizations, and individual developers. Google's release of TensorFlow, Meta's support for PyTorch, and Microsoft's support of Open Neural Network Exchange (ONNX) show that even competitors appreciate open ecosystems' strategic value. Visibility and reproducibility benefit academic researchers, but widespread standardization benefits corporations. This interaction produces a virtuous loop that stimulates innovation faster than closed development.

10.1.2 Challenges, risks, and controversies

Open-source AI software faces obstacles and controversy despite its transformative influence. Misuse of powerful models is a major worry. Large language models, picture generators, and voice synthesis tools can be used for disinformation, deepfakes, automated cyberattacks, and harassment when made public [9]. Open-source generative models have sparked concerns about responsible AI, with critics arguing that democratization without protection could worsen social ills. Managing transparency and responsibility becomes a recurring issue (Figure 10.2).

Sustainability is another issue for open-source AI projects. Major corporations may fund and maintain big frameworks, while many niche but significant initiatives depend on unpaid contributions. Burnout, lack of funding, and low awareness often endanger such endeavors. Although GitHub Sponsors, Open Collective, and community grants exist, open-source AI needs better funding mechanisms to survive. When corporations construct proprietary goods on open-source contributions without compensating the developers, intellectual property issues arise [10].

Reproducibility and quality assurance are challenges. Rapidly published open-source AI code may lack documentation, testing, or verification. Errors, uneven outcomes, and security risks can arise. Poorly maintained repositories worsen the machine learning repeatability dilemma. True openness becomes questionable as models expand in size and complexity, sometimes requiring millions of dollars in

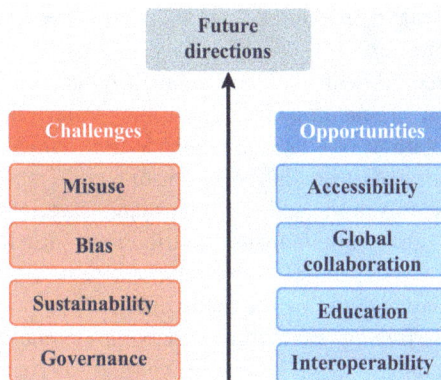

Figure 10.2   Challenges in open-source AI software

computational resources to train. The code is online, but most researchers lack the tools to duplicate or fine-tune such models, making them "open but inaccessible."

Governance and ethics complicate matters. Open-source agreements often handle software freedoms without addressing use. The possibility of AI misuse has generated interest in "ethical licenses" that limit damaging applications. Should developers govern downstream uses, or is openness neutral? Freedom and duty are at odds. Open-source model bias reflects socioeconomic inequalities. Models trained on biased datasets might reinforce stereotypes or discriminate. Consistently adopting training data transparency, rigorous curation, and community supervision is difficult.

Despite its problems, open-source AI software offers huge prospects. Open-source AI fundamentally democratizes advanced technologies. Students in under-developed nations, startups with little resources, and social NGOs can use billion-dollar firms' cutting-edge capabilities. Leveling the playing field encourages creativity in varied circumstances. Medical researchers in resource-constrained situations can use open-source computer vision models to interpret X-rays or detect infections, while environmental scientists can monitor climate change with open-source sensors and prediction models. The portability and versatility of open-source technologies expedite applications in fields that private providers may not target due to low profitability [11–13].

The open-source environment supports education. University curriculum includes PyTorch and scikit-learn for hands-on learning. Tutorials, notebooks, and public datasets enrich AI teaching. Kaggle, fueled by open datasets and colla-borative kernels, shows how knowledge-sharing platforms can train AI practi-tioners. Open-source projects allow students and young professionals to contribute, establish portfolios, and acquire worldwide attention, improving their employment prospects. Another promising direction is interoperability. ONNX lets models learned in one framework be utilized in another, boosting ecosystem collaboration. AI systems increasingly interact with cloud platforms, edge devices, and IoT infrastructures, making interoperability essential. Docker and Kubernetes integrate smoothly with open-source AI frameworks for scaled production deployment. These synergies show that open-source AI is about pipelines, from data ingestion to deployment and monitoring.

Future open-source AI will likely be molded by technological developments and social negotiation. Technology will prioritize efficiency, with frameworks optimized for smaller devices and lower energy use. TinyML and quantization libraries attempt to bring AI to cellphones, sensors, and embedded systems. New social governance models may address ethics and sustainability. Foundations, cooperatives, and DAOs might manage contributions, distribute resources, and ensure accountability. Open-source AI consortia, where stakeholders collaborate to maintain standards, may also define the landscape.

Open-source AI is freeing, hazardous, collaborative, and contested – the con-tradiction of modern technology. How communities, corporations, and policy-makers balance freedom and responsibility, accessibility and security, innovation and ethics will determine their direction. It is apparent that open-source AI software has changed the field. It has sped progress, increased engagement, and provided a shared infrastructure for intelligent systems. As AI permeates society, the open-source ethos of transparency, inclusion, and communal intelligence offers a positive vision of technology as a common rather than a commodity.

10.2 Advantages of open-source AI software

Artificial intelligence has rapidly evolved into a central force in today's technological landscape, shaping industries as diverse as healthcare, manufacturing, education, entertainment, and finance. At the heart of this growth lies a dynamic debate about ownership, accessibility, and innovation. While proprietary AI solutions developed by large corporations often receive widespread attention, open-source AI software has emerged as a powerful alternative that empowers a broader range of individuals and organizations. Open-source AI refers to artificial intelligence tools, frameworks, and models that are publicly available for anyone to use, modify, and distribute. This approach is not merely about free access to code but about fostering collaboration, knowledge sharing, and democratization of advanced technology. Understanding its advantages is crucial to appreciating why open-source AI has become such an indispensable part of the global digital ecosystem [14].

To fully grasp the advantages, it is useful to examine open-source AI across three key dimensions: its role in democratizing technology and accessibility, its capacity to foster innovation and collaboration, and its long-term impact on education, research, and industry sustainability. These dimensions illuminate how open-source AI does not just complement proprietary systems but often drives progress in ways closed models cannot.

10.2.1 Democratization and accessibility

One of the most profound advantages of open-source AI is the democratization of technology. In the past, access to advanced AI tools was largely confined to well-funded research institutions or corporations with the resources to invest in proprietary systems. By making frameworks, libraries, and models freely available, open-source AI has broken down these barriers and given developers, researchers, and organizations worldwide the ability to harness artificial intelligence without prohibitive costs. This accessibility extends far beyond affordability; it levels the playing field by allowing individuals in developing regions, small businesses, and non-governmental organizations to leverage the same advanced resources as large corporations.

Consider the impact on education and academic research. Students who once relied on outdated or simplified tools can now experiment with state-of-the-art frameworks such as TensorFlow, PyTorch, and scikit-learn. These resources allow learners to gain hands-on experience with cutting-edge technologies rather than theoretical approximations. Universities across the globe integrate these open-source platforms into their curricula, ensuring that graduates enter the workforce with practical skills that are directly relevant to industry needs. This exposure also encourages curiosity-driven exploration, as students can access pretrained models, datasets, and interactive tutorials without institutional constraints.

Accessibility is equally critical for organizations with limited resources. For example, healthcare researchers in low-income countries can adapt open-source computer vision models to analyze radiology scans for early disease detection. Environmental groups can use open-source predictive models to monitor deforestation, water quality, or climate change patterns. Non-profits dedicated to social causes, such as literacy or disaster response, can deploy natural language processing tools to build multilingual educational chatbots or crisis-mapping systems. These innovations are possible because the cost of entry is drastically reduced, and the underlying knowledge is openly shared [15].

Moreover, open-source AI encourages inclusivity by supporting a wide array of languages, cultural contexts, and local challenges. Proprietary systems often prioritize global markets with high profitability, leaving smaller or marginalized communities underserved. In contrast, open-source communities frequently adapt models for local needs, whether by training language models for underrepresented dialects or tailoring applications for specific agricultural practices. This global inclusivity demonstrates how open-source AI not only democratizes access but also ensures that AI technologies reflect a diverse set of human experiences.

10.2.2 Innovation and collaboration

Beyond accessibility, open-source AI thrives as an incubator for innovation. The open nature of code and models enables a culture of collaboration where developers, researchers, and organizations can collectively refine and expand upon existing work. Innovation in AI is rarely the product of isolated effort; instead, it emerges through iterative improvement and shared contributions. Open-source projects, hosted on platforms such as GitHub or GitLab, facilitate this by allowing contributors to identify errors, propose enhancements, and build entirely new features [16,17].

One of the most striking examples is the development of PyTorch and TensorFlow. Released by Meta and Google, respectively, both frameworks were intentionally made open-source to encourage adoption and community-driven progress. The result was a flourishing ecosystem of extensions, tutorials, and third-party libraries that expanded the frameworks beyond what their original creators envisioned. Today, these tools form the backbone of countless AI applications, from self-driving cars to language models, precisely because of the collaborative spirit embedded in their development.

Model-sharing platforms such as Hugging Face further illustrate how open-source accelerates innovation. By providing repositories of pretrained models, Hugging Face enables developers to quickly adapt advanced architectures to new tasks with minimal computational cost. A small startup that lacks the resources to train a billion-parameter transformer from scratch can fine-tune an existing model for domain-specific purposes, such as financial sentiment analysis or medical document classification. This capacity for transfer learning, enabled by open sharing, has reduced the duplication of effort and sped up the cycle of experimentation and deployment. Collaboration also extends across institutional and corporate boundaries. Universities, corporations, and independent researchers often work side by side on open-source initiatives. Even competitors contribute to shared standards, recognizing that interoperability and common frameworks benefit the entire ecosystem. Microsoft's support for ONNX exemplifies how open standards create bridges between frameworks, ensuring models developed in PyTorch can run seamlessly in TensorFlow or other environments. This spirit of cooperation not only accelerates technical progress but also creates a culture of transparency and accountability [18].

In addition, open-source AI fosters rapid innovation by enabling reproducibility. Scientific progress relies on the ability to replicate results, yet proprietary systems often limit transparency. Open-source frameworks, however, allow experiments to be validated and extended by others, ensuring that breakthroughs are built upon solid foundations. When errors are discovered, they can be corrected publicly, avoiding the propagation of flawed findings. This openness enhances trust in AI research and ensures that innovation is cumulative rather than fragmented. Finally, the collaborative nature of open-source AI strengthens resilience. Because multiple contributors maintain and improve systems, projects are less vulnerable to stagnation if one institution withdraws. The distributed model of development ensures that progress continues even when funding or leadership shifts. This resilience is critical in a rapidly evolving field where adaptation and flexibility are essential.

10.2.3 Education, research, and sustainable impact

The advantages of open-source AI extend deeply into education, research, and the sustainable development of industries. For education, the benefits are transformative. Open-source AI has become a foundational teaching tool that equips students with practical experience. Beyond formal institutions, online platforms provide free access to courses, notebooks, and datasets built upon open-source tools [19]. This has created a global learning environment where individuals from different socioeconomic backgrounds can gain skills that were once limited to elite universities. Communities such as Kaggle, which combine open datasets with collaborative competition, showcase how open-source principles nurture not only learning but also a spirit of experimentation and friendly rivalry that drives skill development (Figure 10.3) [8].

For academic research, open-source AI ensures visibility, reproducibility, and impact. Researchers can share not only their findings but also the code and data that underpin them, enabling others to replicate or extend their work. This transparency builds credibility and accelerates the dissemination of knowledge. Moreover, when researchers release their models openly, they often receive feedback and improvements from peers worldwide, strengthening the quality of their contributions. The open-source approach thus enhances the collaborative fabric of science itself, moving it toward greater inclusivity and trust.

Advantages of Open-Source AI

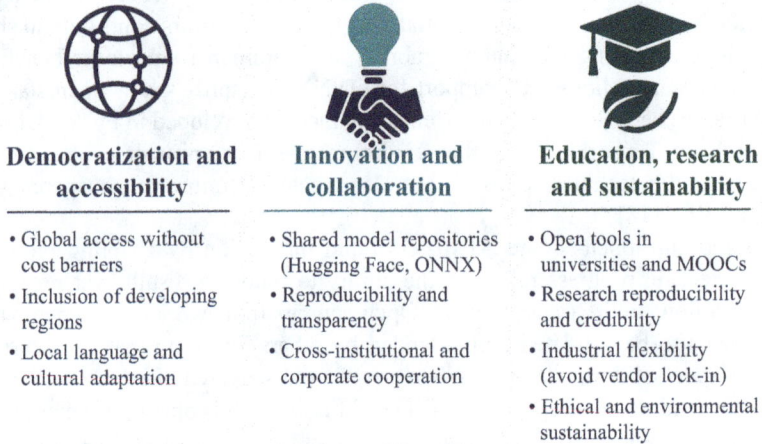

Democratization and accessibility

- Global access without cost barriers
- Inclusion of developing regions
- Local language and cultural adaptation

Innovation and collaboration

- Shared model repositories (Hugging Face, ONNX)
- Reproducibility and transparency
- Cross-institutional and corporate cooperation

Education, research and sustainability

- Open tools in universities and MOOCs
- Research reproducibility and credibility
- Industrial flexibility (avoid vendor lock-in)
- Ethical and environmental sustainability

Figure 10.3   Advantages of open-source AI

Industries also benefit from the sustainable impact of open-source AI. By reducing dependence on proprietary vendors, organizations can avoid vendor lock-in and retain flexibility in their technological strategies. Open-source tools can be customized to specific business needs, integrated into unique workflows, and adapted as requirements evolve. This adaptability lowers costs and encourages long-term sustainability. For small businesses and startups, the ability to access advanced AI tools without licensing fees can be the difference between innovation and stagnation. For larger corporations, open-source frameworks often serve as a foundation upon which proprietary solutions can be built, blending the best of both worlds.

Sustainability also encompasses social and ethical dimensions. Open-source AI fosters accountability by making algorithms transparent and subject to public scrutiny. This transparency is particularly important in high-stakes applications such as healthcare, criminal justice, or finance, where biased or opaque models can have severe consequences. By allowing independent audits and reviews, open-source AI reduces the risks associated with black-box decision-making and encourages responsible development. In addition, open-source communities are increasingly discussing ethical guidelines and best practices, creating a culture where social responsibility is integrated into technical progress.

Looking ahead, the sustainable impact of open-source AI may also include environmental considerations. Training large AI models consumes significant energy, raising concerns about carbon footprints. Open-source initiatives often focus on efficiency, developing tools for model compression, quantization, and optimization that reduce computational costs. These innovations not only make AI more environmentally friendly but also broaden access by lowering the hardware requirements needed to run advanced systems. Taken together, the educational, research, and industrial advantages of open-source AI underscore its role as a cornerstone of future technological development. By empowering learners, enhancing collaboration among scientists, and ensuring sustainable industrial practices, open-source AI builds a framework for long-term progress that benefits society as a whole.

The advantages of open-source AI are extensive and multifaceted, encompassing democratization, innovation, and sustainable impact. By breaking down barriers to access, it ensures that advanced technologies are no longer confined to a privileged few but are available to a global community of learners, innovators, and practitioners. By fostering collaboration and reproducibility, it accelerates the pace of scientific discovery and technological progress. And by supporting education, research, and industry, it lays the foundation for a more inclusive and sustainable future. Open-source AI is not merely a technical approach; it is a social and cultural movement that reflects the values of transparency, inclusivity, and collective intelligence. As artificial intelligence continues to shape the twenty-first century, open-source principles will remain central to ensuring that its benefits are widely shared and responsibly developed.

10.3   Case studies of open-source AI software

Open-source artificial intelligence has increased access to powerful computing tools and changed sector-wide innovation. Practical case studies show how initiatives and communities use the open-source approach to generate sustainable, collaborative, and revolutionary results. These case studies show how open-source AI software affects society, science, and industry beyond its technical features. The following six examples show how open-source AI has been used in deep learning frameworks, natural language processing, computer vision, reinforcement learning, medical applications, and environmental sustainability.

10.3.1   TensorFlow: democratizing deep learning frameworks

TensorFlow, a machine learning framework built by Google Brain and published in 2015, is a leading open-source AI project. Before its launch, only a few large enterprises with resources had trained large-scale deep neural networks. TensorFlow gave developers and researchers a versatile and scalable framework to utilize for free. The project affected academia and industry. TensorFlow quickly became a standard teaching tool at colleges, giving students hands-on experience with convolutional and recurrent neural networks. Integrating with visualization tools like TensorBoard lets researchers monitor and troubleshoot models, speeding up experimentation.

TensorFlow enabled speech recognition and predictive analytics acceptance in the industry. Its early work on AI-powered assistants and translation systems is well known. TensorFlow's modular design enabled extensions and experimentation, resulting in mobile and production pipeline derivative frameworks as TensorFlow Lite and Extended. Open-source projects can make advanced research tools available to everyone, ensuring innovation is not limited to proprietary technologies. As developers worldwide add plugins, tutorials, and pretrained models to the ecosystem, its success shows the virtuous cycle of community participation.

10.3.2   PyTorch and the rise of research-friendly AI

PyTorch, which prioritized researcher flexibility and ease of use, challenged TensorFlow in the open-source AI space. In 2016, Facebook's AI Research lab released PyTorch, which allowed users to alter models during training via dynamic computation graphs. Researchers who needed to quickly test new architectures loved this feature. Thus, PyTorch became the academic framework of choice, enabling advances in natural language processing, computer vision, and generative models.

PyTorch's essential role in BERT and GPT shows its rise. Researchers preferred PyTorch for prototyping complex models because it simplified experimentation and troubleshooting. Since PyTorch was popular in industry as well as academia, the PyTorch Foundation was created to secure its sustainability and governance. Since PyTorch is open-source, enterprises, startups, and universities can contribute modules and optimization methods, bolstering its community-driven reputation. PyTorch shows how open-source AI software may advance scientific discovery and business innovation by prioritizing researcher accessibility and industrial scalability.

10.3.3   Hugging Face and the model-sharing revolution

TensorFlow and PyTorch provide the architecture for constructing AI models, but Hugging Face transformed model sharing, reuse, and adaptation. Hugging Face, a chatbot developer, became a natural language processing platform with the transformers framework. This open-source repository offers pretrained models, including BERT, GPT-2, and RoBERTa, to help developers fine-tune cutting-edge architectures without the massive resources needed to train them.

The benefits of Hugging Face go beyond convenience. A center of thousands of models encouraged academics to share their work for others to reproduce, benchmark, or adapt. This has greatly reduced duplication and accelerated text summarization, machine translation, sentiment analysis, and question answering. Pretrained models allow small businesses to use AI without high costs. Hugging Face now covers computer vision and audio processing, making it interdisciplinary. Knowledge-sharing platforms can transform research and development due to their collaborative nature and open-source license. Hugging Face shows how open-source AI can be a social infrastructure for innovation as well as a technological framework.

10.3.4   OpenCV and the accessibility of computer vision

Computer vision powers facial recognition and autonomous vehicles, making it a prominent AI application. OpenCV, a 2000 open-source computer vision package, is a cornerstone of this discipline. OpenCV, unlike many other deep learning projects, predates the current AI revolution and has developed to stay relevant. The library's image-processing, feature detection, and object tracking techniques are essential for beginners and specialists.

OpenCV is used in education, research, and commercial goods, proving its longevity. Because OpenCV makes it easy to implement core computer vision techniques, students start with it. It is used by researchers to test new algorithms and by companies to build quality inspection systems, medical imaging, and security solutions. OpenCV supports TensorFlow and PyTorch to stay current with deep learning. Its open-source nature lets volunteers worldwide update the library, add documentation, and develop tutorials. OpenCV illustrates how durability, adaptation, and community engagement can survive open-source AI software over decades of technological development.

10.3.5 *OpenAI Gym and reinforcement learning ecosystems*

The reinforcement learning field of artificial intelligence studies how agents learn to make decisions from their environments. With its standardized reinforcement learning algorithm benchmarking environments, OpenAI Gym became a key open-source platform in 2016. Researchers employed diverse tasks and measurements, making it hard to compare study outcomes before their release. OpenAI Gym addresses this by providing a single collection of environments for simple control tasks to complex video game simulations.

The testing arena that democratized reinforcement learning experimentation was OpenAI Gym. To compare algorithms fairly, students, researchers, and hobbyists could use the same surroundings as leading research articles. Technology increased reproducibility by allowing labs to duplicate tests exactly. The modular design of OpenAI Gym enables developers to create bespoke surroundings, making it useful for industrial robots and autonomous systems as well as academic study. OpenAI Gym shows how open-source projects can accelerate specialized industries by combining accessibility and standardization. Newer systems like Ray RLlib and Stable Baselines build on this base to add features and scalability.

Medical Open Network for Artificial Intelligence (MONAI) bridges academic research and clinical practice, making it important. MONAI can help hospitals, colleges, and startups develop AI applications for tumor detection, organ segmentation, and disease classification. Open-source architecture invites medical academics and AI technologists to collaborate, ensuring technically robust and therapeutically meaningful advances. MONAI improves medical research reproducibility, which is crucial to transparency. It also lets smaller medical institutes attempt AI without proprietary systems by eliminating technical constraints. The case study of MONAI shows how open-source AI can improve public health by making powerful medical imaging technologies more accessible and customizable (Figure 10.4).

10.3.6 *Medical imaging and the MONAI framework*

AI in healthcare has long been considered promising yet difficult. NVIDIA and King's College London created the open-source MONAI to address medical

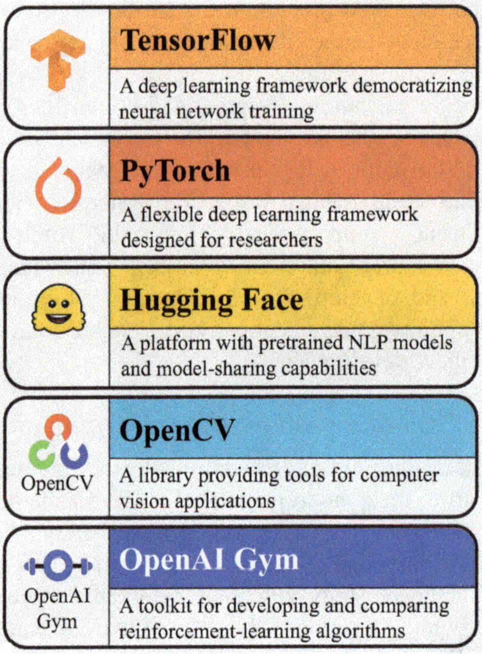

Figure 10.4   List of open-source AI

imaging difficulties. MONAI, released in 2020, offers healthcare data-specific neural network topologies, domain-specific data augmentation methods, and clinical workflow compliance concerns.

These six case studies demonstrate how open-source AI software transforms several fields. TensorFlow and PyTorch show how open frameworks can democratize deep learning and accelerate innovation. Model-sharing platforms accelerate natural language processing in Hugging Face. OpenCV represents longevity and accessibility in computer vision, while OpenAI Gym emphasizes reinforcement learning standardization. Finally, MONAI shows that open-source AI can solve healthcare problems. These examples show how open-source AI advances technology and changes education, research, and industry. Open-source AI promotes inclusive, transparent, and beneficial technological development through accessibility, cooperation, and sustainability. Its evolution will advance artificial intelligence in novel and socially responsible ways (Table 10.1).

10.4   Types of open-source artificial intelligence solutions

Various kinds of AI solutions are available in open source. A few of the more typical ones are listed here (Figure 10.5).

Table 10.1   Case studies of various open-source AI software

Software	Domain/Focus	Key features	Use cases/ Applications	Significance
TensorFlow	Deep learning framework	Scalable, supports CPUs/GPUs/ TPUs, TensorBoard for visualization, modular design	Voice recognition, translation systems, recommendation engines, predictive analytics	Democratized deep learning by making industrial-grade tools accessible worldwide.
PyTorch	Research-focused deep learning	Dynamic computation graphs, easy debugging, strong Python integration	NLP (BERT, GPT), computer vision, generative models, healthcare AI	Became the preferred research framework, balancing experimentation with scalability.
Hugging Face	Natural language processing and beyond	Transformers library, pretrained models, model hub, community-driven platform	Text summarization, sentiment analysis, chatbots, machine translation, multimodal AI	Revolutionized model sharing, enabling rapid fine-tuning and transfer learning.
OpenCV	Computer vision	Rich library of image-processing and vision algorithms, integrates with DL tools	Facial recognition, object detection, medical imaging, robotics, industrial inspection	Sustained relevance for over two decades, foundational in computer vision teaching.
OpenAI Gym	Reinforcement learning	Standardized environments, benchmarks, customizable tasks	Training RL agents, robotics, game-playing AI, decision-making systems	Brought reproducibility and standardization to reinforcement learning research.
MONAI	Medical imaging AI	Domain-specific architectures, healthcare compliance, data augmentation	Tumor detection, organ segmentation, diagnostic support systems	Open-source bridge between medical research and clinical AI applications.

10.4.1   Information systems

The storage, administration, and processing of data are built upon open-source data platforms. The efficient management of massive datasets needed to train AI models is made possible by solutions such as Apache Spark™ and Apache Hadoop®, which enable large-scale data operations. These systems are great for a wide range of AI applications because of their scalability. These data platforms establish ecosystems with other open-source technologies to enable end-to-end AI operations. Businesses can customize them due to their modular architecture.

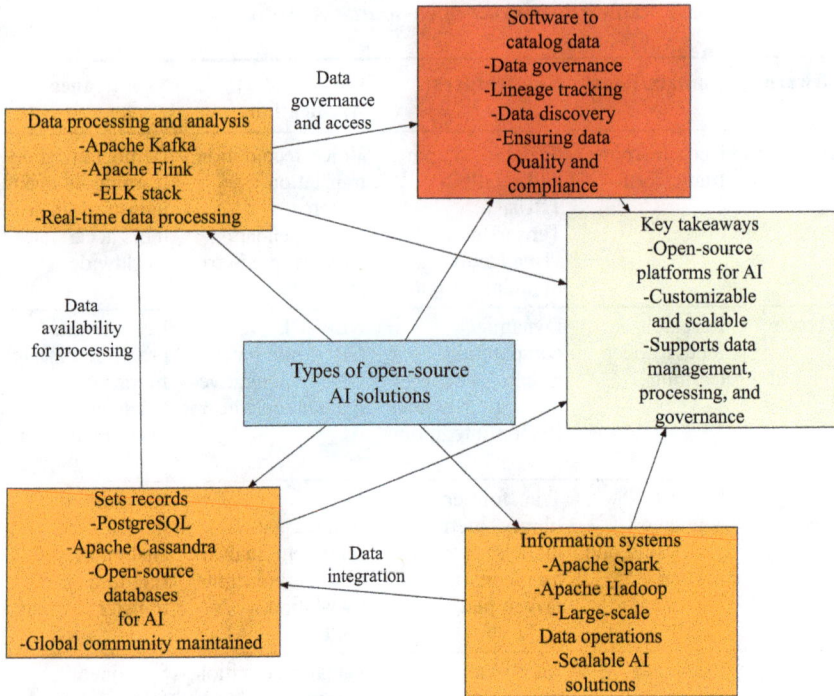

Figure 10.5   Types of open-source artificial intelligence solutions

10.4.2   Sets records

Databases hold organized and unstructured data. For AI data management, PostgreSQL® provides reliable and adaptable database options. Additionally, Apache Cassandra® 5.0 and other open-source vector databases may be utilized with upcoming AI technologies like RAG and LLM. Since these databases are open source, a global community maintains and improves them. Everyone's hard work creates safe, interoperable database systems for processing and evaluating data.

10.4.3   Data processing and analysis software

Data processing and analysis technologies are needed to gain insights from raw data. Real-time data processing in Apache Kafka®, Apache Flink, and ELK Stack simplifies AI model training data preparation. These tools support several data types and sources to make datasets easier to use. Open-source data processing technologies enable complicated data operations, including filtering, aggregating, and enrichment. These resources provide fast processing of enormous volumes of data, essential for training AI models with correct and relevant data.

10.4.4   *Software to catalog data*

Data catalog solutions help organizations organize and manage their data. These governance, lineage tracking, and data discovery solutions provide readily discoverable, traceable, and well-documented data. Enterprise data management should include data catalog solutions to ensure data quality and compliance. These technologies help teams collaborate by making data easy to access and understand.

10.5   The position of open-source AI in ethical AI development

Given that AI technologies are becoming more and more embedded in different sectors, the importance of ethical AI becomes imperative. Open AI is also an important aspect in promoting openness, accountability, and inclusivity; we need to better address ethical considerations (Table 10.2).

- **Transparency and accountability:** Open-source AI facilitate transparency by sharing algorithms, models, and datasets in a transparent manner to be analyzed and audited by the community. Such transparency also means that the AI community as a whole becomes accountable for the systems it is building. Privacy issues such as bias, discrimination, and fairness can be handled more

Table 10.2   Ethical AI development and open-source AI

Aspect	Description	Impact on transparency	Impact on inclusivity	Impact on collaboration
Transparency and accountability	Open-source AI promotes transparency by making algorithms, models, and datasets publicly available, enabling external audits and analysis.	Allows community oversight and external audits.	Ensures that models are publicly scrutinized for fairness.	Promotes shared responsibility for AI systems, ensuring collective accountability.
Inclusive development	Contributions come from a global pool, leading to more representative and inclusive AI systems.	Reduces biases by incorporating diverse perspectives.	Encourages underrepresented communities to participate.	Fosters an inclusive AI ecosystem with contributions from varied backgrounds.
Collaboration for ethical standards	Open-source AI allows for collaborative development of ethical guidelines and ethical licensing models.	Promotes collective effort to ensure ethical compliance.	Involves diverse stakeholders in the ethical conversation.	Encourages the development of ethical standards through community consensus.

effectively with an open-source setup in this context, in which outside contributions can continually maintain and inspect the system.

- **Inclusive development:** Open AI ensures more contributions from more diverse people, rather than these models and technologies being developed in a silo by a privileged few. These donations can also come from people with a variety of cultural, social, and economic lifestyles, which should lead to AI systems that better represent the varied needs and values of our global citizenry.
- **Collaboration for ethical standards:** Collaborative open-source AI can be focused on developing ethical guidelines for AI. Projects such as OpenAI's ethical licensing for models and the AI Ethics Guidelines by open-source communities have already laid important stepping stones to mitigate the worst uses of AI in design, deployment, and beyond.

10.6   Prospective trends of open-source generative AI

With the rise of generative AI, there are a few trends to look for in the open-source world over the next five years. Trends that are centered around democratizing generative AI, making it more sustainable and collaborative (Table 10.3).

Table 10.3   Prospective trends in open-source generative AI

Trend	Description	Impact on accessibility	Impact on innovation	Impact on collaboration
TinyML and Edge AI	Miniaturization of AI models for deployment on smaller devices like smartphones and IoT.	Lowers entry barriers for edge devices and mobile platforms.	Enables innovation on constrained devices with powerful AI.	Encourages collaboration across device manufacturers and AI developers.
AI and climate change	Open-source AI models are used for environmental monitoring, energy optimization, and sustainable management of resources.	Democratizes access to AI tools for climate research.	Drives innovation in addressing climate change with AI solutions.	Promotes global collaboration to tackle the climate crisis.
Decentralized AI with blockchain	Integration of blockchain with open-source AI for data integrity, transparency, and secure model provenance.	Increases trust by making AI models verifiable and traceable.	Facilitates innovation in decentralized AI applications.	Encourages partnerships across sectors for ethical AI development.

(Continues)

Table 10.3   (Continued)

Trend	Description	Impact on accessibility	Impact on innovation	Impact on collaboration
Interoperability	Open-source frameworks like ONNX enable AI models to work seamlessly across different platforms and ecosystems.	Facilitates model sharing across frameworks and systems.	Accelerates innovation through cross-platform compatibility.	Strengthens cooperation between AI developers, frameworks, and cloud platforms.

- **TinyML and Edge AI:** One of the most promising trends in the open-source generative AI space is miniaturizing AI models so that they can be run on smaller devices (such as smartphones, IoT, and edge devices). The enabling technology driving this is TinyML, which empowers generative AI to operate effectively on devices with constrained resources. Open-source TinyML frameworks are evolving quickly, allowing developers to easily run AI models on edge devices.
- **AI and climate change:** Now, open-source AI is being turned to address global problems such as climate change. The utilization of open-source models and datasets will enable them to work together on projects that support environmental monitoring, optimization for energy consumption, sustainable management of resources, and forestry. Open-source technologies will be indispensable to addressing the climate crisis, with creator-led AI-driven environmental platforms that are collaborative as well.
- **Decentralized AI with blockchain:** Blockchain is widely used to implement open-source generative AI, improving data integrity, transparency, and decentralization. By leveraging blockchain for model provenance and building decentralized AI networks, we can design secure and verifiable generative AI applications where ownership and responsibility behind AI models remain transparent and traceable.

10.7   Government intervention and regulation of open-source AI techniques

Open-source AI shows that governments around the world do tech well (and no, it is not particularly controversial). Governments far and wide demonstrate the utility of open-source technology to address security issues. But with open-source AI technologies becoming more pervasive, concerns around the regulation and support of the technology have intensified (Table 10.4).

- **Government incentives for open-source AI:** Tons of other governments are now incentivizing funding for open-source AI projects, particularly ones

Table 10.4   Government intervention and regulation of open-source AI

Aspect	Description	Impact on innovation	Impact on regulation	Impact on security and ethics
Government incentives for open-source AI	Financial incentives such as grants, tax breaks, and sponsorships for open-source AI projects.	Encourages investment in AI projects focused on public good.	Supports ethical AI development with funding for transparency.	Ensures responsible development of AI solutions for societal benefit.
Regulatory challenges	Challenges in regulating open-source AI, especially generative models, for misuse such as deepfakes and misinformation.	Balances the need for innovation with the need for safeguards.	Encourages responsible use while avoiding overregulation.	Addresses risks related to AI misuse and deepfake generation.
Ethical licensing	Introduction of ethical licenses to restrict harmful uses of open-source AI, similar to FDA regulation of pharmaceuticals.	Ensuring innovation is guided by ethical boundaries.	Encourages responsible deployment of AI models.	Reduces risks of harmful AI applications by enforcing ethical standards.

focused on public goods such as health care, education, and climate change. These incentives could be in the form of grants, tax breaks, or sponsorships for shared open-source projects. The European Union's Horizon Europe project, for instance, is funding AI projects that highlight the importance of transparency and ethics in developing AI with a focus on open-source initiatives.

- **Regulatory challenges:** At the same time, governing open-source AI is not straightforward. Although open-source AI has an emphasis on transparency, the abuse of AI models – especially those that are generative – challenges the reliability and veracity of distributed granular information or deepfakes. Governments are starting to debate how to regulate open-source AI, not in an effort to suppress innovation but to establish guardrails for responsible use. Topics like "ethical licenses," which are akin to the Food and Drug Administration controlling what drug companies do with their pharmaceutical products, are rising as part of this regulatory debate.

10.8   Interoperability of open-source AI frameworks

Open-source AI can make a difference in how we work. Interoperability is essential for the broader acceptance of open-source AI. It guarantees that various AI models and apps are designed to work with each other, which is what both researchers as well as industries that use multiple AI systems will need (Figure 10.6).

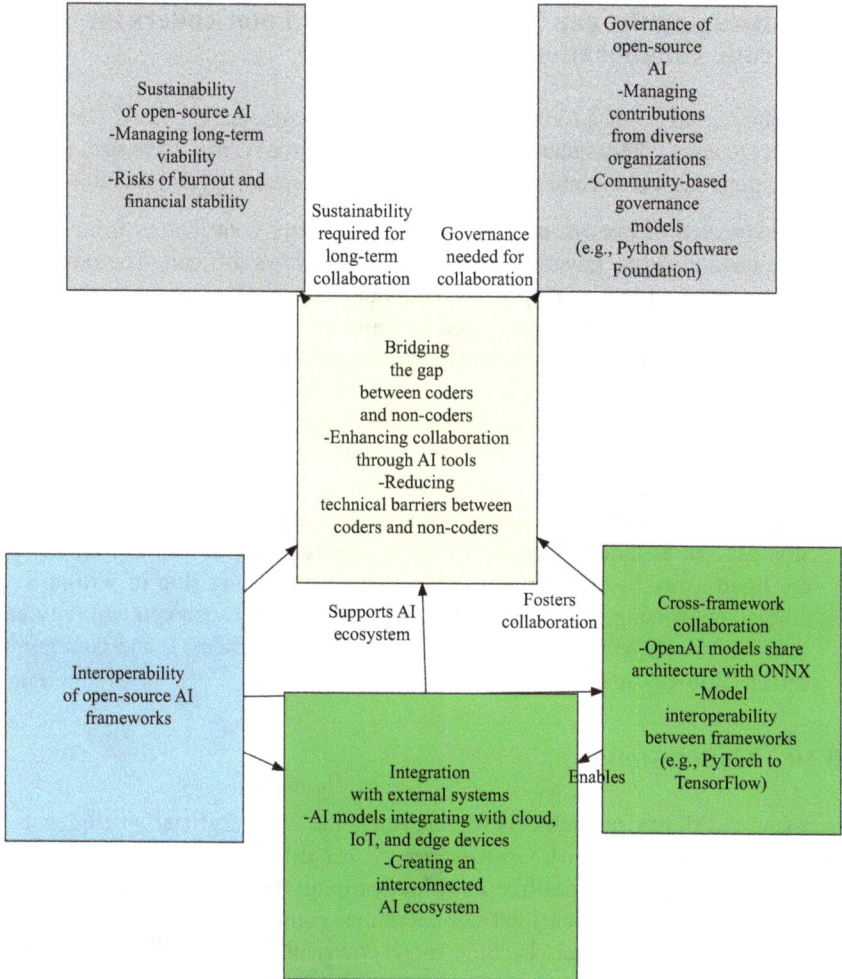

Figure 10.6   Interoperability of open-source GAI frameworks

- **Cross-framework collaboration:** OpenAI, such as models, are addressing this by sharing the model's architecture with ONNX that is designed to allow frameworks to share trained models easily. ONNX has the benefit of making a model trained in one framework (PyTorch, say), deployable immediately on another (TensorFlow), thus allowing organizations to not be locked into any one proprietary system.
- **Integration with external systems:** Another convergence trend is due to the integration of open-source AI with external systems like cloud platforms, IoT, and edge devices; this aids in creating a more interconnected AI ecosystem. The more specialized and context-dependent AI models get, the greater the importance of their abilities to interact with one another, data systems, and external devices will be for them to succeed.

10.9   Bridging the gap between coders and non-coders for code collaboration through AI

Performance analysis of adversarial attacks against segmentation-based features by LG FMN Demons. The collaborative ethos of open-source AI may have sped the pace of innovation, but it also comes with governance, sustainability, and moral issues.

- **Governance of open-source AI:** Given the many contributors from diverse organization types, governing open-source AI grows difficult. The possibility of transforming low-quality or biased inputs into reliable outcomes should not be taken lightly. Community-based governance models, such as those for the Python Software Foundation or Apache Software Foundation, offer valuable best practices when it comes to the management of open-source AI projects.
- **Sustainability of open-source AI:** Open-source AI projects face another obstacle: their long-term viability. A great many high-impact AI projects depend on volunteer contributions, so burnout and money-hunger are major risks. But once you've convinced everyone that it's not going to fail, and not be stomped out as independent development efforts are shut down or employees are lured away by money; that you're here for the long slog of writing corporate sponsorship grants, crowdfunding ventures (because you can only eat: read hire employees if someone is footing their pay checks), and community driven little-guy grants.

10.10   Conclusion

Open-source AI has undoubtedly transformed the way artificial intelligence is being built, shared, and used. Open-source AI has established itself as one of the drivers of innovation in areas like machine learning, natural language processing, and computer vision through joint collaboration, contributions, and transparency. But as generative AI models become more powerful and accessible, they create new ethical quandaries, governance issues, and security risks. Larger and more open, the AI ecosystem will place increasing demands on responsible development, regulation, and cooperation among industries and countries. With continued investment from governments, industry, and communities alike, open-source AI will continue to underpin a democratic, transparent future in an efficient manner.

References

[1]   Lin Z, Ma W, Lin T, *et al.* Open source AI-based SE tools: Opportunities and challenges of collaborative software learning. *ACM Transactions on Software Engineering and Methodology.* 2025;34(5):1–24.

[2]   Dautov R, Husom EJ, Sen S, and Song H. Towards community-driven generative AI. In *FedCSIS* (Position Papers) 2023 (pp. 43–50).

[3] Chen J, and Zacharias J. Design principles for collaborative generative AI systems in software development. In *International Conference on Design Science Research in Information Systems and Technology* 2024 (pp. 341–354). Cham: Springer Nature Switzerland.

[4] Hong S, Ryee H, Jin X, and Yang D. How organizations choose open-source generative AI under normative uncertainty: The moderating role of exploitative and exploratory behaviors. *Journal of Theoretical and Applied Electronic Commerce Research.* 2025;20(3):250.

[5] Hosseini M, Horbach SP, Holmes K, and Ross-Hellauer T. Open Science at the generative AI turn: An exploratory analysis of challenges and opportunities. *Quantitative science studies.* 2025;6:22–45.

[6] Noroozian A, Aldana L, Arisi M, *et al.* Generative AI and the Future of the Digital Commons: Five Open Questions and Knowledge Gaps. *arXiv* preprint arXiv:2508.06470. 2025.

[7] Acion L, Rajngewerc M, Randall G, and Etcheverry L. Generative AI poses ethical challenges for open science. *Nature Human Behaviour.* 2023;7 (11):1800–1801.

[8] Malik A, Onyema EM, Dalal S, *et al.* Forecasting students' adaptability in online entrepreneurship education using modified ensemble machine learning model. *Array.* 2023;19:100303.

[9] Verheijden MP, and Funk M. Collaborative diffusion: Boosting designerly co-creation with generative AI. In *Extended Abstracts of the 2023 CHI Conference on Human Factors in Computing Systems* 2023 Apr 19 (pp. 1–8).

[10] Mackintosh W. Foresighting viable open alternatives to address OER's Existential threat from commercial generative AI: Confronting the unspoken challenge for Pacific Small Island developing states. Available at: https://oer-foundation.org/wp-content/uploads/2025/01/OERF-Pacific-scenarios-for-GenAI-2025.pdf.

[11] Ahuja VK, Clark J, and WurtenBerg J. Impact of artificial intelligence on open-source software development. In *The International FLAIRS Conference Proceedings* 2025 May 14 (Vol. 38).

[12] Bagchi M. Toward generative AI–driven metadata modeling: A human–large language model collaborative approach. *Library Trends.* 2025;73(3): 297–322.

[13] Boussioux L, Lane JN, Zhang M, Jacimovic V, and Lakhani KR. The crowdless future? Generative AI and creative problem-solving. *Organization Science.* 2024;35(5):1589–1607.

[14] Taeihagh A. Governance of generative AI. *Policy and society.* 2025;44(1): 1–22.

[15] Cavanaugh P, Zhang J, and Tenney D. AI-enhanced open educational practices (AIOEP). In *2025 Northeast Section Conference* 2025 Mar 23.

[16] Azoulay P, Krieger JL, and Nagaraj A. Old moats for new models: Openness, control, and competition in generative AI. *National Bureau of Economic Research.* 2024:1–30. http://doi.org/10.3386/w32474.

[17] Dalal S, and Khalaf OI. Prediction of occupation stress by implementing convolutional neural network techniques. *Journal of Cases on Information Technology (JCIT)*. 2021;23(3):27–42.

[18] Lilhore UK, Simaiya S, Dalal S, Alshuhail A, and Almusharraf A. A post-quantum hybrid encryption framework for securing biometric data in consumer electronics. *IEEE Transactions on Consumer Electronics*. 2025;71(3):8289–8297.

[19] Daniel K, Msambwa MM, and Wen Z. Can generative AI revolutionise academic skills development in higher education? A systematic literature review. *European Journal of Education*. 2025;60(1):e70036.

Chapter 11
Future trends in generative AI

Technological change is accelerating thanks to generative AI. Let us look at some fascinating technical advancements that are defining AI's future. Creative professionals may use generative AI's growing intelligence. Consider a technology that lets architects visualize their projects or fashion designers create new trends. As AI technologies improve, artists and designers will have new means to discover and realize their ideas. A designer may utilize AI to test color schemes and fabric textures in real time, pushing fashion boundaries.

11.1 Generative AI applications

Generative Artificial Intelligence (AI) has become one of the most significant technological developments of the twenty-first century. Unlike traditional AI systems that focus on classification, prediction, or decision-making, generative AI creates new data, whether in the form of text, images, audio, video, or even structured code. This capacity to generate content has expanded opportunities across industries, reshaping how people communicate, create, and innovate. By leveraging advanced neural architectures such as Generative Adversarial Networks (GANs), Variational Autoencoders (VAEs), and large transformer-based models, generative AI can produce outputs that rival or sometimes surpass human creativity. To appreciate the depth of its impact, it is useful to examine its applications in six broad areas: creative industries, healthcare and life sciences, education and learning, business and productivity, scientific discovery, and ethics-driven societal transformations [1].

11.1.1 Creative industries and digital media

The creative industries have perhaps felt the earliest and most visible impact of generative AI. Tools based on deep generative models allow artists, designers, and musicians to collaborate with machines in ways that expand their expressive possibilities. Image generators trained on massive datasets can produce original artworks in various styles, from hyper-realistic portraits to abstract digital collages. These systems give professional artists rapid prototyping tools while also granting amateurs the ability to create without formal training. Similarly, generative AI in music composition has revolutionized the production of soundscapes, jingles, and even full orchestral arrangements. By analyzing existing works, AI can generate harmonies, rhythms, and melodies that complement human creativity [2,3].

In film and entertainment, generative AI supports scriptwriting, scene generation, and even special effects. Deepfake technology, while controversial, demonstrates how faces and voices can be convincingly synthesized, altering traditional notions of authenticity in media. Animation studios experiment with generative tools to automate in-between frames, speeding up production while maintaining artistic quality. The advertising industry also exploits generative AI for creating personalized marketing visuals and videos tailored to individual consumer preferences. Across these domains, the technology acts not as a replacement for human imagination but as an accelerant, giving creators tools to explore uncharted artistic spaces with unprecedented efficiency.

11.1.2   Healthcare and life sciences

Generative AI's role in healthcare and life sciences illustrates its potential to address some of humanity's most pressing challenges. One major application lies in drug discovery, where generative models design novel molecular structures with therapeutic potential. Instead of relying solely on laborious trial-and-error methods, pharmaceutical researchers can use AI systems to generate candidate molecules optimized for binding affinity, stability, or bioavailability. This drastically shortens the timeline from hypothesis to clinical trial, potentially accelerating the development of life-saving medicines [4].

Medical imaging also benefits from generative approaches. GANs are applied to reconstruct low-resolution scans into high-quality images, improving diagnostic accuracy while reducing patient exposure to radiation in modalities such as CT scans. In oncology, generative AI can simulate tumor growth under various treatment regimens, helping doctors tailor therapies to individual patients. Virtual patient data generation, another application, allows researchers to train diagnostic models without compromising privacy by synthesizing realistic but anonymized medical records. This is especially valuable in rare disease research where real datasets are scarce [5–7].

Beyond diagnostics and drug development, generative AI supports the design of personalized prosthetics, implants, and biomaterials through advanced 3D generative modeling. By combining patient data with generative algorithms, medical engineers create custom solutions that fit individual anatomical needs. Collectively, these applications illustrate how generative AI not only complements existing medical practices but also opens entirely new avenues for precision medicine and biotechnological innovation [8].

11.1.3   Education and learning

Education represents another frontier where generative AI is reshaping traditional practices. Automated essay writing and text generation tools enable educators to provide students with examples, prompts, or study materials tailored to specific topics. Beyond content creation, generative AI systems produce adaptive learning experiences by generating exercises, quizzes, and explanations personalized to each student's level of understanding. Instead of static textbooks, learners interact with dynamic material that evolves according to their progress.

Language learning has seen a surge of generative AI applications. Conversational models simulate real-time dialog in multiple languages, giving learners immersive practice environments. AI-generated stories and scenarios further enhance comprehension by contextualizing grammar and vocabulary. For students with special needs, generative AI designs customized educational resources that accommodate diverse cognitive and physical abilities. For example, text-to-speech models generate naturalistic audio for visually impaired learners, while text simplification systems provide accessible versions of complex documents [9–12].

At the institutional level, generative AI assists educators in producing teaching plans, syllabi, and course assessments more efficiently. Academic researchers benefit from AI-generated summaries of scholarly literature, enabling them to keep pace with rapidly growing bodies of knowledge. While concerns remain about plagiarism and overreliance on AI-generated content, careful integration demonstrates that generative AI functions best as a collaborative learning aid rather than a replacement for human pedagogy.

11.1.4 Business and productivity

In the business sector, generative AI has become a key driver of efficiency and innovation. One of the most impactful applications lies in content generation for marketing, where AI systems produce tailored advertisements, email campaigns, and product descriptions. These tools enable small and medium-sized enterprises to compete with larger corporations by automating time-consuming creative tasks. Generative AI chatbots and virtual assistants further enhance customer engagement, generating human-like responses that improve satisfaction and streamline support services.

In software development, code generation models are reshaping productivity. By learning from large repositories of programming languages, these systems can generate functional code snippets, debug errors, and suggest optimizations. This not only reduces the workload for experienced developers but also lowers the entry barrier for beginners. Architecture and product design also benefit, as generative algorithms propose optimized layouts, prototypes, or 3D models that meet performance and aesthetic requirements simultaneously.

Financial institutions apply generative AI to model potential scenarios, generate synthetic data for risk assessment, and simulate trading strategies. In manufacturing, generative design systems propose lightweight, efficient structures for components, reducing material costs while maintaining durability. These diverse business applications underscore how generative AI enhances productivity across sectors by automating repetitive work, enabling creativity, and accelerating innovation cycles.

11.1.5   Scientific discovery and research

Generative AI plays a transformative role in advancing scientific discovery. In physics and chemistry, models generate simulations of complex systems, predicting outcomes that would otherwise require costly or impractical experiments. For example, generative neural networks assist in climate science by producing high-resolution weather simulations from coarse data, improving forecasting models essential for disaster preparedness and resource management. Similarly, in materials science, AI generates candidate compounds with desired thermal, optical, or mechanical properties, expediting the discovery of new materials for electronics, energy storage, and renewable technologies.

Astronomy has also embraced generative AI for enhancing telescope images and reconstructing cosmic phenomena from incomplete data. Researchers use generative models to simulate galaxy formations, gravitational wave signals, and other astrophysical events. These simulations help refine hypotheses and guide observational strategies. In computational biology, generative AI models protein folding and molecular interactions, contributing to understanding fundamental life processes and developing new therapies [13].

Perhaps one of the most striking contributions lies in the reproducibility of scientific research. Generative AI can synthesize realistic datasets when real data are scarce or ethically restricted, enabling researchers to validate models under diverse conditions. By lowering barriers to experimentation and providing tools to simulate hypotheses, generative AI accelerates the pace of discovery across disciplines that depend on complex, data-driven inquiry.

11.1.6   Ethics, society, and future transformations

While generative AI offers remarkable applications, its societal impact is intertwined with ethical challenges and opportunities. The capacity to generate convincing text, images, and videos raises concerns about misinformation, deepfakes, and the erosion of trust in digital media. Political campaigns, social media platforms, and journalism face the risk of malicious actors deploying generative AI to manipulate public opinion. Addressing these threats requires robust detection systems, ethical guidelines, and public awareness initiatives.

At the same time, generative AI provides tools for social good. By producing culturally sensitive educational resources, local language translations, and accessible content, it fosters inclusivity and global communication. Humanitarian organizations experiment with generative AI to model refugee movements, simulate resource allocation during disasters, and generate awareness campaigns tailored to diverse communities. Artists and activists also use generative art as a means of social commentary, challenging audiences to reflect on technological ethics and cultural values.

The future trajectory of generative AI depends on how society balances innovation with responsibility. Ethical frameworks, transparent governance, and interdisciplinary collaboration will be essential in ensuring that generative AI remains a force for positive transformation. As the technology matures, its role may extend beyond generating content to shaping new forms of human–machine creativity and collective intelligence, redefining how societies create, communicate, and solve problems (Figure 11.1) [14].

Generative AI applications demonstrate the extraordinary breadth of machine creativity, spanning art, healthcare, education, business, science, and societal transformation. By generating new forms of content, insights, and designs, these systems extend the boundaries of human potential. Yet their adoption requires critical reflection on ethical, cultural, and practical dimensions to ensure that benefits outweigh risks. The case studies across different domains show that generative AI is not a singular tool but a versatile framework capable of reshaping entire industries (Table 11.1).

GENERATIVE AI APPLICATIONS

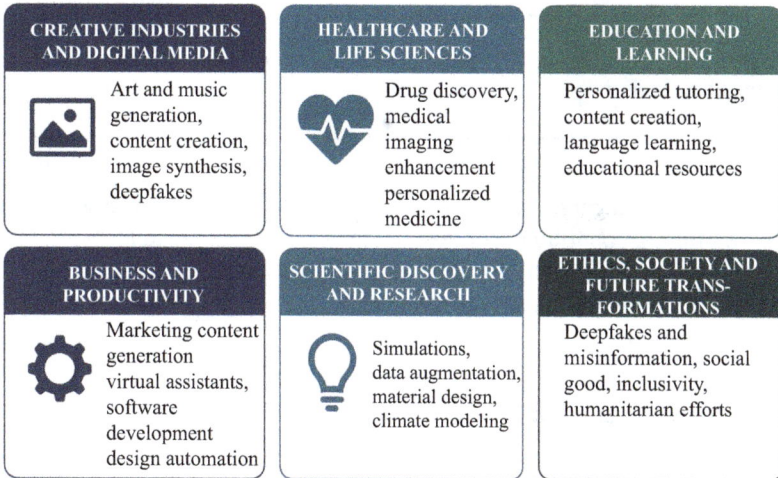

Figure 11.1 Generative AI applications

Table 11.1 Applications of generative AI across sectors

Domain	Focus areas	Key applications	Significance
Creative industries and digital media	Art, music, design, entertainment	Artwork generation, music composition, film scripts, deepfakes, personalized ads	Expands artistic creativity, accelerates content production, enables mass personalization
Healthcare and life sciences	Drug discovery, medical imaging, personalized care	Molecule generation, scan enhancement, tumor simulation, synthetic patient data	Accelerates research, reduces costs, supports precision medicine

(Continues)

Table 11.1   (Continued)

Domain	Focus areas	Key applications	Significance
Education and learning	Adaptive learning, accessibility, content creation	Personalized tutoring, AI-generated exercises, language learning, text-to-speech tools	Enhances inclusivity, supports tailored learning, assists educators
Business and productivity	Marketing, customer service, software development	Automated marketing content, chatbots, code generation, generative design	Increases efficiency, lowers barriers for SMEs, accelerates prototyping
Scientific discovery and research	Simulation, data generation, material design	Climate modeling, protein folding, astronomy simulations, synthetic datasets	Enables reproducibility, lowers experimental costs, fosters breakthroughs
Ethics, society and future transformations	Social good, misinformation, inclusivity	Deepfake detection, humanitarian modeling, inclusive content generation	Raises ethical challenges, fosters responsible use, drives global awareness

Its trajectory suggests a future where generative AI complements human ingenuity, offering opportunities for collaboration, efficiency, and innovation while demanding vigilance against misuse. In this sense, generative AI stands as both a transformative technology and a mirror reflecting society's choices in directing technological progress.

11.2   Future trends in generative AI

Generative AI has transformed the landscape of digital innovation, reshaping how people create, communicate, and problem-solve. Its ability to synthesize new content – text, images, audio, video, and even code – has placed it at the forefront of contemporary technological development. Yet, what is most striking is not merely what generative AI has already achieved, but where it is heading. Emerging trends point toward deeper integration into everyday life, new capabilities in multimodal reasoning, and stronger ties with scientific discovery, business innovation, and ethical governance. As these systems evolve, they will blur the boundary between human creativity and machine generation, challenging established norms in society, industry, and academia. The future of generative AI is therefore not only about technological progress but also about navigating cultural, ethical, and regulatory transformations.

11.2.1   Multimodal generative systems

One of the clearest future trends in generative AI lies in the development of multimodal systems – models capable of processing and generating across multiple forms of data simultaneously. While early models specialized in either text or image generation, the next generation of systems seamlessly integrates vision, language, sound, and even sensory data such as touch or spatial signals. This capacity will allow machines to generate holistic outputs that more closely mimic human perception. For instance, a multimodal model could generate a short film from a text prompt, complete with dialogue, background music, and visual animation. Similarly, scientific models could combine textual reports, numerical data, and visual simulations into unified research outputs.

In practice, multimodality will accelerate innovation across industries. In healthcare, multimodal generative AI could synthesize patient histories, imaging scans, and genetic data to generate comprehensive diagnostic insights. In education, a teacher might request a custom lesson that integrates text explanations, illustrative diagrams, and spoken audio, all produced in real time. Entertainment platforms could evolve into fully interactive environments where users co-create immersive experiences with AI partners. This expansion into multimodal reasoning signals a profound shift, enabling AI systems to transcend the limits of single-domain generation and function as integrative assistants across diverse contexts.

11.2.2 Personalization and human–AI co-creation

Another important future trend is the rise of personalized generative AI, designed to adapt outputs to the specific preferences, contexts, and goals of individuals. Today's generative systems often produce generalized responses, but the models of tomorrow will build detailed user profiles over time, allowing them to refine and align their creations to individual styles. A writer using generative AI may receive drafts tailored to their voice, while a musician could collaborate with AI systems that understand their preferred rhythm, genre, or harmonic style. Such systems will not replace human creativity but will act as collaborators, providing inspiration and accelerating workflows [15].

Personalized generative AI will be particularly impactful in education and training. Students will interact with adaptive learning companions that not only generate practice materials but also recognize their learning styles, strengths, and weaknesses. Business leaders will receive AI-generated reports and strategies tailored to their industries and organizational cultures. Even in healthcare, personalized generative models could simulate treatment plans adjusted to a patient's genetic and lifestyle profile. As personalization deepens, human–AI co-creation will redefine productivity, with machines becoming true partners in creative, professional, and scientific endeavors.

11.2.3 Integration into scientific discovery

Generative AI's influence on science will intensify in the future, making it indispensable for exploration and discovery. Already, generative models are being applied to drug discovery, protein folding, and climate simulations, but the next phase will expand this integration into nearly every scientific discipline. In materials science, generative algorithms will design compounds with precise mechanical, optical, or electronic properties, fueling advances in renewable energy and nanotechnology. In physics and astronomy, generative AI will reconstruct incomplete observational data, simulate cosmic phenomena, and suggest new hypotheses for experimental validation.

One particularly promising frontier lies in generative simulations that accelerate hypothesis testing. Instead of spending years designing and conducting physical experiments, scientists will be able to model scenarios with AI-generated datasets that approximate real-world conditions. In medicine, these models could simulate disease progression in silico, helping researchers test potential therapies at scale before proceeding to clinical trials. In environmental science, generative AI could produce fine-grained climate predictions, aiding policymakers in designing adaptive strategies for global warming. The capacity to generate realistic yet synthetic data will also support reproducibility, enabling the broader research community to verify and expand upon scientific findings. As a result, the next era of generative AI will not merely assist researchers but will become a core instrument of scientific methodology.

11.2.4 Business transformation and Industry 5.0

Generative AI is poised to be a key driver of the emerging Industry 5.0 paradigm, which emphasizes human-centric, sustainable, and resilient industrial ecosystems. Businesses are already exploring generative AI for marketing, product design, and customer interaction, but future adoption will extend deeper into strategic and operational decision-making [16]. Generative systems will automatically create prototypes, financial models, and supply chain simulations tailored to organizational needs. This will reduce design costs, shorten product development cycles, and enhance resilience in uncertain markets.

The retail sector may see AI-driven product personalization, where generative algorithms design clothing, furniture, or consumer goods that align with individual customer preferences [17]. In architecture and urban planning, generative models will propose sustainable layouts optimized for energy efficiency, accessibility, and aesthetic appeal. In financial services, AI will not only analyze risk but also generate investment strategies and portfolio simulations under multiple market scenarios [18]. Importantly, Industry 5.0 emphasizes human–AI collaboration, and future generative tools will be designed to augment human judgment rather than replace it [19]. By automating repetitive tasks and offering creative insights, generative AI will enable workers to focus on higher-level decision-making, aligning technology with human values and long-term societal goals [20].

11.2.5 Ethical governance and regulation

The rapid advancement of generative AI has raised significant ethical challenges, and the future will inevitably involve the development of robust governance structures to ensure responsible use. As systems become more sophisticated, the potential for misuse – such as creating deepfakes, misinformation campaigns, or synthetic identities – will increase. Without adequate safeguards, generative AI could undermine trust in digital ecosystems and amplify social divisions. Consequently, regulatory bodies worldwide are beginning to formulate policies to manage transparency, accountability, and fairness in generative AI.

Future governance is likely to involve multi-stakeholder collaboration, including governments, industry leaders, academics, and civil society. Ethical frameworks will demand that generative systems disclose when content is machine-produced, ensuring that users can distinguish between human and AI outputs. Data provenance mechanisms, such as watermarking or blockchain-based verification, may become standard for authenticating AI-generated media. Additionally, developers will be tasked with reducing bias in generative outputs, ensuring inclusivity across languages, cultures, and demographics. Importantly, governance must balance innovation with restriction, promoting openness for research and education while preventing harmful applications. In the coming decade, ethical governance will not be a secondary consideration but a central force shaping the trajectory of generative AI's development and deployment.

11.2.6 Path toward generalized creativity

The final trend points toward the possibility of generalized generative intelligence: systems capable of applying creativity across multiple domains in a flexible, human-like manner. Current models excel in narrow domains – writing essays, generating images, or composing music – but they remain specialized. The future may bring systems that combine these abilities into unified creative intelligence. Such models would not only generate outputs but also evaluate them, refine them through iterative processes, and transfer insights across tasks. For example, a generalized creative AI might analyze a dataset in climate science, generate visualizations, compose explanatory text, and propose actionable policies, all within a single workflow.

This vision of generalized creativity represents both a technical and philosophical milestone. On the technical front, it requires advances in self-supervised learning, transfer learning, and reinforcement-driven refinement. On the philosophical front, it challenges our definitions of creativity, originality, and authorship. Human–AI collaborations in this context may produce works of art, literature, or scientific innovation that defy traditional boundaries between man and machine. While full generalized creativity remains a long-term aspiration, incremental progress will continually blur the distinction between specialized tools and versatile partners, shaping how society views intelligence and innovation in the age of machines.

The future of generative AI is marked by profound opportunities and challenges. Multimodal systems promise integrative capabilities that merge text, images, audio, and data into unified outputs. Personalized co-creation will redefine the relationship between humans and machines, while integration into scientific discovery will accelerate the pace of knowledge production. Business and industry will harness generative AI as a cornerstone of Industry 5.0, transforming production, design, and strategy. At the same time, ethical governance will be indispensable to ensure that these technologies advance responsibly, addressing the risks of misinformation, bias, and misuse. Ultimately, the path points toward generalized creative systems that combine human-like adaptability with computational power. These trends underscore that generative AI is not simply a tool but an evolving partner in human progress, capable of reshaping culture, science, and industry. The decisions societies make today regarding their regulation, integration, and application will determine whether generative AI becomes a force for inclusion, creativity, and sustainability in the decades to come.

11.3   Generative AI ethics and challenges

In generative modeling, mode collapse occurs when a model cannot capture data diversity, resulting in limited or repeating samples. To address this, numerous methods have been proposed. In particular, Arjovsky *et al.*'s WGAN and WGAN-GP address mode collapse and improve generative model stability. These strategies have greatly reduced mode collapse. Especially GANs, generative models are known for training instability. Several methods have been developed to address this issue. The training process is stabilized by spectral normalization, progressive growing of GANs generates high-resolution images with improved quality and diversity, and self-attention mechanisms improve data modeling of long-range dependencies and training stability. These methods address GAN training instability.

In generative AI, assessing sample quality is difficult. Traditional IS and FID measures are limited. To overcome these constraints, researchers are exploring new assessment methodologies. These possibilities include Fréchet Kernel Inception Distance (FKID) and Wasserstein distance between true and produced distributions. These approaches seek to improve sample quality assessment. Several generative models struggle to capture long-term relationships in sequential data. Many RNNs and autoregressive models struggle to generate cohesive and realistic extended sequences. However, transformer-based models like GPT-3 and DALL-E have shown promise in solving this problem. Models that create extended sequences with enhanced coherence and realism have made substantial progress in addressing long-term dependence issues.

To produce high-quality results, generative modeling requires a lot of data. Generative models may be limited in data-scarce situations. This difficulty is being addressed by research on few-shot or one-shot generative models. In data-constrained situations, these models may produce meaningful content with less data, thereby expanding the value of generative AI. Given its growing strength and capabilities, generative AI raises issues regarding misuse, prejudice, and deception. Addressing these ethical issues requires interdisciplinary teamwork and careful consideration of social impacts. The issues drive generative AI research to build more robust and responsible models and techniques to prevent any harmful effects. As generative AI grows, proper development and deployment are crucial.

11.3.1   *Critical review of current guidelines for generative AI's unique challenges*

Generative AI models like ChatGPT, GPT-3, and other machine learning technologies have raised concerns about their efficient regulation and application. Existing regulations address ethical issues, abuse, and transparency. Comprehensive overview of how these issues are being addressed:

- Generative AI systems can reinforce biases in the data they are trained on. The standards emphasize ethical AI use and demand bias mitigation. These laws seldom include enforcement techniques or criteria for determining bias resolution. This gap permits subjective interpretations of ethical AI, which may lead to contradictions between implementations.
- Health, legal, and finance sectors increasingly want AI systems to be transparent and explainable. Current guidelines encourage AI operations and decision-making openness. However, neural networks' innate complexity makes it difficult to explain decision-making processes, preventing their practical deployment.
- Generational AI systems may need large amounts of data, including sensitive personal information. GDPR in Europe establishes a structure for handling personal data, but AI systems use vast amounts of data, making privacy and security problematic. Existing regulations may not encompass the complexities of data use in AI, including the risk of re-identifying people from anonymized information.
- Generative AI systems can develop content that looks like human-created content, raising copyright and IP problems. AI-generated material presents complex problems to intellectual property laws, often resulting in legal uncertainties and needing new or amended laws. Holding AI systems accountable is difficult. Currently, the rules are under development and often fail to clearly define accountability when AI systems do harm. These technologies are difficult to implement in accountable areas. Avoiding misuse: AI technology might be used to create false material like deepfakes. Although guidelines to avoid and address misuse are needed, existing legislation may lack adequate mechanisms to control or mitigate these concerns.

The existing proposals to address generative AI issues are often not practical, specific, or adaptive to the rapid advancement of AI technology. To ensure responsible and ethical AI development and use, continual study, discussion, and potentially new regulatory techniques are needed.

11.3.2   *Generative AI data privacy and security*

Due to the hazards of misusing AI-generated material and the sensitive nature of model training data, generative AI data privacy and security are important. Figure 11.2 shows potential data privacy and security issues in generative AI. GANs and other generative AI models may sometimes memorize portions of their training data, leading to potential database leaks. This could result in generated

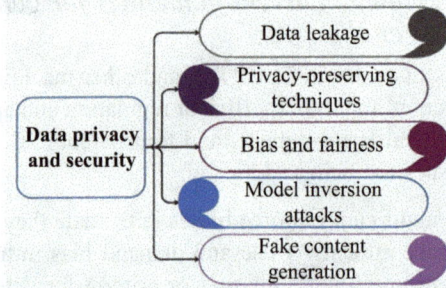

Figure 11.2 Data privacy issues

content exposing sensitive information or Personally Identifiable Information (PII) from the datasets used for training. To address these risks, researchers have been developing privacy-preserving methods for AI model training and deployment. Examples include differential privacy, federated learning, and secure multiparty computation, which help protect data while maintaining model utility.

Another challenge is the amplification of biases present in training data. Generative AI models can inadvertently produce skewed and ethically questionable outputs, raising concerns about fairness and justice in AI-generated material. Alongside this, model-inversion attacks pose a significant risk, as they aim to reverse-engineer generative AI systems to extract sensitive details from training data, thereby violating privacy protections.

Generative AI also has the capability to produce highly convincing fake content, such as deepfake videos and realistic images. While technically impressive, this ability can be misused to spread disinformation, perpetrate fraud, and facilitate social engineering attacks. For the responsible and secure deployment of generative AI, it is essential to address data privacy and security challenges through both technological innovations and strong ethical practices.

11.4 Generative AI IP and copyright issues

Generative AI raises major intellectual property and copyright issues, particularly with model training data and created content. Training data for generative AI models might be difficult to own and protect. Using copyrighted or proprietary training data without permission can result in intellectual property conflicts. When generative AI models produce new material, compliance with licensing and attribution becomes necessary, especially when the training data contains licensed content. Another challenge lies in determining ownership of generated content. It remains unclear whether copyright belongs to the model creator, the user, or the organization deploying the system. Generative AI also raises questions of fair and transformative use, particularly in the context of derivative works. Courts typically

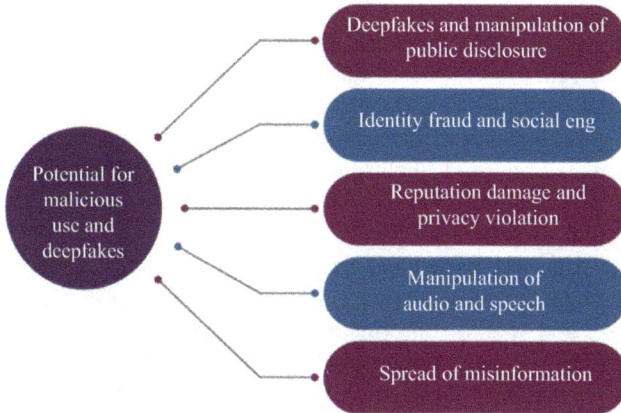

Figure 11.3 Potentials for malicious use

assess fair use by considering the purpose and nature of the use, the proportion and importance of the original work used, and the impact on the market.

Additionally, content generated by generative AI can sometimes closely resemble copyrighted works, raising concerns about plagiarism and unauthorized copying. As the technology advances, legislative frameworks, ethical guidelines, and technical safeguards will be essential to protect the rights of content creators while promoting responsible AI use. Deep learning models such as GANs can also be used for malicious purposes, including deepfakes. These are highly realistic videos or images manipulated to depict individuals performing actions or making statements they never did. Such uses have raised significant concerns about disinformation and harmful applications of generative AI, as shown in related studies and illustrated in Figure 11.3.

Generative AI can make captivating deepfake films of politicians, celebrities, and famous people doing things they never did. Manipulated content can disseminate misinformation and influence public opinion. Criminals can use deepfakes to impersonate someone using convincing fake videos or photos. Social engineering attacks can use impersonations to deceive individuals into revealing sensitive information or committing hazardous activities. Deepfake technology may also leak obscene, libelous, or dangerous material, endangering reputations and privacy. Malicious usage can have long-term effects on victims. Generative AI can simulate speech and sounds. Impersonating or misleading people with this talent can lead to dishonesty and fraud, but it also has innovative potential. Deepfakes may also manufacture fake news clips and realistic media material, spreading disinformation. These behaviors damage trust in media and institutions. Due to the potential of malicious usage of generative AI and deepfakes, synthetic media manipulation and its repercussions require effective detection techniques, public awareness campaigns, and regulatory measures.

For generative AI, justice, accountability, and impartiality are essential. Diversity and representative training datasets, data pretreatment and augmentation procedures, and fairness-aware loss functions are needed to address prejudice and ethics in model building. Additionally, adversarial testing, Human-in-the-Loop (HITL) validation, transparent decision-making, and strong governance and compliance frameworks are used. Inclusive development teams, regular updates, and responsible deployment are all crucial. These steps can create trustworthy, fair, and ethical generative AI systems.

To reduce data bias, varied and representative training datasets are essential. Thus, content may be more varied and inclusive. Preprocess training data to eliminate biases and sensitive information. Data augmentation helps balance datasets and decrease group overfitting. Loss functions that improve fairness and reduce prejudice during model training. Loss functions penalize prejudice and promote fairness. Adversarial testing is necessary to avoid model bias. This examination finds and fixes model performance problems. Human validators review HITL text for biases and ethics. This feedback loop improves model ethics and performance.

Responsible AI development demands openness. Communicating the generative AI model's aims and restrictions to stakeholders and users is key. Disclosure of technical capabilities and biases boosts confidence and ethics. Governance must address generative AI biases and ethics. Ethics are guaranteed via audits and compliance inspections. Inclusive development teams eliminate model design and decision-making biases. Diverse teams offer unique perspectives. The generative AI model must be checked and modified often to overcome biases. Finally, responsible deployment requires assessing the predicted impact of developed content on people and society and implementing controls to prevent misuse and injury.

Overall, the process above promotes justice, openness, and ethics in generative AI model creation and deployment. Researchers, policymakers, business experts, and the public must address generative AI ethics and biases. For ethical AI use, innovation and ethics must be harmonized.

11.4.1   Future generative AI directions and issues developments and issues in generative AI

Several crucial generative AI research areas need attention. All of these fields help create and deploy powerful and adaptable generative AI models. Improved model robustness and generalization are top goals. This requires assuring their robustness in managing complicated inputs. Final goal is to ensure that models can generalize even with unknown data. This prevents inconsistent or misleading results, which might compromise model utility and trustworthiness.

Mitigating biases in generative AI models and promoting fairness in findings are also important. Prevention of harmful preconceptions and inequities in model-generated material is crucial. Research on generative AI model controllability continues. Adding the ability to describe desired properties or features of generated material improves the usefulness and flexibility of these models. Privacy and

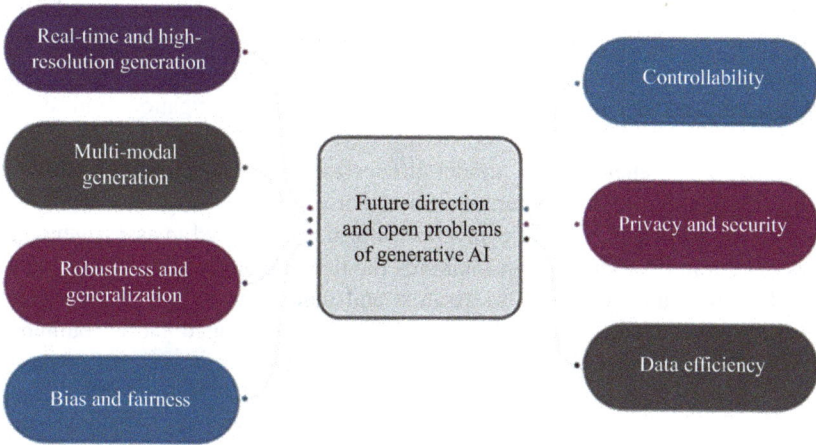

Figure 11.4   Future directives

security of training data and produced content are ongoing issues. This problem emphasizes the necessity for methods and measures to secure sensitive data and content integrity (Figure 11.4).

To reduce data needs for training generative AI models is a crucial effort. This effort attempts to make generative AI more accessible and practicable for additional applications and users. Creative tools and video creation require real time, high-resolution content generation. This region offers great opportunity for innovation and creativity. Finally, research on generative AI models that can handle text, graphics, and audio seems promising. Ensure these models can provide coherent and relevant outputs across multiple modalities to enable multimodal content development.

In conclusion, these study fields improve generative AI models' robustness, fairness, controllability, privacy, efficiency, real-time capabilities, and multimodal capabilities. The development of generative AI and its applications in numerous fields depends on these study areas. Future trends and ongoing obstacles will drive innovation and growth in generative AI. These obstacles must be overcome to responsibly and successfully employ generative AI in many fields.

11.4.2   Dealing with ethics

Generative AI design, implementation, and use must follow numerous ethical guidelines. These ethical rules and frameworks underpin AI activities and should be seamlessly integrated into their lifespan. Responsible AI development relies on public participation. Generative AI discussions and decision-making must engage the public, stakeholders, and specialists. This inclusive method helps identify and address society issues and beliefs throughout development and implementation. For users to understand generative AI models, transparency and explainability are essential. Model openness and interpretability should be improved to help users comprehend the models' decisions and content generating processes. Generative AI development must minimize prejudice and fairness. Preventing damaging pre-conceptions and discriminatory effects requires bias mitigation and content fairness.

Throughout generative AI model lifecycles, data privacy and security are crucial. Both training and generation should use privacy-preserving methods to preserve sensitive data. Effective adversarial testing is needed to assess generative AI model durability. This testing improves the model's dependability by assessing its performance and resistance to assaults and malicious inputs. Responsible AI requires governance and accountability. Effective governance and accountability frameworks are needed to enable responsible and transparent usage of generative AI and promote trust and ethics.

Responsible generative AI development and deployment requires ethical norms, public participation, transparency, fairness, privacy protection, robustness testing, and governance structures. These concerns enable ethical AI practices and appropriate generative AI use across diverse applications and domains. Generational AI can benefit society while reducing dangers by proactively addressing these ethical and cultural issues.

11.4.3   Generative AI research-to-deployment gap

Openly using generative AI research in real-world situations requires closing the gap between research and practice. For practical usage, generative AI research and development need numerous essential problems. First, researchers should create generative AI models that work well in controlled research situations and are scalable for real-world use. This dual focus allows AI models to manage real-world issues and complexities.

User-centric design is essential for generative AI models. End-user needs, limits, and practicalities must be considered for deployment success. User-centric AI solutions better meet user demands. Industries and academia collaborate to progress. Partnerships enable research implementation and industry feedback on research goals. Research-industry partnership improves innovation and impact. exploit transfer learning and pretrained models to speed deployment and exploit past research. Applying knowledge to real-world situations saves model develop-ment time and resources.

Real-world generative AI models require realistic limitations. Data, latency, and computing resources may be constraints. Model design must consider these limits for real-world applications to succeed. Regulatory compliance is important with technology. Generative AI models need legal and regulatory requirements in certain deployment domains. Data privacy and protection must be observed for ethical and legal compliance. Success depends on educating end-users and stake-holders about generative AI's promise and restrictions. User education fosters knowledge and accountability. To ensure generative AI serves diverse real-world applications, these stakeholders must collaborate to easily integrate AI technologies into their processes. These variables support realistic generative AI development. Researchers can responsibly and effectively integrate generative AI into real-world contexts, delivering meaningful benefits across domains, by prioritizing robustness, user-centric design, industry collaboration, efficient knowledge transfer, practical constraint awareness, regulatory compliance, user education, and stakeholder collaboration These methods and the academic community's knowledge and practical ideas can help generative AI achieve real-world benefits.

11.5 Generative AI research and trends

GPT and deep learning architecture are improving capabilities, efficiency, and applications of generative AI. Artificial intelligence systems that analyze text, images, audio, and video are spreading. OpenAI's DALL-E and Google's Imagen can produce images from text, demonstrating how several data modalities boost performance. Model pruning, quantization, and knowledge distillation are being studied to reduce huge AI model training and deployment computing burden. These solutions lower resource demands, making AI models more feasible for real-world application.

Ethics and bias reduction are now priority alongside efficiency. As generative AI improves, abuse and prejudice must be addressed. Identifying, reducing, and managing AI-generated biases requires ethical standards. Researchers are also exploring generative AI's social impacts and responsible use. Additionally, customization is popular. Information, experiences, and user preferences are customized via generative AI. Focus is on AI systems that anticipate user demands. Human-in-the-Loop (HITL) interface enhancement methods are another innovation. AI helpers become more intuitive and responsive with human-like collaboration from HITL. Human interaction improves AI performance in these expanding technologies. Explainability and transparency are essential for AI in healthcare, finance, and law. To defend AI activities to users and authorities, scientists are increasing model interpretability. Generative AI impacts music, art, literature, and design. AI creativity and AI–human artistic cooperation are being enhanced using human imagination and innovation tools. These trends demonstrate a growing industry that might affect technology, society, and culture by changing digital system use and information production. Generative AI must advance across several domains to overcome limits and unlock new opportunities.

GPT-3 needs a lot of processing power, therefore scalability and efficiency are key. Future research will make such models work on lesser hardware without affecting performance. Quantization, model trimming, and transformer efficiency seem promising. As generative AI systems impact society, fairness and bias avoidance are essential. Better frameworks and techniques to identify, assess, and reduce bias and ensure fairness are being explored (Figure 11.5). Explaining and being transparent are crucial. AI models must perform effectively and explain their decisions and findings, especially in sensitive industries like healthcare and finance. Increasing robustness is crucial because generative models might deliver

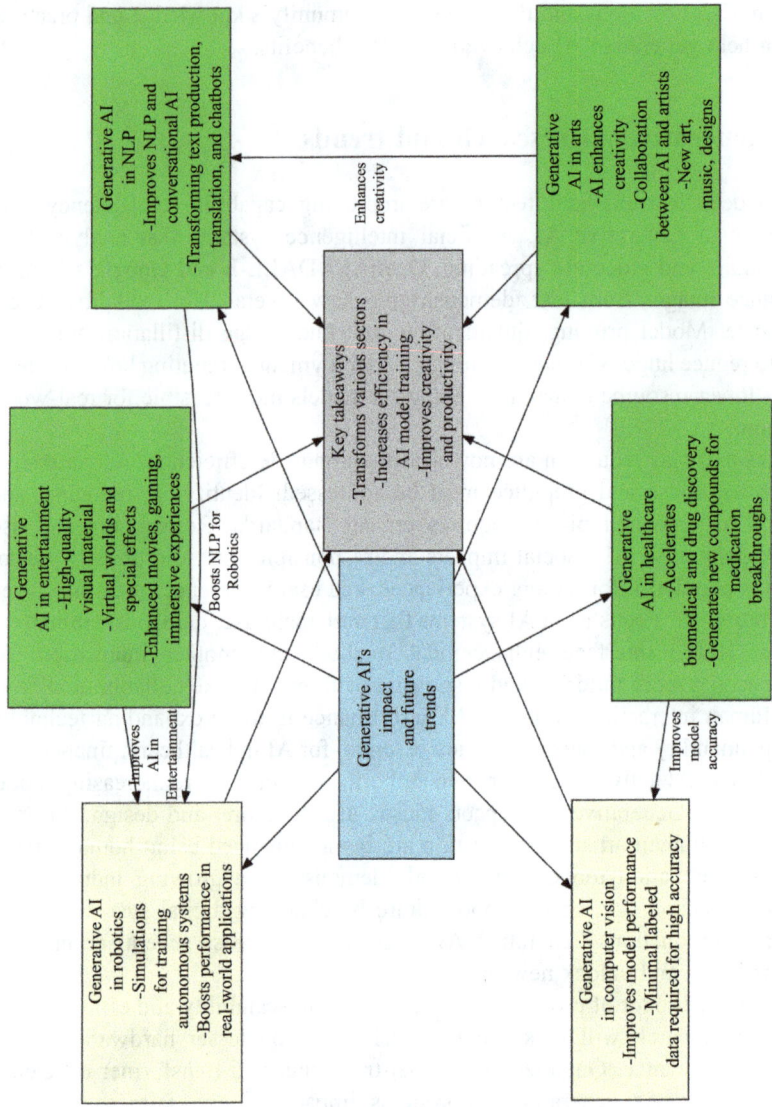

Figure 11.5 Generative AI's impact, trends, and future

inaccurate or harmful information and remain vulnerable to adversarial attacks. AI security research seeks to improve model reliability and abuse resistance.

Generational AI might increase creativity in art, music, design, and literature, according to future studies. Personalization research creates models that adapt to user preferences and provide personalized responses to increase digital assistant and content recommendation system satisfaction. Generative AI combined with reinforcement learning, robotics, or symbolic AI may improve system adaptability and efficiency. Technology necessitates ethical and regulatory standards. Ethics, governance, and policy studies are needed for safe, responsible, and sustainable generative AI implementation. Each topic addresses issues and has the potential to enhance generative AI's creative, technological, and practical limits.

11.5.1   Key generative AI findings and contributions

Generative AI has improved several applications. Powerful GANs may produce lifelike images that are hard to identify. They changed style transfer, super-resolution, and image-to-image translation. A promising area is generative AI models that can create graphics from text. This innovation increased visual creativity in content and design. GPT-like models improve natural language production. NLP and language-based applications have improved due to their text completion, summarization, and dialog synthesis.

Generational AI speeds drug development and chemical generation by creating novel molecules with desired properties. This discovery revolutionized drug development, perhaps enhancing efficacy. Generative AI lets artists and designers experiment with new content and visual art approaches. These technologies enable creativity and research. Researchers have created ways to identify and counteract deepfake material. Digital media integrity and visual and auditory authenticity require this study. Generated AI research values ethics. Since this technology creates ethical difficulties, scientists have recognized the necessity for ethical frameworks. With these research and execution approaches, generative AI improves society and reduces risks. Finally, transfer learning and pretrained models are widespread, allowing generative AI to be efficiently optimized for many real-world applications. This strategy boosts growth and knowledge utilization in numerous domains. Overall, generative AI has improved visual art, drug development, ethics, and technology detection. Recent advancements in creative content generation, scientific discovery, and responsible AI research have influenced various sectors' AI applications.

11.6   Generative AI's impact

Generative AI may transform businesses and improve user experiences. Generational AI is leading many applications and offers disruptive prospects across several disciplines. It empowers creative artists and designers to express themselves in new ways. This combination between human creativity and AI-generated material fuels creative cooperation and new art, music, and designs. Biomedical and drug discovery procedures are accelerated using generative AI. It generates unique compounds with desirable features, opening the way to medication development breakthroughs and enhanced healthcare.

Generative AI models like GPT improve NLP and conversational AI. These models might transform text production, translation, and chatbot interactions. More realistic and human-like AI interactions improve communication and understanding. Using generative AI, media and entertainment companies may develop high-quality visual material, virtual worlds, and special effects. These cutting-edge apps improve movies, gaming, and immersive experiences. Using generative AI, computer vision and speech recognition may be enhanced. It improves model performance with minimal labeled data, boosting AI accuracy and efficiency. In robotics and autonomous systems, generative AI facilitates training simulations. Simulations help robots and autonomous systems learn and adapt, improving their performance in real life. This use might boost robotics and automation.

Generative AI drives innovation and development in many sectors. It transforms industries and opens new paths in creative arts, healthcare, language processing, media, data improvement, and robotics. Generative AI might transform many sectors and improve our lives and technology as research continues.

11.6.1   Generative AI trends and prospects

Several essential aspects of generative AI research are being addressed. More user control over created material is a priority. Researchers are working to give users more control over AI-generated material by letting them choose features and styles. Multimodal generative AI models are also being developed. These models can generate text from photos and vice versa. Interactive and creative applications are expanded by this discovery, boosting innovation across many fields (Figure 11.6).

Few-shot and zero-shot learning are ongoing research priorities. The focus is on equipping generative AI models to learn from little data (few-shot learning) or even without training data in a category. These advances will make generative AI models more flexible and adaptable. The scientific community also studies transfer learning and cross-domain adaptability. Generative AI models that transfer expertise and adapt to diverse domains or datasets streamline model development and maximize information usefulness.

Increasing attention to generative AI has raised ethical and bias reduction concerns. To promote responsible and fair AI deployment, research is constructing ethical and bias-aware generative AI models that actively minimize content biases. Hardware and model architectural advances enable real-time high-resolution content production. Video production and virtual reality experiences, where high-quality, immersive material is in demand, benefit from this growth. The merging of RL with generative AI promises more organized and goal-oriented outputs. AI-generated content becomes more relevant to certain goals and applications due to this synergy. Finally, generative AI research covers user control, multimodal capabilities, ethical issues, real-time high-resolution generation, and RL integration. Together, these research initiatives make generative AI more adaptive, accountable, and effective at tackling many real-world

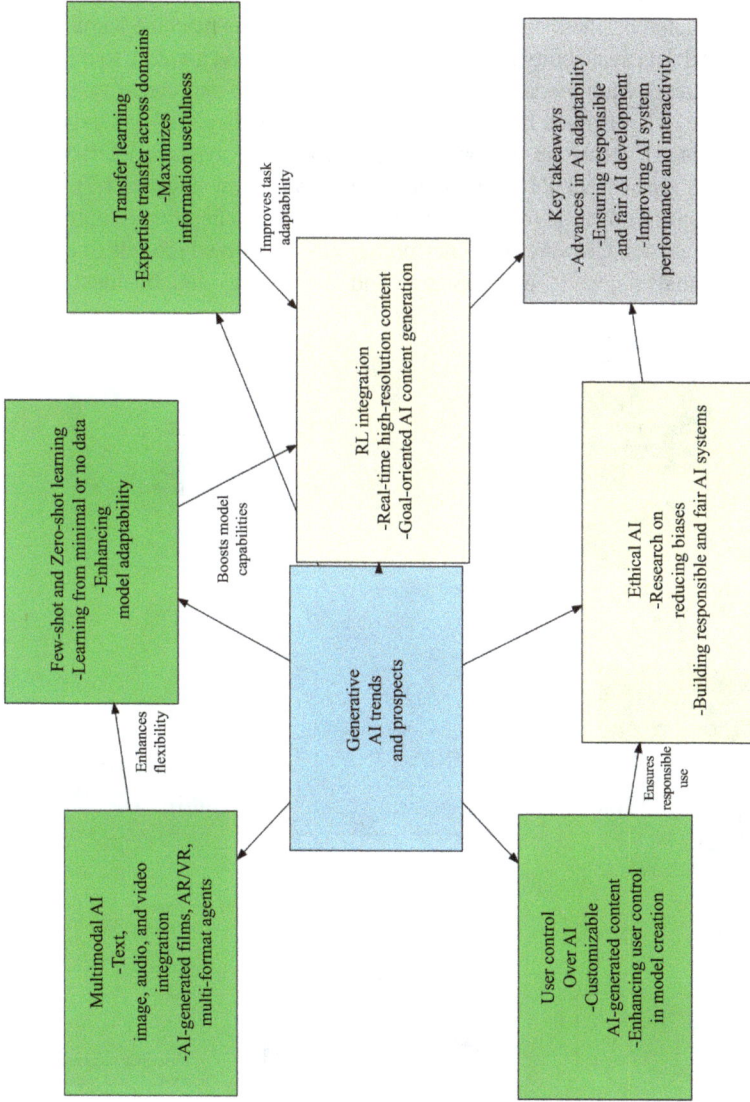

Figure 11.6 Generative AI trends and prospects

concerns and opportunities. Future advances in generative AI will boost creativity, human–computer interaction, and problem-solving. This flourishing field will see exciting advancements from a motivated research community.

11.6.2   Future generative AI trends

GenAI has disrupted business and will continue to innovate as machine learning, computer power, and data availability grow. Moving beyond text and graphics to multimodal AI is a major trend. Multimodal models may smoothly mix and create text, images, audio, and video. AI-generated films from text prompts, improved AR/VR experiences, and multi-format AI agents are examples. Deeper and more dynamic interactions are demonstrated by OpenAI's GPT-4 Turbo and Google's Gemini (Figure 11.7).

A significant trend is the move from single-response generators to autonomous crew-based AI agents. CrewAI combines numerous specialized models to automate research and analysis, code development and debugging, and business process

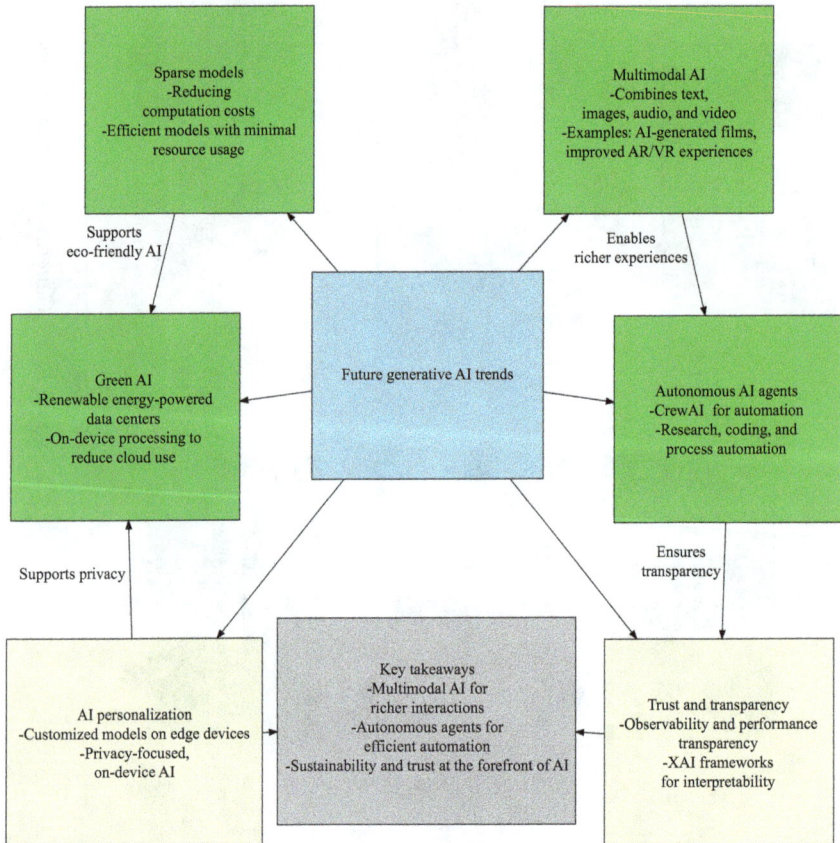

Figure 11.7   Future generative GAI trends

Table 11.2 Generative AI model trends

Trend	Technology	Use case	Main advantage	Challenges
Multimodal AI models	Text, image, audio	AI systems generating multiple media types	More creative, interactive experiences	Increased complexity in training
Few-shot learning	Transfer learning, few-Shot models	Enables AI to learn with less data	Reduces the need for vast datasets	Lower accuracy with minimal data
Zero-shot learning	GPT, BERT	Tasks with no prior training data	Enables broader generalization	Less reliable with complex tasks
Ethical AI models	Fairness constraints, bias mitigation	Reduces model bias and promotes fairness	More equitable AI outputs	Requires continuous updates and validation
AI personalization	Edge computing, AI Agents	Personalized AI assistants	More tailored user experiences	Privacy concerns and data security

automation. Effective AI that optimizes, reduces costs, and is sustainable is increasing in relevance alongside autonomy. Growing demand for large-scale GenAI solutions requires more efficient models that reduce computation costs and preserve performance. This includes using sparse models that activate only useful neurons, quantization for lighter models, distillation for smaller models with near-LLM capabilities, and green AI practices like renewable energy-powered data centers and on-device AI processing to reduce cloud infrastructure use. These techniques make AI developments economically and environmentally viable.

As AI use rises, observability and trust are essential. Organizations require model performance and behavior transparency. Instana, DataDog, and Dynatrace for monitoring, OpenTelemetry for process tracking, and Explainable AI (XAI) frameworks for interpretability are emerging solutions. AI-based personalization is another trend. Customized models that work on edge devices are likely to replace large, centralized systems. This will enable individualized AI assistants, privacy-focused on-device apps, and decreased cloud infrastructure consumption.

Table 11.2 presents the future trends of GAI. GenAI will be shaped by ethics, regulation, and governance. To combat misinformation, prejudice, and unfairness, the EU AI Act was introduced by the government. To construct safer systems, AI watermarking to identify bogus media and ethical AI principles to reduce bias are prioritized. Finally, open-source GenAI models are democratizing AI technology. Companies and researchers are using LLaMA, Mistral, Falcon, and DeepSeek for scalability. These solutions increase transparency, customization, eliminate AI provider dependence, and promote community-driven innovation and security. Companies seeking realistic, large-scale GenAI implementation are drawn to DeepSeek's high-performance models for efficiency and fine-tuning.

References

[1] Batista J, Mesquita A, and Carnaz G. Generative AI and higher education: Trends, challenges, and future directions from a systematic literature review. *Information.* 2024;15(11):676.

[2] Khan A, Jhanjhi N, Hamid DH, Omar HA, Amsaad F, and Wassan S. Future trends and challenges in cybersecurity and generative AI. In *Reshaping CyberSecurity With Generative AI Techniques.* 2025 (pp. 491–522). IGI Global.

[3] Wang N, Li S, Wang C, and Zhao L. Current status and emerging trends of generative artificial intelligence technology: A bibliometric analysis. *Journal of Internet Technology.* 2024;25(3):477–485.

[4] Leong LY, Hew TS, Ooi KB, Tan GW, and Koohang A. Generative AI: Current status and future directions. *Journal of Computer Information Systems.* 2025:1–34. https://doi.org/10.1080/08874417.2025.2482571

[5] Francis Onotole E, Ogunyankinnu T, *et al.* The role of generative AI in developing new supply chain strategies-future trends and innovations. *International Journal of Supply Chain Management.* 2022;11(4):325–338.

[6] Balasubramaniam S, Chirchi V, Kadry S, *et al.* The road ahead: emerging trends, unresolved issues, and concluding remarks in generative AI—a comprehensive review. *International Journal of Intelligent Systems.* 2024; 2024:1–38.

[7] Khan A, Jhanjhi NZ, Omar HA, Hamid DH, and Abdulhabeb GA. Future trends in generative AI for cyber defense: Preparing for the next wave of threats. In *Vulnerabilities Assessment and Risk Management in Cyber Security* 2025 (pp. 135–168). IGI Global Scientific Publishing.

[8] Gatla RK, Gatla A, Sridhar P, Kumar DG, and Rao DN. Advancements in generative ai: Exploring fundamentals and evolution. In *2024 International Conference on Electronics, Computing, Communication and Control Technology (ICECCC)* 2024 May 2 (pp. 1–5). IEEE.

[9] Sharma M, Selvi V, Chauhan R, Khan SA, Siddiqua A, and Balakumar A. The future of business with generative AI models and insights. In *2025 3rd International Conference on Intelligent Systems, Advanced Computing and Communication (ISACC)* 2025 Feb 27 (pp. 386–391). IEEE.

[10] Rana MN, Akhi SS, Tusher MI, *et al.* The role of AI and generative AI in US business innovations, applications, challenges, and future trends. *Pathfinder of Research.* 2023;1(3):17–33.

[11] Cho C, and Baek S. Exploring applications and trends of generative artificial intelligence. *Asia-pacific Journal of Convergent Research Interchange (APJCRI).* 2024;10(6):119–128.

[12] Yu H, Liu Z, and Guo Y. Application Status, problems and future prospects of generative ai in education. In *2023 5th International Conference on Computer Science and Technologies in Education (CSTE)* 2023 Apr 21 (pp. 1–7). IEEE.

[13] Shahzad MF, Xu S, An X, and Asif M. Are generative AI technologies transforming education for the 21st century? Research trends, challenges, and benefits. *SAGE Open*. 2025;15(3):21582440251368594.

[14] Han X. Generative artificial intelligence for future education: Current research status, hot spots, and research trends. In *Proceedings of the 2024 8th International Conference on Algorithms, Computing and Systems* 2024 Oct 11 (pp. 56–61).

[15] Bouguettaya S, Pupo F, Chen M, and Fortino G. A meta-survey of generative AI in education: Trends, challenges, and research directions. *Big Data and Cognitive Computing*. 2025;9(9):237.

[16] Onyema EM, Dalal S, Iwendi C, Seth B, Odinakachi N, and Chichi AM. Management and prediction of navigation of industrial robots based on neural network. *International Journal of Services, Economics and Management*. 2024;15(5):497–519.

[17] Lilhore UK, Simaiya S, Dalal S, Alshuhail A, and Almusharraf A. A post-quantum hybrid encryption framework for securing biometric data in consumer electronics. *IEEE Transactions on Consumer Electronics*. 2025; 71(3):8289–8297.

[18] Lilhore UK, Dalal S, Dutt V, and Radulescu M (eds.). *Industrial Quantum Computing: Algorithms, Blockchains, Industry 4.0.* Walter de Gruyter GmbH & Co KG; 2024.

[19] Dalal S, Seth B, and Radulescu M. Driving technologies of Industry 5.0 in the medical field. In *Digitalization, Sustainable Development, and Industry 5.0: An Organizational Model for Twin Transitions* 2023 (pp. 267–292). Emerald Publishing Limited.

[20] Lilhore UK, Manoharan P, Simaiya S, *et al.* HIDM: Hybrid intrusion detection model for Industry 4.0 networks using an optimized CNN-LSTM with transfer learning. *Sensors*. 2023;23(18):7856.

Glossary of terms

Adversarial attacks	Techniques where maliciously crafted inputs are fed into AI systems to trick them into generating false or harmful outputs. In generative AI, such attacks can lead to deepfakes, manipulated road signs in autonomous driving, or misleading video/audio outputs.
Adversarial training	A defense mechanism in which AI models are trained on adversarial examples so they learn to recognize and resist manipulated inputs.
Analog signals	Continuous waveforms used in audio and speech processing. In generative AI, analog signals are digitized and processed to generate or synthesize new sounds.
Bias in generative AI	The propagation of stereotypes and unfair representations due to biased training data. For example, AI-generated avatars may underrepresent certain demographics.
Case studies framework	A structured method for analyzing generative AI deployments across industries. Dimensions include **purpose, technology, integration, outcomes, and implications**.
Data augmentation	The process of generating synthetic data to expand training datasets, especially where real data is scarce. Widely used in image, video, and healthcare domains.
Data privacy risks	Concerns that generative AI models may memorize and leak sensitive data, such as medical records or financial transactions, during generation.
Deepfake	Synthetic media (video, image, or audio) generated by AI to impersonate real individuals. While useful in entertainment, it raises ethical and political concerns.
Differential privacy	A mathematical privacy-preserving technique where noise is added to data during training to ensure that individual data points cannot be inferred.
Federated learning	A decentralized training approach where AI models are trained locally on devices, and only the model updates (not raw data) are shared. It helps preserve data privacy.

Generative Adversarial Network (GAN)	A generative model consisting of two networks – a **generator** (creates synthetic data) and a **discriminator** (evaluates authenticity). They compete to produce realistic outputs.
Gradient descent	An optimization algorithm used in training generative AI models to minimize error between predictions and actual outputs.
Homomorphic encryption	An encryption method allowing computations on encrypted data without decryption, preserving privacy during AI processing.
Intellectual Property (IP) in GenAI	A critical ethical and legal issue regarding ownership of AI-generated outputs, such as music, art, or code.
Large Language Models (LLMs)	Foundation models trained on massive text corpora to generate human-like responses in natural language. Examples include GPT, Claude, and LLaMA.
Misinformation in GenAI	The use of generative AI to create deceptive or false content, often in political campaigns, news, or social media.
Neural video synthesis	A technique in generative AI that uses deep learning models to create realistic video sequences from minimal input.
Open-source AI	AI software and models that are freely available for use, modification, and redistribution. Frameworks like TensorFlow, PyTorch, and Hugging Face exemplify this ecosystem.
Privacy by design	An approach to AI development where privacy-preserving techniques (e.g., federated learning, SMPC) are embedded at every stage of the AI lifecycle.
Reinforcement Learning (RL)	A machine learning paradigm where agents learn optimal actions by trial and error, useful for adaptive generative systems and dynamic risk scoring.
Risk assessment in GenAI	Systematic evaluation of potential harms from generative AI, including bias, privacy invasion, misinformation, and IP theft, followed by mitigation strategies.
Secure Multi-Party Computation (SMPC)	A cryptographic method allowing multiple parties to collaboratively train AI models without sharing raw data, thereby preserving privacy.
Transformer models	A class of deep learning architectures that leverage self-attention mechanisms for sequence generation tasks such as text, code, and image synthesis.
Variational Autoencoders (VAEs)	Generative models that use encoder–decoder architecture to represent data in a compressed latent space and reconstruct realistic outputs.

Index

www.ingramcontent.com/pod-product-compliance
Lightning Source LLC
Chambersburg PA
CBHW060248230326
41458CB00094B/1530